THE LEOPARD'S TALE

Thames & Hudson

THE LEOPARD'S TALE

Revealing the Mysteries of Çatalhöyük

IAN HODDER

with 137 illustrations,
24 in color

To Shahina

HALF-TITLE: *A paired leopard relief discovered at Çatalhöyük in the 1960s.*
TITLE PAGE: *Reconstruction of Çatalhöyük during the spring flood of the adjacent river.*
CHAPTER HEADINGS: *Stamp seals from Çatalhöyük.*

First published in 2006 in hardcover in the United States of America by Thames & Hudson Inc., 500 Fifth Avenue, New York, New York 10110
thamesandhudsonusa.com

Library of Congress Catalog Card Number 2005906271

ISBN-13: 978-0-500-05141-2
ISBN-10: 0-500-05141-0

Printed and bound in China by Midas Printing Ltd

Contents

Prologue

Each time I walk onto the 21-m (69-ft) high mound at Çatalhöyük (pronounced approximately Chatalhuyuk) in central Turkey I feel a thrill of excitement. Even though I have worked at the site each summer since 1993, I still feel a tingling in my feet as I tread over the ground. After all, the soil beneath me is filled with fascinating details about a town that was lived in by 3,000 to 8,000 people some 9,000 years ago. The town extended over a massive 13.5 hectares (33.5 acres). It was inhabited for about 1,400 years between 7400 BC and 6000 BC.[1] There are 18 levels of occupation as people abandoned old houses, filled them in, and built new ones on top. So the mysteries of Çatalhöyük include its great size and duration at a very early date – when people had started settling down into permanent villages and had begun domesticating plants and animals.

When the site was first found and excavated by James Mellaart in the late 1950s and early 1960s, the world was stunned by his findings. Working from Britain, Mellaart was a young scholar setting out to show that the earliest farming villages not only occurred, as had been thought, in the Levant and adjacent areas in the Middle East, but also in central Anatolia. In each occupation level at Çatalhöyük he excavated up to 30 buildings – overall about 160 of them spread over the different levels (the excavation of part of Level VI is shown in Figure 1). The current project which I direct has excavated or planned a further 80 buildings. What Mellaart and we have found was a site that had been inhabited by people much like us today – not only the same species, but also growing their food and hunting animals, and making tools and buildings. Each building was probably lived in by a family of 5 to 10 people. There was a main room for living, craft activities, cooking, eating and sleeping, and there were side rooms for storage and food preparation. This was all fairly standard for a site of this time period, even if it was especially large.

1 James Mellaart's extensive excavations at Çatalhöyük in the 1960s.

But there were also some distinctive characteristics of Çatalhöyük, and it was these that so astonished Mellaart's audiences. The buildings in which people lived were tightly packed together so that there were few or no streets. Access to houses was across roofs and down stairs into interior spaces. The interiors were packed with a rich art – mural paintings, reliefs and sculptures. There were remarkable images of women that some thought indicated a Mother Goddess cult. People buried their dead beneath the floors. By finding this site, Mellaart had not only shown that early farming centres existed outside the Levant and Mesopotamia, but he had also discovered a site filled with mysteries and elaborate symbolism. Despite excavating for four years between 1961 and 1965, Mellaart only uncovered a small part of this huge site, and the excavations which I have directed at the site since 1993 have only pushed the amount of the site exposed up to 5 per cent. So I know, as I walk over the mound that there are literally thousands of unexcavated buried buildings beneath my feet, full of art and symbolism, waiting to be explored, providing keys into the way these people lived their lives and thought about the world around them so long ago.

I will introduce the site more fully later in this prologue and in subsequent chapters, but for the moment I want to provide a concrete example of the riddles that face archaeologists as they excavate this remarkable site. The table of data that

I want to start with also allows me to introduce the leopard which is an important component of the art and symbolism of Çatalhöyük and is at the centre of my tale. The table below was prepared by Nerissa Russell and Stephanie Meece, who work on the faunal remains from the site. They were part of the team that studied the finds that were excavated between 1995 and 1999.

The table has four columns of data. The first column shows the proportions of different mammalian taxa in the paintings found on the walls of the buildings at Çatalhöyük. The main reason why the site is so well known and has been so widely celebrated is that it has an amazing concentration of wall art. The walls of the houses were frequently replastered with a white soft plaster, and this plaster was often painted in figurative scenes as well as with geometric patterns. The main theme in the paintings is wild animals – including bulls, equids, deer and wild goat. The high proportion of leopard paintings is recorded in the table because there are also scenes of people, in some cases bearded, wearing spotted skins (for an example see Plate 1) with apparent tails. Because there are other, clearer images of leopards (see below), and because leopards were still to be found in Turkey until recently, these garments are usually interpreted as leopard skins. There are also clay and stone figurines of people, including women, wearing spotted clothes which can again be interpreted as leopard skins or garments which have been made to look like leopard skins.

As well as the paintings at Çatalhöyük, there are animal shapes moulded onto the walls. These reliefs are often then themselves painted. The second column of

Table 1 Percentages of mammalian taxa found across different media at Çatalhöyük.

	Paintings	Reliefs	Installations/Deposits	Faunal Remains
Hedgehog	0%	0%	0%	<1%
Hare	0%	0%	0%	1%
Wolf	0%	0%	1%	<1%
Dog	1%	0%	2%	5%
Fox	0%	0%	1%	2%
Bear	1%	0%	1%	<1%
Mustelid	0%	0%	1%	<1%
Wild cat	0%	0%	0%	<1%
Leopard	65%	35%	0%	0%
Equid	6%	0%	1%	8%
Boar	3%	0%	13%	3%
Fallow deer	1%	0%	1%	<1%
Red deer	12%	0%	1%	1%
Roe deer	0%	0%	0%	<1%
Cattle	1%	46%	54%	15%
Goat	10%	0%	11%	9%
Sheep	0%	19%	13%	56%

2 Pair of leopard reliefs showing one of several layers of painted 'spots'. This pairing was discovered by James Mellaart on the west wall of a building he called 'Shrine VII.44' in the excavations in the 1960s.

3 Bench inset with wild cattle horncores. Originally the cores would have been covered in horn and so would have been considerably larger.

data shows the proportions of different animal types in these reliefs. Here too the leopard is well represented, even though cattle reliefs are more common. The leopard reliefs occur as pairs of animals head to head, as in Figure 2. In some of the cases found by James Mellaart, there were many layers of painting on the leopards. The spots would change at each repainting even though the relief form remained the same. All of the work done by Russell and Meece had to struggle with the issue of how to identify animals in paintings and reliefs. These pairs of spotted animals have generally been accepted as leopards, but the depictions are not accurate. Their stylized form would allow them to be interpreted as cheetah (which formerly ranged through the Middle East[2]) or even spotted dogs or 'decorated' lions.

The third column of data shows the importance of different types of animals in installations. The buildings at Çatalhöyük also contained bull and animal heads, horns, teeth, tusks and so on set into walls and placed on pillars (e.g. Figure 3) and modelled in plaster. In particular, cattle skulls were brought into houses, the heads were plastered, and the resulting 'bucrania' as they are called were placed on the wall (as in Plate 17). As we shall see, leopard bones were virtually never brought onto the site and so there are no leopard installations.

One of the main types of data that we find when we are excavating at Çatalhöyük is animal bones. These are found in open refuse or 'midden' areas between houses together with sweepings from hearths and other refuse such as stone tools, figurines, pottery, grinding stones and so on. Animal bones are also found in houses as we shall see later. The fourth column of data in the table deals not with representations of animals, but with these actual bones of animals that we have unearthed in the excavations. Once the bones have been brought out of the ground they are identified and studied in the faunal laboratory at the site. At the time of producing this table, the faunal team at Çatalhöyük had studied 24,190 animal bones which they could identify to taxon. And yet they found not one bone of the leopard (*Panthera pardus*). In fact they found no bone from any of the large cats. This seems especially remarkable given that it is plausible that the inhabitants of Çatalhöyük were bringing leopard skins onto the site to wear, as suggested by the paintings. When animal skins are brought onto a site they often contain the feet bones. But not even the feet bones of leopard have been found.

So here is a puzzle seen in a table of data. Why should there be so many depictions of leopards but such a marked lack of leopard bones? Russell and Meece are careful to point out that there are many ambiguities and uncertainties in their analysis and quantification. Many animal depictions are hard to interpret and the counting of taxa proved fraught with difficulties. As I have already pointed out, it is possible that the leopard reliefs actually show cheetah, or lion or even a symbolically decorated dog. However, it is most likely that at least one of the large wild cats is represented. So even if the reliefs have been misidentified as leopards, there is still a very clear puzzle: some big wild cat seems depicted but no big wild cat bones have been found. And there are very sharp contrasts with other animals. Sheep, for example, dominate the faunal assemblage, but there is not a single painting of an unambiguous sheep.

So how can we interpret this pattern? What tale can be told? A number of factors could be seen as relevant. First of all, perhaps leopards were never killed, but were a central part of myth. To support this claim, there are several aspects of the art at Çatalhöyük, as we shall see, that do not represent reality so much as myth and memory. Perhaps the leopard was such a central part of myth that it was never killed. Another possibility is that leopards were killed and skinned and the bones not brought onto the site. It is likely that humans competed with leopards (or other wild cats) as hunters and scavengers of large prey. They would have met and perhaps killed these animals in order to protect their own food. Carrying a full-sized leopard or other large wild cat back to the site would have been difficult but we know that they did bring back wild cattle and horse. Skinning the animal away from the site and just bringing back the skin would have saved effort. Other fur animals at the site have the head and feet bones present as these tend to be left in the skins. So if the leopards were killed off site and the skin brought back, the carcasses were not just skinned but thoroughly processed away from the site. A third possibility is that the inhabitants did not want to lose the meat of a large animal they had killed. Perhaps they did bring the animal to the site, used it for skin and meat, but then dealt with the bones in such a way that they left no trace in the archaeological record. For example, the bones might have been discarded off site or burned to such a high temperature that they became ash. Archaeologists are unable to identify the species in bone ash.

The most likely scenario is perhaps a mixture of these three possibilities. We know that leopards (and other wild cats) occurred in Turkey into historic and recent times. It seems highly likely that, as in the second option, the inhabitants had to compete with leopards, and vultures, for carcasses of large game. But a special symbolic status for large cats (as in the first option) may have involved some sort of taboo against bringing the bones and meat back onto the living space. We know that people at Çatalhöyük did burn bone, as part of cooking, but it would be difficult to burn bone so fully, as suggested by the third option, without leaving some trace of the bones (such as the thicker articular ends of the bones). A further possibility is that the leopard and its skins were rare and the bones heavily curated so that they did not get into archaeological deposits very frequently. There remains a difference, however, between the rarity of the bones and the frequency of depictions in the art.

There is much else in Table 1 that we will return to later. There are many other differences between the bones found on the site and the representations in the wall paintings. But the contrast between the paintings and the bones seems starkest for the leopard or large wild cat. This suggests some special status for these animals. While we may never be able to detail precisely what beliefs and myths surrounded the leopard at Çatalhöyük, we can go some way down the road of making sense of a set of values, taboos or restrictions. To make sense of this and other puzzles at Çatalhöyük will be the aim of this book. As more and more pieces of the jigsaw are brought into the argument, I hope to convince you that an elaborate symbolic world from 9,000 years ago can be reconstructed – certainly with many ifs and buts, through a glass darkly. But progress can be made and mysteries revealed, if only partially and tentatively.

Why is working out this puzzle important? Why is Çatalhöyük and its rich and complex symbolism important? I gave a preliminary answer to these questions at the start of this prologue, but in order to answer them more fully we need to look into the discovery of the site and at the various communities to whom it has become important.

Archaeologists often talk as if their discovery of a site was 'the' discovery. But Çatalhöyük, like many sites, while new to western scholarship, had long been known by the local community. It was named by them. The term 'Çatalhöyük' means 'fork mound', probably referring to the fact that the path from the town Çumra to the south divides into three at the mound. One path turns left to the nearby village of Küçükköy that we will return to and from where most of the local people that work on the excavation come. One path turns right. As it does so one notices that Çatalhöyük is in fact two mounds (Figure 4). The main, famous

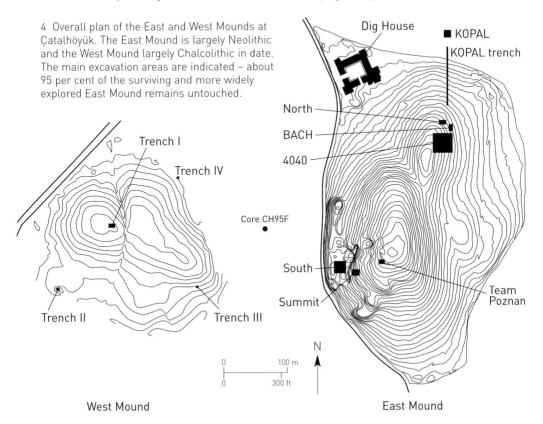

4 Overall plan of the East and West Mounds at Çatalhöyük. The East Mound is largely Neolithic and the West Mound largely Chalcolithic in date. The main excavation areas are indicated – about 95 per cent of the surviving and more widely explored East Mound remains untouched.

Dig House

■ KOPAL

KOPAL trench

North

BACH

4040

Core CH95F

South

Summit

Team Poznan

Trench I

Trench IV

Trench II

Trench III

0   100 m

0   300 ft

N

West Mound

East Mound

mound is Neolithic in date and is known as the East Mound (Plate 2). The West Mound, locally termed Küçük Höyük (small mound), follows on from the East Mound and is Copper Age or Chalcolithic in date. So this second path turns between these two mounds and continues to the village of Karkın. A third used to cross the East Mound in the gully between its northern and southern eminences or hills, but this path was blocked when the East Mound was fenced off after the excavations in the 1960s.

A young ethnographer David Shankland has carried out research in the village of Küçükköy in order to ascertain the local knowledge of and understanding about the site.[3] He found that some of the villagers believed that their village had descended from classical remains known as Eskiköy (old village), near to Çatalhöyük. The mound was seen as other mounds – as a place to picnic, or for grazing. But it was also known as the place of burial of a 'wayward' woman, and as a place surrounded by superstitions. At night it is thought that the 'souls of those past' could be seen as little lights moving between Çatalhöyük and other mound sites in the region.

To Turkish and western scholarship, however, the site was unknown. During the 1950s there was little evidence to suggest an early development of the first farmers and the first towns and villages outside the Fertile Crescent – that is the area stretching from the Levant, up into southeastern Turkey and northern Syria and across into the Zagros area of northern Iran. It was in this area alone that the first Neolithic farmers were thought to emerge, on the hilly flanks where wild cereals – the ancestors of wheat and barley – grew, and where there were wild sheep and goats to domesticate. In 1956 Seton Lloyd, who became the Director of the British Institute of Archaeology at Ankara, was able to write that 'the greater part of modern Turkey, and especially the region more correctly described as Anatolia, shows no sign whatever of habitation during the Neolithic period.'[4] He put this lack down to the 'extreme cold of the Anatolian winter.'[5] But, as noted by Roger Matthews when he later became Director of the Ankara Institute, at the time that Seton Lloyd wrote James Mellaart had already spotted the mound of Çatalhöyük at a distance.[6] James Mellaart, David French and others had identified prehistoric material in their surveys of the Anatolian plateau between 1951 and 1958.[7] The Çatalhöyük mound was noted in the distance in 1952,[8] but could not be returned to until 1958. In November that year James Mellaart, David French and Alan Hall reached the site just before nightfall. They immediately realized the importance of the East Mound as it had mud-brick buildings with Neolithic pottery at both the top and the base of the huge mound.[9]

However, Mellaart was at the time excavating at another site called Hacılar, and it was not until 1961 to 1965 that he excavated at Çatalhöyük.[10] His excavations were mainly confined to the East Mound in the southwest (the area shown as 'South' in Figure 4), although two small trenches were also dug on the Chalcolithic West

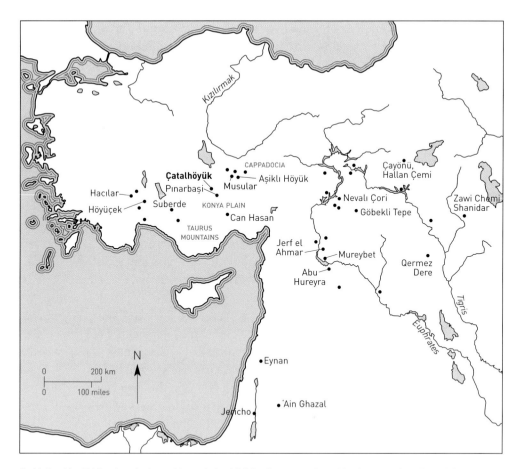

5 Major Neolithic sites in Anatolia and the Middle East mentioned in the text. Çatalhöyük is now seen as just one element of a much wider pattern of Neolithic settlement in the region.

Mound. Mellaart's publications resulted in very widespread interest in the site. Initially the importance of the site was recognized as its large size at an early date, and its location outside the supposed 'cradle' of civilization in the Middle East as noted above. But a major factor for its prominence was undoubtedly its art which, in his foreword to Mellaart's 1967 book Sir Mortimer Wheeler[11] described as a 'curious and sometimes a trifle macabre artistry' which nevertheless distinguishes a site which 'represents an outstanding accomplishment in the upward grade of social development'.

Much has changed in our knowledge of the Neolithic in Anatolia since the 1960s. In some ways Çatalhöyük is no longer so exceptional. In terms of date, we now know that there are many earlier village- or town-like settled sites in eastern and central Anatolia (Figure 5) and in the Levant and some of these are very large – as large as or larger than Çatalhöyük. We also know that the domestication of plants, sheep and goat was well under way in these areas thousands of years before

6 James Mellaart found well-preserved and tightly packed houses at Çatalhöyük, many of which were richly decorated with sculpture and paintings. The features in the foreground can be seen in greater detail in Figure 66 and Plate 17.

the time of Çatalhöyük. In fact, as is clear from Figure 19 and the box feature on page 20, Çatalhöyük is late in the Neolithic sequence.[12]

But there are ways in which Çatalhöyük remains distinctive. For example, the narrative character of the wall paintings remains unparalleled in Anatolia and the Middle East at this date. And the sheer amount of the art – its concentration in so many houses in one site – remains particular. Indeed, the main mystery of Çatalhöyük remains the question of why all this art and symbolism, this flowering of imagery, should occur in this place at this time. But perhaps the most important way in which the site can claim a special status regards depositional processes and building survival (seen in Figure 6 and Plate 6). Through much of its sequence, Çatalhöyük provides a richly textured record of the minutiae of daily life. Rather than making hard lime floors that could be used over decades (as in many sites in Anatolia and the Middle East), at Çatalhöyük the floors were mostly made of a lime-rich plaster that remained soft and in need of continual resurfacing. Thus on an annual or even monthly basis, floors and wall plasters were resurfaced with extremely thin layers. Within 10 cm (4 in) of floor or wall deposit it is possible to find hundreds of layers of replasterings. These provide a detailed record of daily life inside buildings, like rings in the growth of a tree. Middens too are finely layered, so that individual dumps of refuse from the hearth can be identified.

And then, on abandonment of a house, paintings were covered over, and ovens and other internal features were sometimes carefully filled with earth. The upper walls were demolished and the lower half of the house often carefully filled in with fairly clean soil. In these ways the lower parts of the house were well protected and preserved. A new house was constructed using the lower halves of the walls of an earlier house as a base for new walls. Gradually the 21-m high mound was built up as house was constructed on house (Plate 4). Together with the soil conditions that lead to good survival of carbonized plants, animal and human bone etc, these depositional processes result in a remarkably well preserved site with much detailed information covering long periods of time. Difficult to excavate because of its complexity, the rewards in terms of detailed information are high.

Mellaart excavated quickly. His large-scale work established the importance of the site. No further work was carried out at the site between 1965, when Mellaart's work stopped, and 1993 when the project I direct began. Given that the site had been extensively excavated in the 1960s it was incumbent on us to use the latest scientific techniques available to conduct intensive and detailed studies to throw further light on the large-scale results obtained by Mellaart. So the ideas that I will be exploring in this book are the result of two very different types of work at the site – the extensive work carried out by Mellaart and the more intensive work of the current team.

A wide range of scientific techniques is used by the large number of specialists who work at Çatalhöyük. These techniques will be explained as we meet them in the course of the book. They include radiocarbon dating, micromorphological analysis of soils in order to work out what activities took place in buildings and refuse areas, and chemical analysis of human bones in order to reconstruct the diets of people living at Çatalhöyük. The techniques include the study of residues left in pots to work out what people were cooking, and geological study of obsidian, the volcanic glass from which tools were made, in order to understand ancient patterns of trade and exchange. All these, and other, scientific techniques provide the information that is weaved together in this account.

But before I embark on the tale that I wish to tell, it is important to recognize that the site has a significance beyond the narrow confines of those specialists that spend their time digging up the Neolithic of Anatolia and the Middle East. In broader terms, the Neolithic period in which Çatalhöyük is situated, albeit towards its end, was the time that anatomically modern humans perhaps went through the greatest change in their existence on earth. This was the time people moved into villages and towns, adopted farming, and began to accept greater degrees of social domination. Although Çatalhöyük occurs towards the end of this seminal period, the detail of the excavated remains and the richness of the site do allow us to understand more fully what it meant to live in an early settled agricultural town. This book will also be about the theories which purport to make sense of the shift of societies to an agricultural settled life in the Middle East and Turkey.

The essence of a new approach that I wish to explore takes us back to the mysteries of the elaborate symbolism at Çatalhöyük. We have already seen that by comparing the depictions of animals in the art with the numbers of actual animal bones found on the site, we can gain a glimpse into a set of beliefs that seem to focus on wild animals. Despite the fact that Çatalhöyük occurred well after the initial domestication of plants and animals, and despite its economic dependence on domesticated plants and animals, the symbolism focuses on wild animals. The contrast between the symbolic focus on wild animals like the leopard, and the lack of symbolism surrounding the domestic sheep is stark.

Throughout centuries of attempts to explain the origins of agriculture, an event-like set of causal connections has been sought. Thus climatic or technological change led to population increase and thus to agriculture and settled villages. Different authors give different weight to these different factors, but always there is an event-like causal sequence. Over recent decades, more emphasis has been placed on the non-determinant interaction between several variables – multilinear and multicausal processes. But even in these there remains something of an event-like causality.

Another type of causality is social, especially when people argue that the whole process is pushed along by increased political centralization and power. Certainly this has an important role, but many have recognized that there must be wider changes for inequality to be sought and tolerated. There must be wider changes in everything from the technological to the conceptual to allow these things to happen – changes in a way of life in a more general sense.

Recent detailed work at Çatalhöyük allows us to see how people were living. We see how their daily activities were gradually changing as part of a wider process that I will come to describe as 'distributed' – that is the process was dispersed through many different areas of life. This set of changes did not just involve events such as climate change and more intensive plant gathering or increased social ranking. It also involved how one cooked, slept, ate, defecated. It involved how one understood time, how one related to others, how one related to the spirit world and to animals. Each small event, however mundane, contributed to an overall process that was thoroughly distributed. But more than just 'distributed' it was also 'orientated' – it involved looking at and being in the world in a certain way. Thus it was a 'discourse' that was built up from the tiny movements that make the millennial changes we identify as the 'origins of agriculture'.

Using the data I will try and describe this discourse and explore how it was built up from multiple small acts that led to the way of life we see at Çatalhöyük. I will also argue that it began in the Upper Palaeolithic and continued on into later periods – a long slow flow of change in which no particular event or act was significant – rather all acts were. This is a prehistory of the mass.

I will also argue that it was almost unnoticed. This may seem a strange claim for such a major event in human history. But many archaeologists have come to accept that the changes previously termed the 'Neolithic revolution' were spread over a very long period of time. Work on the genetic changes associated with the domestication of plants and animals has suggested that some of these were swift – but also that they could have occurred without intentionality, as an offshoot of other processes. This is all part of the 'distributed' idea. But in particular, Çatalhöyük shows that at least some people in society placed great social emphasis on hunting and gathering even millennia after the first plants and animals were domesticated in the Middle East. The art at Çatalhöyük, plentiful as it is, makes little reference to domesticated plants and animals. It shows an over-riding concern with wild plants and animals. So I will argue that this great revolution was produced by people whose social concerns were mainly about obtaining and distributing wild resources. Çatalhöyük covers a small and quite late part of this process, occurring well after the first farmers and the first settled villages in the Middle East and Turkey, but the detailed understanding of daily life and symbolism at the site allows a new insight into the slow, long-term processes that preceded Çatalhöyük and followed on from it.

Most of the chapters that follow this prologue deal with the details of daily life and symbolism in Çatalhöyük. They attempt to understand the mysteries of the site. But having reached a level of understanding from all the detail, it will be possible to return in Chapter 11 to the larger picture of how the richness of information from the site allows us to reconsider some of the major debates about the Neolithic.

My goals in this book are to understand some of the puzzles of Çatalhöyük (such as the contrasts between the depictions of animals and the faunal remains) as a way of making sense of what life was like at the site, and what it was like to be a person there 9,000 years ago. In doing so, I also aim to provide a perspective on the long-term processes that lead up to and follow on from the start of domestication, settled life and the formation of large complex sites in the Middle East.

CHRONOLOGIES OF THE FIRST FARMERS IN THE MIDDLE EAST
The Neolithic of the areas of the Middle East bordering the eastern
Mediterranean is conventionally divided into phases that were worked
out in the Levant. In broad terms, the long period of hunter-gatherers
in the Ice Age or Pleistocene ended in Upper Palaeolithic and then
Epipalaeolithic cultures with distinctive types of stone tools, and
some tendencies towards aggregations of small groups and a more
sedentary lifestyle. By the time of the Natufian culture in the Levant
(dated from the 12th to 10th millennia BC) there were more settled
and larger villages with intensive exploitation of animals and plants
that were still morphologically wild. In the Levant, the Natufian is
followed by Pre-Pottery Neolithic (PPN) cultures which have
increasing evidence of dependence on domesticated plants and
animals and sites become large and sedentary. These cultures are
normally divided into phases PPNA (approximately 9300 to 8400 BC),
PPNB (8500 to late 8th millennium BC), and PPNC (late 8th and early
7th millennia BC). Pottery is then introduced so that the Pottery
Neolithic (PN) begins in the early 7th millennium BC.

Attempts are often made to use this same chronological scheme in
neighbouring areas of the Middle East and Turkey, with varying
degrees of success and with varying degrees of adoption by local
archaeologists. In central Turkey attempts have been made to use a
similar scheme that separates an Aceramic Neolithic (at sites such
as Can Hasan III and Aşıklı Höyük and the early layers of Çatalhöyük)
from the Ceramic Neolithic (as seen in the main sequence of levels at
Çatalhöyük).

A map of the main sites in these periods is shown in Figure 4 and the
chronological positions of the sites and periods are shown in Figure 19.

Whether one uses the Levantine or the central Anatolian terminology it is clear that the Neolithic Çatalhöyük East Mound (7400–6000
BC) occurs towards the end of the Pre-Pottery or Aceramic phases,
but is mainly in the Pottery or Ceramic Neolithic. The Chalcolithic
Çatalhöyük West Mound has started by 6000 BC and continues into
the early 6th millennium BC.

CHAPTER ONE

A Journey Back Through Time, and Some Fellow Travellers

One way to approach the notion of a distant time is to use the trope of travel. The idea of time travel into the future has become commonplace, and Disneyland-type 'time cars' take one back in time at museums such as Jorvik, where one travels back to a frozen moment in Viking York. Visitors to Colonial Williamsburg in America are met by people dressed in another time. There are also academic texts that discuss how people travel to the past as if to another country.[1]

Overplayed as this idea of time travel to the past has become, I think it is a useful device. So let us take a trip in a time car to the destination Çatalhöyük 9,000 years ago. And let us concentrate on how the daily ways we live our lives have changed. And we can think of it as travelling back to the generations that have come before us. If we take a generation as about 25 years, then to travel back 9,000 years – in fact to 7400 BC when Çatalhöyük began – we will have to travel back 376 generations.

But it will be enough to start with our own grandparents' time. I only knew my father's parents, and they certainly seemed from a different world. Born at the end of the 19th century, they talked in a very clipped and formal way, and had a whole series of attitudes about how one should behave that seemed quaint and out of place in my world at the end of the 20th century. In fact it is well recognized that many aspects of how we see ourselves have changed since then. Ideas of self, intimacy, and emotion have changed.[2] For example, I was taught by my mother and grandparents not to think of myself – and indeed I felt rather uncomfortable as a young person seeing an image of myself in a mirror. After the 'me' generations such attitudes do seem quaint and anachronistic.

But as we go even further back – to my grandparents' great-great-grandparents at the start of the 19th century, we see even greater change. As the historian Michel Foucault's work has shown us, the ways people lived changed dramatically in the late 18th and early 19th centuries. For example, before that time in France Foucault describes public executions in which people were tortured and dismembered in the streets in ways that today we find stomach-turning. And yet by the mid-19th century prisoners were being treated humanely and public torture had come to be seen as unacceptable in France. What had seemed quite appropriate in the 18th century, had come to be seen as contrary to the rights of individuals in the 19th century. Today most countries in the west think that even the idea of the death penalty for murder is heinous and unacceptable. How much things have changed over just eight generations.

So onwards back to earlier generations and we find ways of living that seem even more bizarre and unacceptable. Another historian, Norbert Elias, has catalogued the numerous ways in which behaviour changed from the medieval to the post-medieval period in Europe.[3] So let us look back to the 13th century in England. This is still only 30 generations ago, but the differences are stark – in the most basic aspects of life. Elias shows, for example, how spitting, flatulence and belching happened at dinner. I can remember spittoons in trains in England when I was a boy. And it could be argued that a certain amount of passing of air has returned as acceptable in some quarters today! But on the whole, Elias shows how such behaviour gradually came to be seen as unacceptable. The very way in which our bodies work has changed. This is what I mean by saying that the ways in which we live our lives have changed. Of course, there has been the introduction of new technologies, from the car to the aeroplane, but it is also basic concepts about the self, the body and how to behave that have changed radically. To be in your body was quite a different experience 30 generations ago.

Similar points can be made about the Roman and Greek worlds – different attitudes to children, to the gods, to death, and so on – and yet we are still less than a quarter of the way to our destination. We know much about the ancient Egyptians 3,000–5,000 years ago, their very different views of life, death, self, 'marriage', love and so on. And we can read the first writing in Mesopotamia and learn of their myths and beliefs.[4] And still we have 4,000 years to go. We step out into the open expanses of prehistory. With the later prehistoric civilizations of the Middle East we can still say a lot about how they lived their lives. As we go beyond them, into deeper prehistory, it is less easy to see clearly what life was like – and we still have 3,000 years to go of this deeper prehistory before we get to Çatalhöyük. And then finally we come to Çatalhöyük, our destination, 9,400 years ago and 376 generations back. Here there is a bit of light, an insight into another world. We can suddenly see again, however dimly. This book is the story of what we can see.

I have emphasized the differences and the strangeness as we travel back and meet earlier generations. I am talking about a very long time ago. But of course there would also be things that we recognize. People had to eat, defecate, have children, punish wrong-doing and so on, just as we have to do today. People had to build houses, wear clothes to keep warm, make weapons to kill animals, harvest the crops and so on. But I have tried to emphasize that even though people may have been doing things we recognize, they 'lived' in a very different world in that they saw that world differently and made sense of it in different ways. They even felt differently in their own bodies. Let me give one final example. I get a very strong 'tingle factor' when I listen to 19th-century Romantic music played by a large orchestra – music written by composers from Beethoven to Mahler. And that sense of the Romantic is a very important part of my outlook on the world. I do not get that particular tingle at the base of my spine in any other context. So my sense of myself and my body is at least partly dependent on the invention of certain types of instrument and large orchestras and on the emergence of composers for those orchestras in the 19th century. I do not think I could have that bodily sensation without that technology and set of circumstances. I couldn't be 'me' prior to the 19th century. Of course there are aspects of me and my physical body that are the same as the 19th century, or any earlier century since the appearance of anatomically modern humans, but the way of being in the world and how I experience my body, that is my embodiment, have changed.

It would be wrong to assume that as we travel back in time things get more and more different – just because of the difference in time. We cannot assume some linear evolutionary process. But if ways of feeling and living are related at least partly to technologies, as in the orchestra example, then ways of living would have been very different in the ancient technologies used by our forebears 376 generations ago, before the wheel, before domesticated cattle, before metal tools, and before the use of wool.

In this book I want to show how we can gain some glimpse of how different it was to be a person inhabiting Çatalhöyük. I want to try and take you there so that you also can get some sense of what it was like to be there. Working at Çatalhöyük is tantalizing. The preservation is good because of the infilling of abandoned houses. The frequent replastering of walls and floors in houses traps traces of earlier activity. Even some cloth fabric is preserved in burials, and there are the traces of baskets, wooden containers, and the impressions of mats on the floors. All this makes people feel that they can almost touch the past – really travel there and collapse time; come face to face with our 376th ancestor (Figure 7). It is partly this that draws so many people to this remarkable site. And yet, it all

7 Face to face with our 376th ancestor – this plastered skull is one of the most remarkable new finds from Çatalhöyük. It was coated in several layers of plaster, each of which had been painted red.

seems so strange, so unfamiliar – even disturbing. People seem to have slept on the platforms where their parents and grandparents were buried. What strange attitudes to the dead must have existed to allow this? And sometimes they dug down and cut off the head of a relative and kept it. Certainly we may know of our parents or grandparents, or we may have heard of people, that kept the ashes of their kin in an urn on the mantelpiece, but this seems a long way from sleeping just above the rotting remains and then cutting off and keeping the head. How can we begin to make sense of such very different behaviour?

They brought in the skulls of vultures and stuck them in their house walls, looking into the interior space. They did the same for weasel and fox teeth and the tusks of wild boar. They brought in the horns of wild bulls and placed them in installations on walls. And of course, they depicted leopards or other wild cats. Why depict these dangerous wild animals in the house? And why cover the abdomens of some bodies buried beneath the floors in carnivore excrement? Emma Jenkins who has done her PhD on the microfauna from the site, has studied the excrement and I will discuss such cases further in Chapter 8. She found that the material sometimes placed over the body had been digested and excreted by some sort of small carnivore, perhaps including a weasel. The excretions or scat contained large numbers of small mammal teeth and bones – such as the teeth of the mouse which had been hunted and consumed. Is there some parallel here with the weasel and fox teeth brought into the house and placed on the walls? How can we begin to make sense of such things?

But there is also a danger – that we impose on our destination ideas that we bring from our own world. When things look familiar, we have a tendency to assume they really are comprehensible. One of the challenges of travel to distant times and places is to be sensitive to difference and to be critical of the assumptions we too easily make in confronting other worlds. I have often found when working at Çatalhöyük that people easily jump to conclusions. They assume people must have been disgusted sleeping just above their dead, or that they must have felt cramped living in these small rooms, without recognizing that other people, including other people in contemporary societies today, can have very different attitudes to the dead and to space than are found in developed Western nations.

In 2004 I came across a particularly good example of this tendency to jump to anachronistic conclusions. In a foundation grave beneath a platform floor in Building 42 we discovered a skull that had been removed from its body and on which some facial features had been modelled (Figure 7). The skull was held in the arms of a complete female skeleton. I will discuss this interesting case in Chapters 6 and 9, but for the moment what is of relevance is that most people, when viewing this burial scene, expressed a sense of empathy. They interpreted the scene in terms of some sort of romantic attachment between a woman and a relative or someone close to her. It was assumed that the woman had 'kept' the lost person as a plastered skull – and that she had wanted to be buried with that person. This interpretation in terms of loss, sentiment and nostalgia is very much a product of the modern era in the West. Most of these ideas, at least in the terms we understand them, are relatively recent historical products.[5] In Chapter 6 I will use all the available evidence to provide a very different reading of this evidence – one that situates the plastered skull in the context of lineage status and ancestry. In this reading, the skull gives power to the woman. In our journey back in time we need to be suspicious of our assumptions and sensitive to the radical differences that we find.

One way of helping us to see such differences is to study present-day or recent societies that have similarities with Çatalhöyük. Thus we might compare Çatalhöyük which is distant from us in time, with a society living today in Africa which is distant from us in terms of space and technology. Here we are assuming that travel over space is similar to travel through time. As anthropologists have shown,[6] it is wrong to assume that travel to countries designated by some as 'less-developed' is equivalent to travel backwards in time. The use of ethnography is dangerous if it implies that some people have stopped in time. Contemporary non-western or 'less-developed' societies too have been going through their journeys over the last 9,000 years. They are not frozen or static. Also, most large settlements in contemporary non-Western societies have been influenced by capitalism, and so parallels with the pre-capitalist past are difficult.

And yet there may be similarities between past and contemporary societies based on factors such as size and level of technology and environment. North American pueblos are a possible parallel with Çatalhöyük (Figure 8). These are agglomerated settlements with activities on roofs, but the social system seems to be rather different in that there are ritual buildings or kivas separate from houses. Large agglomerated settlements or towns occurred and occur in West Africa, but they are usually linked to trade and/or imperial contact. For example, the Dogon settlements in Mali in West Africa look quite similar to Çatalhöyük in their bustling density (Figure 9), and the arrangement of the architecture has been studied from an archaeological point of view by Paul Lane.[7] But there are many differences from Çatalhöyük. For example, Dogon houses are separate, storage is large scale, food is prepared collectively, and buildings are used in sequence – in other words there are different types of buildings and one uses different buildings at different times as one moves through the life cycle. And of course there are many other differences in social system, religious belief, technology and so on.

For me, an experience that was important in influencing my interpretation of Çatalhöyük was fieldwork that I did amongst the Nuba in Sudan in the late 1970s and early 1980s.[8] Here round houses are grouped around covered courtyards. As one steps into the courtyard space through narrow entrances from the outside, one's eyes gradually become used to the dark and the smoke. The fire in the courtyard gives some light and slowly one becomes aware of elaborate painted and relief art on the

8 Taos Pueblo in the American Southwest in 1900. Although entrances were in side walls, the overall aspect of the pueblo may be compared to a part of Çatalhöyük.

9 A large and densely clustered Dogon village in Mali, West Africa.

walls (Figure 10). There are even the horns and skulls of animals. All Mesakin Nuba compounds have such art, which is also found on bodies, calabashes (gourds), and so on. This experience showed me that elaborate art could be part of daily domestic life. In this way the Mesakin Nuba look rather like Çatalhöyük, but there are also radical differences. The Nuba 'villages' are dispersed amongst the agricultural fields, and there are very large grain stores showing a heavy dependence on intensive agriculture. Each house and space in a compound cluster has a different function (storage, food preparation, eating, sleeping), showing a degree of specialization not found at Çatalhöyük – and of course house entry is at ground level.

Throughout the book I have used a lot of quotations from the anthropologist Raymond Firth's work on the Tikopia[9] – a society far from Çatalhöyük in time and space, located in what is now Polynesia. This is a small-scale society of some 1,200 people on an island, with simple hoe agriculture, and with loose villages. Kinship is an important aspect of social life, domestic production predominates, and people live in independent domestic houses with the dead buried below the floor (Figure 11). Residence is patrilocal and descent is patrilineal (that is, people live amongst and reckon their descent through the father's family line), but affiliation through the female line is important. There are larger kinship groupings and clans in which cohesion depends primarily on the tie of recognized descent from common ancestors. Its members may be spread out through various residential units – but they are linked back through ancestry to ancestral house sites.

10 Symbolism on house walls inside a Mesakin Nuba courtyard in Sudan. The two horns were for holding a pot of water for washing or showering. The courtyards are covered and it is normally difficult to see the paintings and installations. The paintings include images of frightening beings and objects.

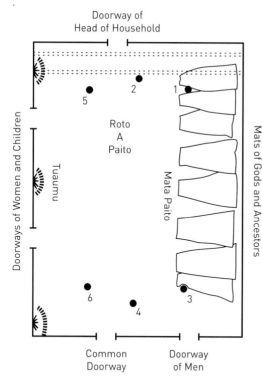

Doorway of
Head of Household

Roto
A
Paito

Mata Paito

Mats of Gods and Ancestors

Doorways of Women and Children

Tuaumu

5

2

1

6

4

3

Common
Doorway

Doorway
of Men

11 Drawing by New Zealand anthropologist Raymond Firth of the interior ground plan of a Tikopia house. From his work on the island in the 1920s, he was able to identify six different focus points within the house: 1) a post for offering; 2) the seat of the chief (the titular head); 3) the seat of a guest; 4) the seat of the eldest son (the head of the house); 5) the seat of a younger son; and 6) the seat of a son or guest. Ancestors are buried below the mats to the right.

We do not know whether society at Çatalhöyük was patrilocal and patrilineal. I will discuss some evidence to suggest that both patrilineal and matrilineal descent may have been important. But certainly many of the other aspects of this brief description of the Tikopia suggest strong similarities with Çatalhöyük. There are, as ever, also many differences, such as the greater role of centralized authority and chiefs in Tikopia, their heavier dependence on agriculture, their dispersed villages, larger houses and smaller society.[10]

Nevertheless, I have been struck by the way in which Firth's account of the Tikopia often seems to illustrate my interpretations based on the Çatalhöyük data. The ethnographic depth and detail he provides seem to add to the archaeological picture. So I have provided excerpts from Firth's accounts throughout this book. The aim of these is not to draw precise parallels, not to strengthen my argument through analogy. I have simply wanted to illustrate the types of behaviour that are found in small-scale societies like Çatalhöyük and the Tikopia, especially as so many people find some of the evidence at Çatalhöyük, like burial beneath floors, so very strange. By referring to cases like the Tikopia where burial beneath the floors is routine, it may be easier to envisage the Çatalhöyük data. So I have used the excerpts from Firth to provoke and for contemplation.

There is extensive use of wild resources at Çatalhöyük – from wild cattle to wild boar, deer, equids, bear, as well as wild plants, birds, bird eggs and fish. In interpreting Çatalhöyük I have also used ideas from hunter-gatherer societies. In particular, I have made use of the work of David Lewis-Williams on the San Bushmen of southern Africa. Lewis-Williams claims that his work has applicability to many hunter-gatherer ideological systems. He has also used his knowledge of the San and shamanistic practices to make quite specific interpretations of the Neolithic world and the art at Çatalhöyük.[11] He shows how the art at the site can be seen in terms of a three-tier cosmos, and that the installations on the walls of the houses can be understood in terms of the movement of animal spirits from the lower world through the house walls and into the house. Shamanic practices may facilitate the movements between daily life and the world of spirit animals. For example, they may assist the flow of power from the sacred eland (or bull in the Çatalhöyük case) to people in their daily lives, or they may provide knowledge of sacrifice and ritual that can ward off the anger of the animal spirits.

Çatalhöyük appears dimly through these comparisons. Parallels can be drawn, but understandably there are always differences. In this book I will use such comparisons to open up the past to more possibilities than might exist in our own Western imaginations. The site and its art have too often been interpreted in terms of later civilizations such as in Egypt or Classical Greece and the Aegean (as in the use of the term Cybele for the figurines of women). As we have seen, there is a very long period of time between Çatalhöyük and these historical societies. We need to branch out and look at alternative models. But in the end we have to try and understand our destination in its own terms.

I have so far been talking about using very specific ethnographic parallels for Çatalhöyük. But it is also possible to use general anthropological understanding – that is, the conclusions used by anthropologists who have studied and compared a large number of societies and developed general theories. It is always necessary to be critical of such generalizations and to contextualize them in the specific data from the site. But they remain important in stimulating ideas and thoughts about the deep past. I will use such generalizations throughout the book, but one example concerns interpretation of the violence which seems just beneath the surface in much of the Çatalhöyük art. However much the leopard or feline might be tamed by the woman with her hands on its head (Plate 24), it remains an animal of violence. It kills its prey by sinking its canines behind the wind pipe and asphyxiating the animal. It then has to compete with hyaenas or wild dogs that might approach, and it pulls the carcass up a tree to consume it. The leopard is only one of the wild, dangerous or carnivorous animals that seem so central to the Çatalhöyük art, as they are to the art of earlier sites such as Göbekli.[12] As previously outlined, there are examples at Çatalhöyük of vulture skulls being placed in walls, as if protruding out from them, as well as the tusks of wild boar (Figure 12), the teeth of fox and weasel, and the claws of bear placed in walls or plaster features.

One person whose general thinking on the symbolism of powerful violent animals may be useful is Georges Bataille.[13] His work seems particularly useful for archaeologists since he engaged in a detailed interpretation of Palaeolithic art – which again focuses on wild animals. In his work on violence, sex and death, Bataille argues that there are moments of transcendence. He notes the frequent links

12 Hand paintings and protuberances on the wall in 'Shrine VI.8'. When James Mellaart removed the protuberances he discovered that the lower jaws of wild boars were set within them.

between violence, sex and death and suggests that one link is that each of these involve moments in which there are movements away from the here and now. Such movements beyond everyday experience allow humans to cope with the restraints and limitations of social life. They create a sense of timeless unity that can be used in ritual to create social bonds and a sense of social commitment. The link between violence and death is seen at Çatalhöyük in the imagery of vultures associated with headless corpses. Even if the immediate role of these images was in terms of shamanism or travel between worlds, for Bataille there is a deeper meaning associated with the construction of society and coping with restraint. Bataille's writing seems initially attractive as it appears to make sense of the role of violent imagery as people settled into large villages. However, his view often seems rather inadequately reductionist – there is clearly more to the violent art than simply its function to help deal with constraint.

Another approach to this issue is provided by anthropologist Maurice Bloch in his book *Prey into Hunter: The Politics of Religious Experience.*[14] Bloch explores the role of violence in ritual across a wide range of different societies. He takes a rather different stance to Bataille's philosophical explorations, one that relates violence more satisfactorily to the political and social context.

As many have argued, ritual often involves inversion, turning things inside out in some 'other' world 'beyond'. Ritual often involves going to such a place and then returning. Bloch particularly concerns himself with initiation, where the initiate

13 A stag is surrounded by bearded men in this wall-painting from a building excavated in the 1960s. The deer is large in relation to the smaller human figures, who seem to be pulling the tail, tongue and snout of the animal, and otherwise arousing or annoying it.

returns into a different stage of life, and he is concerned with the way in which initiation often involves a symbolic 'killing' of the initiates. So rather than birth leading to growth and further reproduction, movement to a new stage in life is achieved through violence, death and rebirth.

Bloch argues that this violence is a necessary part of the movement into another world. He sees most human societies as understanding that there is a permanent framework to social life that transcends the natural transformative processes of birth, growth, reproduction, ageing and death. The violence and symbolic killing takes the initiate beyond process into permanent entities such as descent groups. By leaving this life, it is possible to see oneself and others as part of something permanent and life-transcending.

He goes on to argue that the vitality that is gained on the return from this transcendental state is often obtained from outside beings, usually animals; and that, having become part of permanent institutions, the initiate returns in conquest, perhaps involving also consumption.

All this fits remarkably well with Çatalhöyük. The scenes of bearded young men teasing or baiting wild animals (e.g. Figure 13) can be linked to the evidence of trophies (skulls and horns of cattle, tusks of wild boar, antler of deer) from the animals in the houses. Such teasing and baiting could well be part of initiation ceremonies, and the trophies could well represent both the movement into another world and an incorporation into the descent groups that seem so central to Çatalhöyük life, as we shall see. And we shall see evidence that the consumption of wild bulls was an important component of feasting.

These ethnographic, anthropological, even philosophical ruminations help us to make sense of the strangeness and 'otherness' of our deep-time destination. They provide ways of thinking about Çatalhöyük even if, in the end, we have to try and understand the site in its own terms and allow its radical difference to have an impact on us. Our concepts of violence, for example, are particularly rooted in our own traditions. Not all deaths are violent, and many wild animals may not be seen as violent in ways that we might presume. It is important to use ethnographic data carefully and critically, and to be cautious in applying general ideas and assumptions to Çatalhöyük.

But one of the things that is so distinctive about travel, is that one's fellow travellers often seem to get such different experiences out of destinations. They get absorbed by quite different things, notice different things, feel affronted by different things. And much the same is true of time travel. Here again, different groups of people in the present get very different experiences out of their interaction with the past. We need to recognize that the past is seen differently by different communities and it has different values for them. It is becoming increasingly important in archaeology, museums and heritage to realize that the Western scientific archaeological community has to have dialogue with and interact with these divergent communities. In what follows I want to show how travel to Çatalhöyük needs to be a shared experience, one in which different views and perspectives are accommodated. Indeed the development of scientific knowledge about Çatalhöyük needs to engage with the interests of various communities. In what follows I will discuss the different communities and stakeholders with an interest in the site, and show how the various themes in the book have partly come about through interaction with these different groups.

FELLOW TRAVELLERS: THE COMMUNITIES INTERESTED IN ÇATALHÖYÜK

The Turkish public interest in Çatalhöyük has never ceased to amaze me. Whenever we hold a press day at the site, up to 50 newspapers and television channels send their reporters and photographers. They swarm over the site and write lengthy articles, and still come back for more. The international press is less evident, but every year we have several television companies, from Canada to Australia, making films or documentaries in some way. Of course, there is undoubtedly a good story. There is the fascination with burial beneath the floors. Or the wonderment that people should have their entrances in their roofs. Or the story of the powerful imagery of women. Or the vultures picking flesh from headless corpses. All this radical difference of a distant time makes the site endlessly fascinating, and the journey worthwhile. In addition, there is all the excitement of the discovery of the site by James Mellaart in the 1960s, and his colourful personality. And then there is the presence of a large multinational team to report. Underlying all this for Turkey is the reputation of the site as the origin of Anatolian civilization, expressed clearly in the main museum in Turkey in Ankara, and in numerous publications.

The media interest in the site is certainly one of the factors that attracts some of the communities that have an interest in how it is managed and interpreted. For the first group which I will mention as having an interest in Çatalhöyük, this media focus is crucial. Politicians show a special engagement with the site since, at press events, they are able to gain wide media coverage. Of course, they each have their different claims to make, but for all, the pay-off is publicity in the context of an international project working at one of the most important early sites in Turkey. I wish to limit this discussion to two contrasting groups of politicians – the local regional politicians and the European politicians. As we will see, they use the site in very different ways. To what extent can the archaeology engage in a dialogue with such political interests? To what extent can it respond to the questions the politicians raise?

Çatalhöyük is situated one hour southeast of Konya in central Turkey, in a region known for its religious fundamentalist and/or nationalist politics. It is also a centre for Islamic companies and traditional rural Islamic attitudes towards women regarding social and economic behaviour. When politicians such as the local mayor (from Çumra, the local town), or governor, give talks in front of the press at the site, they talk about the importance of the locality and the region. The name Çatalhöyük has been appropriated by the local town and village. They say that the presence of Çatalhöyük demonstrates the special nature of the region. Of course, they admit that the site is pre-Turk and pre-Islamic, but they nevertheless say that it shows the importance of the land and its traditions. They point also to the international character of the project and the visitors it attracts. Again this shows the importance of the region. Some try at times to make links to the migrations of the Turks themselves (for example that the people of Çatalhöyük were Turks who then moved to central Asia before returning in the historical migrations), but most are content with rather vaguer connections between past and present.

There is undoubtedly a political and local interest in the question 'who were the people that lived at Çatalhöyük?'. Local people ask us this question all the time. 'Were they related to us?'. To what extent can archaeologists respond to this question? One obvious contemporary method is through ancient DNA analysis. The human burials discovered in the excavations at Çatalhöyük have been the subject of two ancient DNA projects. The first was undertaken by the Leeuwen laboratory in

Belgium, and the second by Stanford University.[15] So far this work has only been able to suggest that there may be some ancient DNA present in the human bones. Much more and very intensive study will be needed before anything can be said about the similarities between the ancient and modern populations in central Turkey.

There clearly is considerable local interest in trying to understand the genetic links between Çatalhöyük and present-day populations, and so the project will continue to try to find ways of continuing this ancient DNA research. Another response would be to focus on historical studies which show how the local villages in the Çatalhöyük-Çumra area are made up of migrants from the Balkans, and such research is part of ethnoarchaeological work being carried out by Nurcan Yalman[16] (Figure 14). Yet another response is to show ways in which Çatalhöyük is part of a regional tradition. It has long been assumed that the agricultural revolution spread through Anatolia and Europe after originating in the Fertile Crescent. Contemporary versions of this view will be discussed below. But recent comparative research by the Turkish archaeologist Mehmet Özdoğan[17] has suggested the importance of regional continuities in central Anatolia. Certainly the evidence from Çatalhöyük shows connections across a wider zone reaching into the Levant and middle Mesopotamia. For example, a hard lime plaster is used on the floors in the earliest levels of Çatalhöyük and such floors have parallels in the PPNB in the

14 Local ethnoarchaeological research in the Konya area is being carried out by Nurcan Yalman. Especially in the hill villages, roofs are used for a wide range of activities.

Levant. Plate 18 (see also Figures 87 and 110) shows a relief figure with upraised arms and legs. Similar depictions are found at Göbekli (Figure 89) and Köşk Höyük. And more generic traits such as the bull heads and female figurines and burials beneath floors are widely found. Plastered skulls from Çatalhöyük and Köşk Höyük recall those from the Levant. On the other hand, Özdoğan points to distinctly regional traits in central Anatolia such as the lack of centralized author-ity.[18] There are undoubtedly distinctive characteristics of the Çatalhöyük evidence that suggest a local process of development, even if influenced by the Middle East.

Such evidence says nothing, of course, about the continuity between the past and the present, but it reinforces the interests of local politicians in the distinctive contributions of their region. As archaeologists we have to resist, however, those politicians who wish to take the evidence towards an extreme interpretation in terms of cultural or racial superiority. The archaeological and historical evidence indicates a long period of cultural mixing between local traditions and outside influence. Even the DNA evidence will not resolve the issues of 'who we are', since answers to that question are as much social, cultural and historical as they are genetic. The important point is that archaeologists are able to enter into a debate with local politicians about issues in which they show a prime concern.

From time to time, a very different type of politician visits Çatalhöyük. For example, the Ambassador of the European Union makes very different speeches when he speaks to the press at the site. His aim is to speak to those in Turkey who, in contrast to the nationalist politicians, wish to take Turkey into the European Union. The Ambassador talks of the fact that there was no boundary between Europe and Asia at the time of Çatalhöyük. He refers to the evidence we have dis-cussed with him for cultural contacts between central Anatolia and southeast Europe in the Neolithic. He is fascinated when we describe to him the work of Colin Renfrew[19] on the spread of Indo-European languages and on the relation-ship between that language dispersal and the spread of farming from Anatolia into Europe. He takes this as proof of his view that 'originally' Turkey was part of Europe, and he seems less interested when we say that many archaeologists take the view that there are difficulties with the notion of a large-scale spread of Indo-Europeans associated with the spread of agriculture. We point out the evidence, described above, for regional sequences, but he looks at the evidence through his own political lenses.

It does seem possible, then, to direct archaeological research so that it responds to, interacts with and counteracts issues raised by local politicians. Indeed, I would claim an ethical duty to respond not simply because of responsibility towards one's hosts, but also because the politicians use the distant past to make claims about origins and identities. These claims need to be tempered by the archaeological evi-dence, or at least the archaeologist needs to provide the opportunity for competing

15 Schoolchildren as well as tourists are frequent visitors to the Visitor Centre at Çatalhöyük.

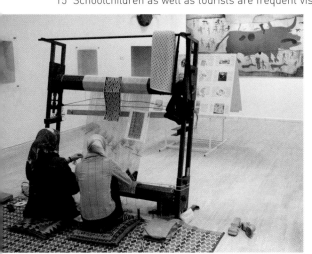

16 (left) Kilim production takes place in the Visitor Centre.
17 (right) The local community is involved in post-excavation study at the site.

points of view to be taken up. The site and the data that are made known by the archaeologist will be used in one way or another to support political claims – in my view it is unethical for the archaeologists to wash their hands of this process and to remain disengaged.

The central political interest in Çatalhöyük is the nation state of Turkey. The national guardianship of the site is in the hands of the Ministry of Culture and Tourism, and the primary concern is preservation. One central aim of the project, developed in consultation with Turkish officials, is to provide the Turkish Ministry of Culture and Tourism with a well-planned heritage site. This was certainly one of the main reasons that led to the decision to allow renewed work at the site in the 1990s. During the 30 years after the first excavations had been stopped in the 1960s, the excavation trenches were left exposed and the mud-brick walls and plaster had suffered severe damage. Although protected by a fence and guards, the site was of little interest to tourists and had no facilities. Since the original project had been British-based, the Turkish authorities felt that a new British project should restore the site. Certainly a central aim of the current project is that the site and its architecture should be properly conserved and protected, and that visitors should be able to experience the site in a number of ways. A site management plan has been completed funded by the European Union, and as a result of this the Turkish Ministry of Culture and Tourism is putting the site forward to the UNESCO World Heritage Site list. A conservation laboratory has been built and the latest techniques applied.[20] A long-term goal is that the conserved wall-paintings, sculptures, textiles, wooden and ceramic artifacts could be placed on display in an on-site museum. Some reconstructions of the paintings have been and will be placed back in conserved houses on the site. Parts of the site have been covered (Plate 4) so that the ancient houses are protected and so that visitors can gain some sense of walking around a Neolithic village. An interpretive Visitor Centre has been constructed as part of the on-site 'dig house' (Figure 15). By providing a range of visitor experiences the full heritage potential of the site can begin to be exploited.

Another important community with an interest in the site is the local farmers, village and town. The Turkish men and women who work on the project come mainly from the local village of Küçükköy (1 km (0.6 miles) from the site) and from the local town of Çumra (15 km (9.5 miles) from the site). They work in a variety of capacities from labourers to guards and guides to flotation assistants and heavy residue sorters. Increasingly the site has been visited by local people from other neighbouring villages and towns and from the regional centre at Konya. What types of questions are these stakeholders interested in, and how can we contribute to their interests in and understanding of the site?

Many of the local rural inhabitants are farmers with low incomes and limited education. Their knowledge about the site is obtained from primary school and from folk traditions. In general, they have little detailed knowledge of the history and prehistory of Turkey and the Konya region. Their interests in the site thus include more practical concerns, such as how to benefit economically from the project, the site and its tourists. A villager from Küçükköy has built a cafe and shop outside the entrance to the site, and the women from the village sell embroidered cloth at the dig house. We have started, in consultation with local groups, to develop a Çatalhöyük brand and to undertake craft production and training at the site (Figure 16). The project has also contributed to the digging of a new well and the provision of a new water supply. It has helped to persuade regional officials to build a new school in the village, and it has contributed a library to the village.

Finding out what the local communities want to know about Çatalhöyük is a specialized task and the ethnographers who work with us have been involved in various schemes to educate and engage the local communities in the site and the project. For example, Ayfer Bartu has given talks about the project in the village.[21] She has also assisted the women from the village to set up a community exhibit in the Visitor Centre at the dig house. In this exhibit, the women chose to concentrate on the plants that grow on the mound – these are important as herbs and medicines. Another perspective on the site is provided in a book manuscript written by Sedrettin Dural entitled 'Memoir of a Çatalhöyük Guard' (Çatalhöyük Bekçisinin Anıları). Sedrettin Dural worked at the site as a guard through much of the lifetime of the current project and publication of this book is awaited. The book presents a very different voice about the site and the project.

In 2001, a group of men and women from the village were asked to take part in our post-excavation studies (Figure 17). They were paid to contribute to discussions about the interpretation of the site, based on the most recent analytical results that were explained to them. These discussions were put on video and their comments have been used as verbatim quotes in the publication texts. The types of question to which they could most effectively contribute were those that related to the experiences and practices of living in the central Anatolian environment. Thus they were able to contribute to issues of how ovens of different shape and made of different clays could be used. They knew the effect of the dominant winds on the location of fireplaces in houses. They contributed to issues regarding the difficulties of life in the winter. One question that most interested them was 'why here?'. They were particularly interested in why this particular bit of land was chosen for the site. They were interested in the specifics of the locality, and how it was used for agriculture and food. Our answers to these questions are discussed in Chapter 3.

We can, then, attempt to answer some of the local questions about the site. But it is also important not to promote the view that somehow the local communities are distant in time, leftovers from prehistory. It is not surprising, perhaps, that the local farming community is most interested in locality and land use. But it would be wrong to assume that there is some continuous connection between past and present. Historically there has been much in and out migration. There has been massive social and cultural change over the last nine millennia. It would be wrong to assume that the local communities are an 'other' that is somehow closer to prehistory than 'we' are.[22] The local communities contribute to the project and ask questions of it that relate to their knowledge of the environment and its soils. They do not have some privileged knowledge based on cultural continuity. To claim that would be to 'museumize' the local communities. They are heavily involved in global processes (and some have lived as guest workers in Germany).

Another set of communities interested in the work of the project at the site focuses on the figurine shown in Plate 24 and on other female imagery. Groups on Goddess tours visit the site from the USA, Germany, Istanbul and elsewhere. They come to pray, hold circle dances, and feel the power of the Goddess. There is a great diversity of such groups from Gaia groups, to Ecofeminists, to Goddess New Age travellers. Individuals are often visibly moved by the experience of visiting and it is undoubtedly the case that for many the existence of the Goddess at Çatalhöyük is important for their personal sense of identity. The project has entered into dialogue with some members of the varied Goddess groups on its website, it has worked collaboratively to produce an exhibit in the Visitor Centre that responds to Goddess and spiritual interest in the site, and some of the research directions being taken result from these interactions.

One specific offshoot of the interest in the site from women's movements was a fashion show staged in Istanbul by Bahar Korçan, a Turkish/international dress designer. She based an exhibition on the theme of Çatalhöyük and 'women of other times'. The clothes were inspired by the site, the catwalk was 'in' a model of Çatalhöyük, and slides of the site and its art were shown in the background as part of a multimedia experience. In fact, the show was a major press and television event, with the top popular singer at the time, Tarkan, making an appearance. The press coverage extended globally, to France, Japan and beyond.

The varied Goddess groups with an interest in Çatalhöyük ask different questions of the site. Some take a strong line regarding the role of women in the past, arguing that women were dominant and that the society was peaceful and without violence. Others want simply to engage with the site from a spiritual and religious point of view. Others have an educated interest in the evidence for the role of women at the site 9,000 years ago.

It is not possible for archaeologists to contribute to the religious view that the Goddess is present at Çatalhöyük. But it is possible to try and respond to those women's groups that want to know about the role of women at the site. Was the European archaeologist Marija Gimbutas[23] right in arguing for a powerful position for women, even a matriarchy, at these early sites? Can we identify the roles of men and women? These issues are discussed in Chapter 9. Many followers of the Goddess have engaged in dialogue and have been able to see that new evidence can be incorporated into a revised perspective – for example, one in which women were powerful for reasons other than mothering and in which some equality existed in practice. Thus it is possible to ask questions that are of interest to particular groups, and then to enter into a dialogue that can contribute to changed perspectives on all sides.

The final interest group that I wish to introduce consists of a variety of artists. These again vary in terms of specific motivation and interest. They include those who create works or performances about the site at other venues, and those involved in installation art at the site. There is also some overlap with the Goddess groups as several of the artists are inspired by the notion that women at Çatalhöyük had a more powerful role than in contemporary society.

One example is Jale Yılmabaşar, an artist working in Istanbul. She held an exhibition of paintings in Istanbul that referred to paintings from the site. The pianist and composer Tuluyhan Uğurlu gave a concert in Istanbul inspired by Çatalhöyük. His music is popular and it mixes a variety of styles including Turkish motifs. He decided to write music about Çatalhöyük because of its global and New Age associations, but also because he came from Konya, the nearest city to the site. One of the main parts of the concert centred on a poem written by Reşit Ergener, a Turkish economist and tour guide, and co-organizer and leader of many of the Goddess tours to Çatalhöyük. The concert also used slides and images taken from the project website. The music acted as a 'frame' around the slides, which he watched as he played and partly improvised to.

Örge Tulga, who had a gallery exhibit of her gold and silver jewelry on display in Istanbul in 2002, explained how her designs were inspired by and based on the art of Çatalhöyük, especially the Goddess imagery. She also said how much she wanted to visit the site: 'I want to come and feel the atmosphere. I want to live there a little.' The 'atmosphere' referred to here is partly spiritual. This linking of performance, art and spirituality at the site itself is seen particularly in the work of Adrienne Momi. Again an organizer of Goddess tours, and based in California, she has constructed installation art at a number of prehistoric sites in Europe. In 2001 she made a spiral at Çatalhöyük. She worked closely with the archaeological team, learning about the current interpretations of the site. She engaged local people and schoolchildren in her art – which involved making paper on site, then making stamps based on the art from the site, and then printing these designs onto the paper and sticking the paper on a large paper spiral laid out on the grass slope of the Neolithic mound. She was careful to get official permission and throughout worked in a consensual way. The spiral and the art were meant to provide a channel of communication with the subconscious of the site. She called her installation *Turning through time: communication with the distant past at Çatalhöyük*.

There are various ways in which artists can be engaged in the archaeological project. Another example involves the artists employed by the project itself to illustrate the finds and architecture. John Swogger has been working as an on-site archaeological illustrator at Çatalhöyük since 1998. He adamantly identifies himself as an illustrator rather than an artist, but as an illustrator who is pushing the rigid boundaries of archaeological illustration.[24] By defying the strict, but what he sees as artificial, boundaries between the media considered to be the domain of the 'artists' and the domain of 'the archaeological illustrators', he suggests that all these media can be seen as a 'tool - a mechanism or process for recording and presenting archaeological information in visual form'. He also argues that such an expansion and broadening of the definition of what archaeological illustration is gives the illustrator the freedom to embrace different types of media and styles that will enable exploration of different aspects of archaeological information. What he does is to create reconstructions based on the evidence provided by different specialists at the site. These sketches, drawings and reconstructions provide means of visualizing various findings, interpretations, hypotheses and theories. As Swogger points out, 'combined with a process of exploring new modes of visual expression and looking carefully at the way "art" can illustrate the data of "science", there could be here the potential for creating a powerful and important tool for managing on-site interpretation and analysis.'[25] His illustrations and reconstructions have been integrated within the recording, analysis, and public presentation of the findings from the site. Several examples are reproduced in this book.

Another artist, Nessa Leibhammer, also works as an illustrator, but she uses more straightforward artistic conventions and does not attempt to use detailed measured drawings.[26] She feels that the 'scientific' codified drawings do not capture the full sense of what is seen. Her more interpretive and aesthetic drawings complement the more scientific depictions. In contrast to Swogger's illustrations, Leibhammer's images are artistic and personal interpretive drawings that focus on the visible, physical aspects of archaeology such as walls, rooms and spaces, rather than reconstructions that attempt to incorporate all the evidence from the site. But her drawings have also enriched and become part of the archaeological archive of Çatalhöyük. Her drawings and paintings provide a fuller sense of depth and volume in the complex wall plasters, and they are more successful at this than the measured line drawings.

So, one way of involving artists in the archaeological project is to engage them in the process of recording and expression. But another response is to attempt to answer the questions they ask about the role of 'art' at Çatalhöyük 9,000 years ago. The artists bring their contemporary assumptions about aesthetics, framing and specialist production. And yet can we talk about the symbolism at Çatalhöyük in these terms? Was this 'art' at all? And what was the role of the 'art' – how can we interpret it? Our engagement with these issues is discussed in Chapter 8.

In a globalized world, archaeologists increasingly work with multiple communities. I have tried to provide examples of some of the problems and issues that are raised in such a context. I have tried to suggest that rather than archaeologists just setting their own agenda, going on their own journey to the past, it is possible to negotiate research questions with a number of fellow travellers. It is possible to collaborate with these groups in relation to the answers given and the interpretations made. At times the interactions may be difficult, and the travellers may feel a need to part company. I am very aware at Çatalhöyük that there are many tensions. For example, the Goddess groups have attitudes to the roles of women that seem diametrically opposed to the religiously informed attitudes of the local Konya community. There are potential tensions between the nationalist focus on the site and the project's international team and commercial interests. Often I find myself as an archaeologist having to take a stand and trying to prevent the site being used in ways that contradict the evidence or my ethical role as a professional archaeologist.

These can all be difficult interactions, but in the end the ethical responsibility is to use the specialist archaeological and conservation knowledge to respond to the interests of one's fellow travellers. I have not mentioned some of the other groups that focus on the site – such as those that believe the site is the origin of the kilim (a type of Turkish carpet). Çatalhöyük fascinates so many people. What I aim to do in this book is make some sense of the site, and I hope in doing so to answer some of the questions that are asked by my fellow travellers.

A Brief Overview of Some Techniques

The project that started work at the site in 1993 is a research excavation with numerous aims. The primary aims deal with conservation, site presentation and management, but also with the attempt to place the art into its full social, economic and environmental context. The methods we have been using are described in a specially devoted volume,[27] and I will only briefly summarize them here.

There are a number of different excavation teams that work at the site – we have had teams from Britain, the United States, Greece, Poland, Konya and Istanbul. These all use some version of an excavation method called 'single context recording' which means that every context (we in fact call them units) of soil that is excavated (a layer in a pit, a floor in a room, a brick layer on a wall) is described and planned separately. The different soil contexts or units are then tied back together again in the analysis stage after the excavation. The relationships between layers are worked out on a Harris matrix (a system for representing and analyzing the temporal sequences of units devised by Edward Harris in the 1980s). This type of approach is important on a site with extremely complex stratigraphy. The method was originally worked out for large urban sites in Britain[28] but it is very well suited to Çatalhöyük with its multiple, complex, interweaving lenses and layers.

During the excavation, all soil is passed through a dry sieve or screen with a 4 mm (0.16 in) mesh. In addition, up to 30 litres of soil are taken to the 'flotation machines' for water flotation. The lighter material that floats (mainly charred plant material) is the 'light residue', and the 'heavy residue' is the material which sinks onto a 0.5 mm (0.02 in) mesh. The heavy residue is then dried and sorted into three fraction sizes of >4 mm (0.16 in), <4 mm (0.16 in) and >2 mm (0.08 in), and <2 mm (0.08 in) and >1 mm (0.04 in). Each fraction is studied to find densities of 'micro-artifacts'. All visible artifacts on floors and all other 'small finds' are 3-dimensionally plotted as 'macro-artifacts'.

In our recording system, units are grouped into 'features' which are sets of closely related units such as an oven with its wall and fill units. Features are then grouped into 'spaces' which are spatially bounded entities of some kind, such as a room. These spaces are then grouped into 'buildings'. All these categories are numbered such that Unit 4571 (or just (4571)) may be in Feature 273 (or F.273) and Space 391 which may be in Building 47. Units are also grouped temporally. Thus a series of units and features may constitute a phase of use within a building. These phases are then numbered (as Phase 3B). The site has also been divided into 18 levels which are given Roman numerals counting from the top – such as Level VIB or VIII. Mellaart used a different referencing system for buildings. He thought that the more elaborate buildings on the site were shrines rather than houses (a distinction which we have been unable to make, as will be discussed in Chapter 5). So Mellaart labelled buildings either Shrines or Houses, and then gave terms describing level and location – thus his Shrine E.VIB.10 would refer to a building called Shrine 10 in Level VIB in his E area.

In the current project, each unit of soil is sampled in a variety of ways. As well as the dry and wet sieving and water flotation, samples of soil are taken to keep as an archive, and also for chemical analysis and phytolith analysis, and objects are sampled for isotopic analysis of bone, radiocarbon dating (a basic timeline based on this is shown in Figures 18 and 19), and for the analysis of shell, microfauna, beads, figurines, clay balls, obsidian and so on. Individual objects found on the site are sometimes given their own 'x' number – thus 1871.X1 refers to an object given the number 1 specially recorded in Unit 1871.

To encourage close interaction between all those excavating on the site and the archaeologists and scientists interested in the analysis of particular types of materials, nine laboratories have been built on the site, covering topics such as faunal analysis, archaeobotanical analysis, conservation, computing and data management, human remains, pottery, groundstone and obsidian analysis, micromorphology and so on (Figure 20).

The project is organized so that after periods of three to four years of excavation, emphasis shifts to analysis and writing up for publication. Again this is done in as collaborative way as possible, and the first set of volumes are in various stages of production.[29] The excavation results are linked back into the types of data that require long and slow laboratory analysis such as the study of charred plant remains

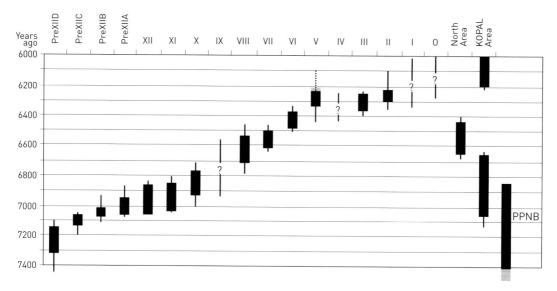

18 Overall radiocarbon dating timeline for the levels at Çatalhöyük.

19 The dating of Çatalhöyük in relation to other sites in Turkey and the Middle East. The dating of most sites in the area has now been confirmed and refined by radiocarbon dating.

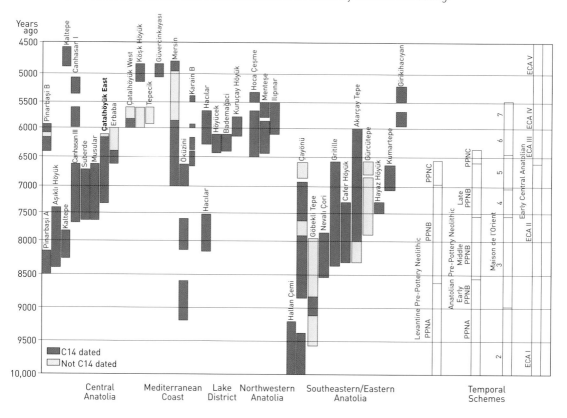

20 The dig house at Çatalhöyük. The dig house contains laboratories, living accommodation and the Visitor Centre.

or the chemical analysis of the sources of the obsidian that came to the site. This book is mainly based on the research published in the 2005 and 2006 volumes.

From 1993 to 1995 we worked on the surfaces of the Neolithic East and Chalcolithic West Mounds, making topographic maps, collecting surface sherds, sampling the surface with scraped trenches and geophysical prospection, and redrawing the eroded sections or profiles left by Mellaart. From 1995 to 1999 excavations were undertaken in two main areas (Figure 4). On the northern hill of the East Mound, Building 1 and, beneath it, Building 5 were excavated and the area was called the North Area. Nearby, Building 3 was excavated by the BACH (Berkeley Archaeologists at Çatalhöyük) team and these results will be reported on separately by Ruth Tringham and Mira Stevanovic, although they are referred to where appropriate. These northern excavations were undertaken to find out whether the types of buildings discovered by Mellaart in the southwest of the mound would also be found elsewhere. In the South Area we chose an area within Mellaart's excavations and continued down to find the base of the mound, which we did in 1999. A team led by Neil Roberts excavated to the north of the East Mound in order to examine the deposits in the plain off the mound, and they dug a long narrow trench on the north flank of the mound in order to study site formation processes (i.e. the processes that led to the formation of the cultural deposits at Çatalhöyük). These trenches were termed KOPAL (Konya Plain Palaeoenvironmental survey). From 2000 to 2002 the teams concentrated on post-excavation study and publication. In the meantime, a team from Poznan in Poland began excavating the TP (Team Poznan) area near the top of the southern eminence of the mound in order to study the latest levels of the site. Excavation was also undertaken on the West Mound by a team led by Jonathan Last and Catriona Gibson.[30]

In 2003 and 2004, a new phase of excavation started. This involved opening an area 40 m by 40 m (130 ft by 130 ft), called the 4040, on the northern eminence in order to look at large-scale settlement organization (Plate 5). In the South Area a large shelter has been built (Plate 4) and excavations are continuing to dig down to explore the lowest levels of the site.

CONCLUSION

Çatalhöyük is undoubtedly a site of deep mysteries. The high level of preservation appears to take one close to a very distant and different world. And yet the strangeness of it all is confronting and distancing. It intrigues and baffles us.

It does this to us now, and I am going to argue in this book that it did something somewhat similar to people 376 generations ago. Its symbolism, ambiguity, and strangeness drew people in then just as they do today. Of course the specifics were different, and I will try to detail these. But for them and us there was a fascination – to the revealing of mysteries.

Today many different communities are drawn to the site, for different reasons and with different expectations. As an archaeologist I consider it a professional duty to engage with such communities and mediate their involvement. We shall see that it is possible that people from different communities were sucked into Çatalhöyük 9,000 years ago. For example, in Chapter 3 I will refer to a regional survey by Douglas Baird which suggests that as Çatalhöyük grew, the numbers of nearby sites decreased. One interpretation of this evidence is that people were drawn into Çatalhöyük from different communities. If this is correct, these different communities had to find a way of living with each other. Whatever their origin, this book is the story of how large numbers of people managed to live together.

It is thus also an attempt to answer one of the greatest mysteries about the development of anatomically modern humans. Why, after hundreds of thousands of years living as mobile hunter-gatherers did humans settle down and form large 'towns' in the period after the end of the Ice Age or Pleistocene? This 'settling' is a process that happens in many parts of the globe at different times after the end of the Ice Age. Can the process in Anatolia and the Middle East, and can the data from Çatalhöyük, contribute to an understanding of this wider transformation? As noted in the Prologue, Çatalhöyük occurs well after the formation of settled agricultural life in the Middle East, but I believe it can show, because of the detailed preservation at the site, how 'ways of living' changed through the process of settling down. I will argue that the transformation to settled agricultural life in large dense sites was not just about climate change and subsistence change, important as these shifts were. The transformation was also about how people lived their daily lives, their notions of self, body and time.

CHAPTER TWO

The Leopard's Puzzle

I want to return to the puzzle that I started the book with in the Prologue and to continue on from there. I will describe some of the bits of the puzzle that I have been mulling over for years. One might have thought that the rich survival of evidence at Çatalhöyük would make solving puzzles about the past easier – because the more pieces of the puzzle one has, the easier it should be to see the picture. But it doesn't seem to work like that. What happens instead is that the more bits and pieces one has, the more one realizes how complex the picture is. The reality that one is trying to reach does not provide neat and simple answers. The more one knows, the more complex the puzzle becomes.

We can see this by following further the same lead that we began with in the Prologue. In Table 1 we saw that leopards (or other big cats) are common and central to the art, but at the time of writing this book not a single leopard bone had been found on site (see Epilogue). On the other hand, there is an under-representation in the art of animals that were domesticated at the time – sheep and goat. This emphasis on wild animals in the art in contrast to the heavy dependence in the diet on domestic sheep and goat is part of a more general pattern: the art emphasizes wild animals, and often dangerous or powerful parts of wild animals.

For example, the tusks and mandibles of wild boar and the antlers of deer are brought onto the site and used in installations on walls. Boar tusks are made into necklaces worn by women, and some are later buried with individuals under house platforms. The presence of head and foot bones of deer and boar on the site suggests that their skins were being used. But the rest of the deer and boar body (their other post-cranial elements) are relatively rare throughout much of the site's history (although in the earliest levels all parts of deer carcasses were brought onto the site). Cattle bones, especially skulls and horns, are used frequently in installations even

21 This wall-painting features two water birds – possibly cranes, which would fit with other evidence from the site.

though they are not a major part of the faunal remains. Analysis by Mike Richards and Jessica Pearson of the chemical isotopes in human bones also shows that cattle were not a major part of the diet.[1] We have found the paw of a bear on site, and Mellaart found the jaws of wild boar and the skulls of fox and weasel embedded in house walls. Burials have been found covered in the excrement of small carnivores.

So there is much fascination in the art and symbolism with wild animals, and especially with the hard, dangerous or powerful parts of wild animals, at the expense of the other parts of those animals and with domesticated animals. Plants also play very little part in the art; although they were an important part of the diet, and although there are a few depictions of trees, overall the plant world is rarely depicted. In particular, although people must have spent large amounts of their time tending fields of cereals and pulses, and although they must have spent much time processing and preparing these crops, there are few or no clear depictions.

As we shall see, the paintings and installations occur in the domestic context of houses. And yet it is not that domestic world that is depicted. Rather it is an outside world of wild animals. Much as one might try not to impose modern notions about separations of domestic and wild, it is difficult not to accept that some version of such a distinction is being expressed here. However we look at it, it seems clear that wild and domestic animals, as we define them today, were treated differently in the past at Çatalhöyük.[2] As we shall also see, there is a preference for the use of wild bulls in feasting, with a more general emphasis on cattle (all the cattle are the very large wild animal termed aurochs or *Bos primigenius*) and especially sheep in daily consumption.

Even when we look at the bird bones and the depictions of birds we find puzzling patterns. There are few paintings of birds (Figure 21) and few unambiguous bird figurines. The vulture is the most commonly depicted bird (Figure 22), but there are also cranes and perhaps another water bird.[3] Vulture skulls occur in installations on walls. But the bird bones found amongst the faunal remains on site are dominated by smaller water birds such as geese and ducks.[4] Çatalhöyük was situated in a wetland environment so the prevalence of the bones of water birds is hardly surprising, but the contrast with the emphasis on vultures in the art is clear. The vultures in one case have human legs and could be interpreted as hybrid creatures or people dressed up as vultures. There is evidence of crane wings being used as part of a costume.[5] All this suggests particular symbolic emphasis placed on large waders and vultures, the latter also associated with death (for the associations between headless human corpses and vultures see Figure 22).

We notice some other parts of the puzzle if we shift from the art to pottery. Pottery starts to get used as a container in about Levels XII to X (approximately 7050 to 6800 BC), but is not used for cooking until Level VI (approximately 6500 to

22 A wall-painting showing a vulture pecking at a headless human corpse – the most common bird scene in the art at Çatalhöyük. Vulture skulls have also been found in some installations. For a clearer transcription of a similar scene, see Figure 57.

6400 BC). From 6500 to 6000 BC when Neolithic Çatalhöyük ends, we often find pots placed near the hearths and ovens mainly in the southern parts of houses. In fact pots are sometimes set in hollows near the oven – and one function they seem to have had was to contain the fat of small ruminants, probably sheep and goat.[6] So they are very much associated with what one might define as the domestic world. It is thus of interest that the pots are not decorated and do not for the most part show all the elaborate symbolism seen on the house walls. Of course, as our ceramicist Jonathan Last[7] has pointed out, the pots are burnished, and this could be seen as artistic. But in comparison to later periods when, as in the Chalcolithic West Mound, pots are elaborately painted using themes similar to those used on the Neolithic walls, the pots on the Neolithic East Mound are not being given a heavily symbolic load.

It is of interest too, then, that pots are never found in burials. Certainly some broken sherds do find their way into the soil placed back into graves, but whole pots are never placed as offerings in graves. Burial tends to occur in the northern parts of the house where most of the wall decoration and installations are found. The art concentrates on wild animals – and also on death, in the images of vultures pecking the flesh from headless corpses (although, as we shall see, we have no evidence that human bodies were treated in this way in reality). So we seem to be able to see a general set of distinctions between wild animals and death on the one hand, and an undecorated less overtly symbolic world of domestic and domesticated life on the other.[8]

Clay balls which were used for cooking in the early levels in the site occur rarely if ever in intentional deposits in graves. They are closely associated with ovens – indeed the floors of ovens may be made of layers of broken clay balls, and there are often medium to large caches of balls near ovens.[9] The round ones at least, which are the most clearly used in cooking in houses, are rarely and minimally decorated. Grinding slabs occur in oven areas of houses, and they are not decorated and do not occur in burials. There are a couple of miniature greenstone axes from burials and also polished stone maceheads.[10] Stamp seals on the other hand are used to make designs on bodies, skin or cloth.[11] They occur mainly in the upper levels of the site and they frequently occur in graves. Thus, things associated with the oven and domestic production area usually do not get placed in graves, but items of personal identity or status do.

We can follow this pattern (southern versus northern, undecorated versus decorated, oven versus burial, lower dark floors near ovens versus higher whiter floors with burials and so on) through in other data. The pattern was not something we had expected before we started digging. It just became obvious as we dug – something that we could not ignore. The pattern became summarized loosely and colloquially as a difference between 'clean' floors and 'dirty' floors. Everybody came to recognize as they dug that there were these two types of quite different

23 Densities of small bone (between 2 and 4 mm (0.08 and 0.16 in)) in Building 1 in Phase B1.2C showing concentrations in the western room and around grinding and bin areas in the south of the main room. Such statistical analyses help to confirm that apparent trends spotted by excavators in the field are real and not imagined.

context. In addition, there turned out, in the post-excavation analysis, to be statistical support for what we had noticed in the field. There is a wide range of quantitative data which can be plotted and tabulated in order to show distinctions in the ways in which different types of artifact are deposited in different places in the houses (see Figures 23 and 24 for examples). From such data we can see that the floors in the southern, oven-related areas of houses are very different from the white plastered floors in the northern parts of houses and on the platforms under which burial occurs.

Clay figurines too are often deposited in midden and oven-related contexts, but they are never found in burials. The situation with obsidian – a black volcanic glass which produces razor-sharp edges for cutting – is less straightforward. Obsidian is found cached in pits or scoops near the ovens and in abandonment pits as intentional deposition, and there is much debris from obsidian knapping in the areas near ovens. But, by way of contrast, in the excavations of the current project we have rarely found obsidian in graves. Mellaart[12] does record cases of obsidian blades in graves, for example wrapped in a bundle by the leg of a male skeleton, and he also found obsidian mirrors in graves. He also records other examples of obsidian and flint daggers, knives and projectile points found in graves.[13] It is difficult to know at this stage whether such occurrences indicate a shift in practices

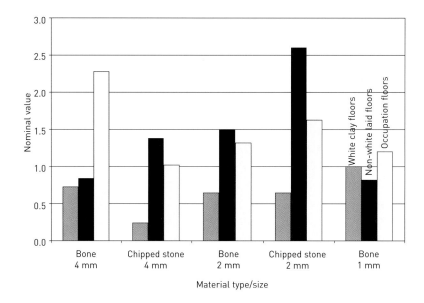

24 Median densities of bone and chipped stone in different types of floor in the North Area at Çatalhöyük. We can see that, for example, density of all bone and chipped stone is lower in the white clay floored areas, whilst higher densities of material tend to be found in other floor areas.

over time, or some special role or function for individuals buried with these obsidian items. It does seem to be the case that everyday obsidian tools, flakes and blades which dominate in the oven areas of houses rarely made their way into graves, but other more elaborate obsidian objects (large blades, points, mirrors) clearly did.

The pattern breaks down still further if we consider the evidence of baskets. For example, we have found much evidence of baskets or small round mats sitting round the oven area and in storage areas. But baskets do occur in burials – young people especially may be placed in baskets, and adults also may be treated in this way. Bone artifacts too complicate the picture. There is much evidence for the manufacture of bone tools such as awls and bone decoration such as finger rings in the oven areas of houses. But some of the rings for example, then get deposited in burial as part of personal adornment.

What I realized as I tried to make all the different parts of the puzzle fit together in some way, was that the puzzle was very complex, but that one could discern some order, at least in some spheres of activity. There seemed to be a complex interweaving of symbolic and practical realms. The symbolism of cattle was linked to the practices of feasting for example. The symbolism of leopards was linked to practices of exclusion of their bones from the site. But the relationships and links were often inverted or even contradicted as one moved from one sphere to the other. Thus, things common in the oven area often did not get into graves, but baskets, for example, did move across into burial. There seemed to be a lot of restrictions in how one behaved. One could not put a pot in a grave. One could not take a leopard bone onto the settlement. One could not bury an adult by the oven. All these restrictions were both symbolic and practical. But they were also often contradictory and complex.

In fact it seemed possible to identify from the puzzle of all these restrictions and interlinkings four spheres of activity which had some degree of separation but which also interweaved and intersected each other. I wish to introduce these four spheres briefly now and then use them as a basis for the discussion in the rest of the book. These different spheres of life could be described in many ways. They could be described as domains, fields, discourses, or networks. I wish at this stage just to sketch them out using the neutral term 'spheres' and then later in this chapter to discuss a way of conceiving them. More detailed evidence of each sphere will be discussed throughout the book.

The first sphere is that of **domestic production**. It is identified in the everyday discard near hearths and ovens (Plate 7) and in middens – the areas of refuse between groups of houses (see Chapter 4 for a full discussion). It is possible to see in the middens fine lenses of material discarded from the hearth and oven area. The midden material is charcoal-rich and with small flecks of plaster as well as with a full range of bone, obsidian and other material like that found near the ovens. Although the middens do have some characteristics of their own,[14] they seem to be largely composed of domestic refuse from the houses. Part of this suite of items found in oven and midden contexts is not found in burial and there are not domestic oven-related scenes in the wall art. Many of the objects involved are undecorated and often are deposited in an undecorated part of the room.

The material includes small figurines, pottery, carbonized seeds, and animal bones especially of sheep and goat. It includes obsidian, baskets and clay balls. This sphere also has evidence of bead production and bone tool production. These objects, while not themselves decorated, are used for bodily decoration and some do occur in burial, but pottery, figurines, seeds, animal bones and clay balls rarely if ever are placed in burials.

Perhaps pottery is especially associated with this domestic sphere because of the way it was involved in the practices of the house. The earliest pots in Levels XII and above were organic tempered and there is no evidence they were used for cooking.[15] They were probably used for keeping and serving food. From Level VI onwards, the pots are grit tempered and took over the role of cooking from clay balls (Figures 25 and 49). They were mainly associated with cooking involving the fat from sheep and goat, and they were often set in emplacements or pits near the oven. Thus they became intimately connected with food preparation by the hearth/oven. In the earliest levels, cooking was achieved by heating clay balls which could then be placed in a basket or other container in order to heat liquids and food. While cooking with heated clay balls is quick and efficient in terms of

25 A well-preserved example of a grit-tempered pot from the site. From Level VI onwards, these vessels took over the role of cooking from clay balls.

heat transfer, the process requires continual supervision as the balls are replaced and reheated. Once cooking shifts to the use of pots on a fire, there is less need for minute-by-minute supervision as the food cooks. People are thus freed to spend time on other tasks. Indeed, as one goes through time at Çatalhöyük, there is increased evidence for specialization of production in the domestic context – for example, both pottery and lithic technologies change around Level VI (approximately 6500 to 6400 BC) and become more specialized.[16] So the shift to the use of pottery rather than clay balls for cooking may have been linked to an increasing need to schedule time and tasks in the domestic context. In a sense, then, people came to depend on their grit-tempered pots. The pots did the cooking for them as they did other tasks. Thus one could say that people became entangled with pots in the domestic context. It is not so easy to make quite such a strong case for close entanglement between people and baskets and wooden containers, although of course people were dependent on these too.

So the sphere of domestic production includes a series of locales. The most important was the area around the oven in the south part of houses. Analysis of segments of fallen roof suggests that some domestic activities took place on roofs. There must also have been other locales such as where pottery was made. I will describe later other activities, such as brick production and lime production that seem to have been on a largely domestic scale but which took place outside the house. This sphere has a clear social component – the domestic unit. And it has a clear set of social and symbolic restrictions – material is often undecorated and burial of adults does not occur, but obsidian caches are buried here – and so on.

There is much evidence for the production of bone beads in the domestic oven locale, but if we follow their path into consumption we arrive at two spheres of affiliation: **exchange** and **ancestry**. If we first of all consider these two spheres together we can see that they deal with the place of the person in relation to others. The objects that indicate these spheres include baskets, wooden containers, cloth, beads (made of stone, bone and clay), copper, shell, amber, obsidian and geometric art, all found in or near burial, as well as other contexts. Many of these things are bright and shiny and are clear examples of 'technologies of enchantment' or of material 'entrapment', using the terminology of Alfred Gell in his book *Art and Agency*. Even the cloth that is found in burials may have been stamped with designs using the stamp seals found in the upper levels of the site. Gell argues that our attention gets drawn by objects that have complex designs, or glitter, or in some other way engage us. He shows how such enchantment is a central part of value in exchange – and how it is linked to status and power in exchange. I will discuss later other ways in which the objects in these spheres of affiliation come to be enchanted, but for the moment it is important also to note that many of the items in this sphere deal with personal appearance. These are items associated with the body – they are what define the person and so are buried with the person. They link the domestic sphere with society at large.

But within this sphere of affiliation we can see a separation of two forms, one based on ancestry and the other on exchange. The sphere of **ancestry** is based on the passing down of ancestral rights, material things and memories. I will discuss this sphere particularly in Chapter 6 which deals largely with archaeological evidence for human burial (Figure 26) and the retrieval of animal installations. The evidence for this sphere is seen in the circulation of skulls and animal parts. There are examples of the retrieval of human skulls and animal reliefs and of their reuse and handing down from generation to generation. This type of handing down could just be seen as a form of exchange – but it is of a particularly inalienable form. People may receive ancestral objects and in exchange give their labour to the social group which is linked together by joint ancestry. But the objects themselves may themselves constitute the rights and membership of the group – they cannot easily be 'given away'. Affiliation through the passing down of inalienable objects creates social units that probably link those in houses and groups of houses together. Status distinctions are created between some houses and others in terms of their ancestral ties. But there is no clear division with the sphere of exchange (or with other spheres). Burials, which are central to this ancestral sphere, also contain objects which may have been involved in more alienable forms of exchange.

The sphere of **exchange** is identifiable archaeologically in a wide range of artifacts that will be

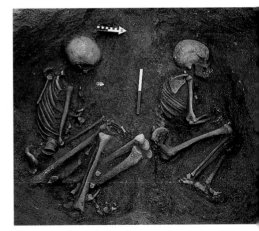

26 A twin burial found in Building 1. Most burials were of bodies that still had all their flesh and had been flexed, although skulls were sometimes later retrieved.

discussed in Chapter 7. Long-distance movement is seen, for example, in the obsidian that was obtained from Cappadocia (170 km (105 miles) away), in the timber from the Taurus Mountains to the south, shell from the Mediterranean and baskets from the Red Sea. In addition to these long-distance movements and exchanges, there were local movements of clays, stones and animals. Most of these items are at one point or another brought into the house. Thus, obsidian was brought from Cappadocia as roughed out forms and stored in small pits near the oven (Figure 71). It was then taken out and knapped as needed before being used or exchanged as a finished form. The items obtained through exchange were used in all the other spheres (for example, animals used in domestic food consumption, or shell beads used and passed down to create ancestral links). Similarly, objects produced as part of domestic production near the oven, such as beads, were passed on in exchange.

The sphere of the **community** is seen in a number of areas of material culture that will be discussed in Chapters 3 and 4. The very practices of living in the large settlement at Çatalhöyük would have created community interactions. Dealing with drainage, water supply, refuse and so on must have required a scale of community cooperation in a population somewhere in the 3,000 to 8,000 range (at the upper end of this range for some of the site's duration) and in a settlement 13.5 hectares (33.5 acres) in size. But there is also evidence of a scale of community organization larger than the domestic unit. For example, wild bulls were used in collective feasting. In the art there are groups of people seen in the animal baiting scenes. Some degree of collective action must also have been involved in the wider use of the landscape for hunting, herding and farming. There must have been some regulation of rights for access to land and trackways and resources. There is little evidence for centralized ceremonies, central social dominance, or central elites at Çatalhöyük, but there may have been groups of elders that made collective decisions. The site as a community is seen in the overall site restriction on bringing leopard bones, and parts of deer and wild boar on to the site. It is seen in all the site-wide rules about how to do things: where to put an oven, how to make a bone ring. It is seen in the repetition of art motifs, and the common symbolic repertoire at the site. It thus involves seamless links between practical activities and symbolic worlds.

There has been much discussion in the literature concerning Çatalhöyük about which of these spheres, which I have very briefly introduced here, is dominant. Some have argued that the question of why Çatalhöyük emerged can be answered by its importance in the regional exchange of obsidian. Others have argued that the key is overall community organization. In my view, all the spheres played a central role in the emergence and maintenance of the settlement and its art. There were multiple strands in a distributed process. But I will in this volume place a central emphasis on the domestic sphere. Despite the importance of exchange, ancestry and community, I believe that a good case can be made for the largely domestic scale of many aspects of life at Çatalhöyük. I will make this case in some detail in Chapter 5. But one key piece of evidence concerns storage (Figure 27). We know that the bins in the houses were used for storing agricultural produce such as lentils and wheat. All houses seem to have storage bins of some form, and all houses have generally similar storage capacity. There is no evidence of a scale of storage beyond the domestic scale. Equally, we do not have evidence of large containers that could store food for units beyond the domestic unit. We shall also see in Chapter 5 much evidence for production at the domestic scale. It is fascinating too how rare it is to find party walls – even though houses may be just a few centimetres apart, people built and maintained their own walls. Overall the evidence suggests that individual houses were fairly equivalent and self-sufficient. As indicated in the Prologue, one of the main puzzles at Çatalhöyük is why people concentrated together at all.

27 Storage bins at Çatalhöyük. Most such bins occur in side rooms and were used to contain a range of types of plant food.

Changing Tensions Between the Spheres

I have argued that there are close interactions and interdependencies between the four spheres. But we also started with a series of restrictions in the associations and depositions of groups of artifacts – around ovens, in burial, in the art, in the faunal remains and so on. What is it that creates these restrictions and avoidances?

It could certainly be argued that there are social tensions that lie behind the avoidances. Little of the art relates to agricultural production, and indeed to the first sphere at all. The social focus in much of the art, symbolism and ritual is on hunting, exchange and ancestry. It is almost as if the agricultural side is hidden or downplayed. This suggests that social power is about an interlinked set of ideas to do with ancestry, large-scale feasts, taking the heads off wild animals and people and passing them down, large-scale animal teasing events, exchange of high-value shell and beads, and so on. Even though society at Çatalhöyük is largely organized at the domestic scale, the other spheres are the focus of most art and symbolic ritual and reproduce themselves through the exchange of valuables and through ancestry. So there is potentially a tension here, between the first sphere and the other three.

It is indeed this tension that is most evident in the arrangement of activities inside buildings – the separation between the 'dirty' oven area and the 'clean' burial platforms. But there are also other tensions between the emphasis on the overall community and the emphasis on the ancestral lines of individual houses or groups of houses. These various tensions are also seen very clearly if we shift away from the rather static picture I have so far outlined and consider change through time. At major earlier sites in Anatolia, there is a very clear emphasis on the collective. There are specialized ritual buildings at Göbekli, Çayönü and Aşıklı Höyük[17] (for the locations of these sites see Figure 5 and for their dates see Figure 19). At Aşıklı Höyük, which is on the edge of the Konya Plain and covers the millennium prior to Çatalhöyük, there is less symbolic and productive evidence in houses, less burial beneath house floors, and a very clear overall sense of larger collectivities in the layout of houses into zones. There is also clear evidence of large-scale community feasting at nearby Musular. A strong sense of collective organization is also seen at the immediate and spatially proximate predecessor of Çatalhöyük at Can Hasan III. At Çatalhöyük, on the other hand, it is as if everything is brought into the house. It is possible that more specialized buildings will be found in as yet unexplored areas of the site, but even if such finds are made, the houses at Çatalhöyük have brought things inside. For example, burial occurs in houses more frequently at Çatalhöyük than elsewhere. The art motifs that are found in public buildings at Göbekli occur in the house at Çatalhöyük.

This shift will be discussed at some length in Chapter II. For the moment, very crudely and over-simplistically one could argue that an initial focus on the community scale in many of these earlier sites shifts to the house or groups of houses at Çatalhöyük. In the earlier levels so far excavated at Çatalhöyük the emphasis on the ancestral sphere is clear – there is a focus on burial and paintings referring to death, the use of 'art' referring to feasting in the house or in groups of houses. But through the sequence of occupation at Çatalhöyük things change and the individual domestic unit takes on more of a focus. In the upper levels of the site and in the ensuing Chalcolithic West Mound, the houses become larger, multi-roomed and multi-functional.[18] This may indicate an increased social emphasis on domestic production, and there is decreasing emphasis on ancestry at the house level. There is a focus on the exchange of decorated pottery between house units, although we shall see that there is no simple sequence.

I have simply wanted at this stage to introduce the idea that it would be wrong to think of Çatalhöyük society as thoroughly holistic, integrated and unchanging. While it may have been more integrated than many others, and I will make that case in later chapters, it was also a divided society with internal tensions that led to change. There were changing relationships between the spheres. Through time the role of burial shifts from being associated with the house and with groups of houses to being associated at later sites like Çatalhöyük West with burial outside houses (there are no burials beneath the floors at Çatalhöyük West – and in sites of this later period cemeteries for the community as a whole may emerge, as probably at Hacılar). Similarly in the upper levels at Çatalhöyük pottery, which had been an undecorated part of the domestic sphere, shifts to being increasingly decorated – and in Çatalhöyük West this change is completed as the symbolic elaboration that had been reserved for house walls at Çatalhöyük East shifts to pottery (Figure 107) that could be moved between houses.[19]

Spheres of Entanglement

I raised earlier the issue of how these different spheres are to be understood. What did they represent in the realities of peoples' lives? In answering this question I want to suggest that the spheres are comprised of groups of activities that involved sets of entanglements in social, material, productive, symbolic and other realms. They were webs of interests and engagements and rather different networks made up the different spheres. The relationships between the spheres of entanglement changed through time as the result of minor shifts and reactions in the practices of everyday life.

The detailed evidence from Çatalhöyük allows some insight into the dense network of dependencies and intersections that make up the entanglements. One example has already been given above in the discussion of how changes from clay balls to pottery in cooking were linked to many other changes in the ways people lived their lives.

It may be helpful to explain more fully what I mean by entanglement[20] by considering another example, again from the domestic sphere. The inhabitants of Çatalhöyük made the decision to live in mud-brick houses, and for a whole set of reasons they decided, at least in the middle layers of the site, to plaster the floors and walls with a fine mud plaster, rich in lime (Figure 28). At least one of the reasons for plastering floors may have been to limit infestation from mice. Emma Jenkins[21] has found many examples of mouse bones and mouse activity in the houses, and they must have constituted a nuisance

28 Multiple layers of plaster. The very fine lines probably represent seasonal or monthly replasterings, and the groups of lines probably indicate yearly resurfacings.

resulting from the dense packing of houses, grain storage and sedentism. Whatever the reasons, it was decided to plaster the floors and walls. But where to get the lime muds from? Around the edges of the site we have found marl extraction pits. These were dug down through alluvium in order to get to the Pleistocene lake marls which were fine and lime rich and could easily be processed to make the plaster for the walls and floors. So it was necessary to get the tools to dig the holes, and the containers to carry the mud. And there had to be agreement about who could dig where off the edge of the mound; and about which time of the year would be best for plastering. And there would be the social effort of getting enough plaster collected; and also different types of plaster for the different types of platform in the houses. It turned out that the fine plasters themselves did not stick well on the walls so that rougher foundation layers needed to be put on first with more organic temper. So now people had to be organized to get different types of clay, and to collect and prepare the temper. In order to get a group of people together for all the digging and carrying of different types of clay, all at the right moment, it is likely that some sort of exchange would be offered – say a small feast. So that meant getting an animal killed and prepared. And a plastering tool was needed; worked cattle scapulae may well have been used in this way,[22] but that meant the group of people plastering had to have access to a cow, or to someone that had a scapula.

And so on. My point here is simply that one material act (plastering a floor) involves a network of entanglements – with the properties of materials, but also

29 This scapula was left resting on a hearth when Building 1 was abandoned – perhaps because it had some special significance.

with a web of social relations. There were also beliefs and symbols involved – perhaps cattle scapulae had some special significance. Certainly they are deposited in very distinctive ways in relation to hearths during house abandonment (Figure 29). So the entanglements extend into a network which is material, social and conceptual. But they are also networks in which people become heavily dependent on non-humans, which come to delegate for other humans. Thus people become dependent on pots in the cooking case outlined above – they cannot complete their schedules in the house unless the pots help them. And they become dependent on the plaster – it may help with mice infestations or with protecting the inhabitants of a house from the effects of decaying bodies beneath the floors. We also see how the entanglements involve moves between the spheres I have identified – for example a move from domestic activities to exchange and ancestry.

I would like to take another example from the ancestral sphere. As people settled down in more permanent settlements at the end of the Pleistocene and in the early Holocene in the Middle East, there were a number of practical implications of the emerging way of life. While burial certainly occurred amongst hunter-gatherer groups, it must be presumed that many bodies were left out away from settlements, to decay and be consumed by animals, or were buried away from settlements. As settlements became larger and as people moved around from place to place less, leaving out the body or burial away from the settlement may have been seen as both more difficult and less appropriate. People began to develop a closer relationship with the settlement, the house and its community. Memories and associations with place became stronger in relation to settlement and house. So burying close kin near to the house and settlement may have seemed both practical and appropriate. But burial beneath the house floor would have had a whole series of implications. For example, in the early (Pre-XII) levels at Çatalhöyük a hard fired lime plaster floor was used and in the Levantine PPNB thick solid plaster floors occurred. It would have been difficult to dig down through such plasters. But in the area around Çatalhöyük there were marls that had a high lime content and could be used as soft plasters, and there were reeds available in the marsh to make mats. So there was a shift to softer plasters, although that itself had implications for labour – the plasters wore away and had to be renewed frequently. Another implication was that it became possible for people to associate specific memories and individuals with specific burials – the ancestors would not go away and they could be named and identified. The bones became delegates of the dead and intruded themselves into daily life. One response would have been to use lime plasters to protect against putrefaction and smell. But it turned out that the best lime clays were not readily available. So one ended up with categorial differences between different types of plaster – the better lime plasters kept for burial platforms, some others used for work areas, and so on. We can see the endless webs of material entanglements which are practical, social, ritual, mythical and so on. And again we can see the moves between spheres.

I wish to introduce two more brief examples from the other spheres. In terms of the sphere of exchange we can look at obsidian (Figure 30). Its value may have been partly linked to its shiny surface. This 'enchanted' or 'entrapped', and could be used to make mirrors. But the value of obsidian also depended on the complex exchange networks that existed at the time,[23] on distance travelled from the sources in Cappadocia, and on the practical use of the sharp volcanic glass in making tools, points

30 An obsidian point from the site. These fine bifacially flaked tools were made of obsidian (volcanic glass) obtained from Cappadocia. Obsidian was highly valued for its sharp cutting edges, but it could also be ground and polished to create a mirror (see Figures 101 and 102).

and weapons. The value of the obsidian probably changed when it had been brought into the house and buried beneath the floor near the oven. This was an area where pots too were often inset into the floor, and small pits containing animal bones or just rounded stones or clay balls have also been found here. Children too are sometimes buried beneath the floor near the oven, and more generally the floors (but mainly the northern floors) are used for burial. So it is possible that the burial of the obsidian gave it added, house-based meanings, so that it became less alienable. Once dug up again and made into points or tools it had house-based associations, and the end product depended on the knowledge and skills of those in the house regarding stone knapping. We think that much of this knapping was carried out in the oven area where many other productive tasks also had to be scheduled. The shatter created areas that might have needed covering with mats. But if successfully achieved, the resulting obsidian tools could be used again in exchange or in further productive tasks such as woodworking. So the exchange and circulation of obsidian take us along a complex network of interlinked material, social, symbolic and aesthetic relationships.

As a final example, in the sphere of community, we could consider the entangled webs involved in the practicalities of getting water off the site, or the practical problems of moving around on roofs, or of dumping personal faecal material into middens and so on. Let us take the apparently simple issue of moving the location of a hearth or oven. In fact all the houses that we have so far excavated show much evidence of restless movement of oven location. Normally the oven moves around close to the south wall, but on rare occasions it may move to the west or even the north wall. We are not sure why these changes are made so frequently from phase to phase. Ovens seem to have worn out quickly, and most have been frequently re-floored, but the shifts often seem linked to wider changes in the arrangement of buildings. If an oven does move location, the layout of the stairway and roof entrance also presumably had to change as both the stairway and oven smoke used the same roof hole. Changing the hole in the roof would have effects on the layout of the rest of the house. For example, we find puddling below stairs resulting from rain coming through the entrance hole. So the stairs cannot be near the sleeping platform. Also changing the entrance hole location will change the way in which smoke escapes through the roof. This could in turn have an effect on the arrangement of activities on the roofs of adjacent buildings. We know that a range of activities including those associated with ovens and hearths took place on the roofs of houses. Changing entrance hole locations would have also affected the overall pattern of pathways and access routes on the roofs, and thus the locations of activities. So an apparently minor change within the confines of one house has effects on the community at large.

Imagine the same analysis extended over a wide range of activities that emerge in the Neolithic – making pots, polishing stone axes, making bricks, storing grain, looking after the herds. The degree of entanglement implied by all this is massive. And yet there is no reason to see this entanglement as without its own local fields and tensions. In a distributed system, even though everything is ultimately connected to everything else, there remain disconnects, faults and fissures. Thus there may be quite different sets of interests involved in maintaining the ancestry sphere in comparison to the domestic production sphere. One may be based on lineage and the passing down of rights by elders, whereas exchange may be linked to social and economic relations that partly cut across ancestral ties. An emphasis on constructing community ties may occur in group initiation ceremonies in which wild animals are teased and then feasted on. Such activities may be relatively unlinked to domestic production based on sheep and goat.

So it is possible to argue that the restrictions and avoidances in the puzzle that I started with in this chapter relate to the faultlines within the entangled webs of social, economic and cultural life. It may be in the interests of ancestry and community to emphasize the teasing of, and feasting on, wild animals and bulls, as the animal heads are passed down from generation to generation. But there may be rather separate countervailing interests that focus on domestic production. As a result, it was thought inappropriate to place pots (associated with domestic production around the oven) in graves which focus on ancestral ties. It was thought inappropriate to bury adults near ovens or under 'dirty' floors with much domestic refuse. And it was thought inappropriate to show domestic activities in the art on the walls since the latter deal predominantly with wild animals, ancestry and the collective.

So the leopard's puzzle has started to be pieced together. The tale is complex and I have only introduced it here. But we can begin to see how the restrictions, such as the avoidance of leopard bones on the settlement, relate to the ways in which people managed their practical lives. People were entangled in somewhat different spheres of activity. These different sets of entanglements involved practical, symbolic, economic and aesthetic dimensions in a seamless web. But they nevertheless involved slightly different sets of activities and interests.

Ultimately, in the main sequence at Çatalhöyük, there is a shift towards the centrality of domestic production and exchange, as I will explore in Chapter II. There is a shift towards the increased practical and symbolic importance of the productive potential of the 'house'. This shift occurs very slowly indeed – taking millennia to occur. This shift provides an example of what I meant in the Prologue by the 'prehistory of the mass' – the slow movement caused by the small changes in the daily practices of large numbers of people. It is in the distributed processes of daily life that small acts come to have large consequences. To move the location of an oven may not seem like much, but in its entanglements such a change can have broad impact. Or the change from organic to grit temper in the pottery may not seem like much, but in the entanglements of pottery the shift allows a change in cooking, changes in the scheduling of tasks within the house, and thus changes in the numbers of tasks that can be undertaken within the domestic sphere.

In this chapter I have attempted an initial solving of the puzzles that Çatalhöyük poses. In the remainder of this book I will explore the different components of the puzzles, the different spheres of entanglement, in greater detail, and explore their changing interactions through time more closely. I will begin with larger-scale community questions, and then focus on the house, ancestry and exchange in Chapters 3 to 7. This gradual exploration of various sets of evidence will then allow me to discuss some general themes in the way people lived their lives at Çatalhöyük. In Chapters 8 to 10 I will examine the idea of 'art' at Çatalhöyük, gender relations and notions of selfhood. I will then be able to return in Chapter 11 to the question of change through time, and to the larger issue of how understanding of the way people lived at Çatalhöyük may throw light on the long-term processes of domestication and population concentration in the Neolithic of Anatolia and the Middle East.

1 Wall-painting of a running figure grasping a curved implement (possibly a bow) in one hand and wearing a possible leopard skin at the waist. This is just one of many similar figures that have been found at Çatalhöyük.

2 (above) Aerial view of the East Mound as seen from above the West Mound, looking out eastwards across the Konya Plain.

3 (right) Reconstruction of Çatalhöyük and the surrounding landscape during the spring flood.

4 View looking across the multiple levels that have been conserved under the spectacular South shelter. The people standing in the distance are on Level IV, while the photograph is taken from a building in Level VII. The shoring to the right is in buildings of Levels IX and X.

5 Excavations in the 4040 Area in 2004. This area was opened up in 2003 on the northern eminence of the East Mound in order to record and analyse settlement organization at a larger scale.

6 Building 5 during excavation.

7 The interior of Building 3 at a late stage of excavation (with north to the right). The southern and western areas have ovens, storage and evidence of food preparation, and the northern and eastern areas have whiter platforms with burials beneath.

8 Symbolism and daily life within the house at Çatalhöyük were very closely associated.

CHAPTER THREE

A Mysterious Attraction

The Turkish men and women who work on the project come mainly from the nearby village of Küçükköy (1 km (0.6 miles) from the site) and from the local town (15 km (9.5 miles) from the site) of Çumra. As noted in Chapter 1, one of the main questions about the site that interests them is 'why here?'. They are particularly interested in why this particular bit of land was chosen for the site. They are interested in the specifics of the locality, and how it was used for agriculture and food. The types of question to which they could most effectively contribute in our discussions with them were those that related to the practices of living in the central Anatolian environment, but even with such detailed knowledge about the local environment, the location of Çatalhöyük remained a mystery.

The people who have lived for some time in the local villages and towns remember sightings of leopards, especially in the upland areas of the Taurus to the south. As noted earlier, the leopard is a solitary animal that prefers to ambush its prey and then carry the prey up a tree – at least the leopard acts in this way in sub-Saharan Africa where it has to protect its prey from competitors such as hyaena.[1] The main competitors for the leopard in Anatolia at the time of Çatalhöyük are likely to have been packs of wolves,[2] and of course humans. The leopard is likely to have roamed in areas with some tree cover on the flanks of the uplands and along water courses.

The aims of this chapter are to outline a picture of the environment around Çatalhöyük, and to describe how that environment was used by the inhabitants of the site. This will help us to understand the community at Çatalhöyük and what held it together. Right at the start we need to be careful not to consider the environment simply as a physical resource, and we need to be wary of reducing the existence of the community at this particular point on the landscape to physical needs. For example, 'to the Tikopia nature does not work independently of man;

fertility is not merely a concatenation of physical factors but depends on the maintenance of a relationship between man and spiritual beings…. Towards individuals of the natural species an attitude of respect, sometimes amounting to reverence, is exhibited by members of the human group.'[3] The environment at Çatalhöyük was embedded in a complex symbolic world that extended into the lives of those dwelling there. For example, we have seen that the leopard was part of a set of myths and meanings that might have prohibited leopard bones from being brought onto the site or might have given special value to this rare animal. Many animals in the environment can be shown to have had some symbolic significance at the site.

The notion that the whole landscape was linked into the type of symbolism seen at Çatalhöyük has been shown recently by Douglas Baird and Trevor Watkins in their work at Pınarbaşı.[4] This site is a shelter in the Karadağ hills, about 25 km (15 miles) from Çatalhöyük. Here there are occupation levels contemporary with Çatalhöyük, and they have some unexpected parallels with it. In one trench Baird and Watkins found lumps of plaster with broken animal bone inside. This association between plaster and animal bones perhaps recalls the plastered animal installations at Çatalhöyük. Whatever the specific interpretation, these symbolic or ritual objects show that the whole landscape may have been linked through symbolism as much as it was linked through economic and social ties. Another example of perhaps a similar process is James Mellaart's record that natural limestone concretions, stalagmites and stalactites were found on site, and some were crudely made into suggestive human and other forms.[5] It is possible that these objects are simply by-products of the carving of figurines from limestone collected in caves, but even if that is all that is going on here, the use of stalagmites for figurines is of interest. There is also some evidence that would suggest that the inhabitants of Çatalhöyük brought distant natural stone into their symbolic worlds. In a grave recently excavated in the 4040 Area on the north hill of the East Mound, a smooth and veined natural piece of white calcite was found in a burial (Figure 31). While some markings were visible it was essentially a natural piece of stone from afar that had been incorporated into the grave accoutrements. Someone had noticed this unusual stone, brought it to the site, given it significance, so that it ended up being placed in a grave.

This chapter deals with the 'mysterious attraction' of Çatalhöyük – its place in the landscape. Other work by Douglas Baird involved a regional survey of the Konya Plain in which Çatalhöyük is situated.[6] While sites could be found in the survey that were earlier than Çatalhöyük, and other sites could be found that were later, there were no sites on the plain clearly contemporary with the main ceramic occupation at Çatalhöyük East. In fact Çatalhöyük seems to have drawn in population (as well as perhaps repelling some) from a wide area. What pulled people in? There is no evidence that people had to congregate to make use of a very localized resource. In fact a very wide environment was used. So the question is underlined –

31 A curious piece of stone emerges from a burial containing some very decayed human bones, found at the surface of the 4040 Area in 2003. This unusual, but natural stone was given significance by the inhabitants of Çatalhöyük.

what pulled people in to create the dense community at this place? Since people were using the landscape so extensively, both symbolically and as a resource, what brought them to live in such overcrowded conditions, so that there were no streets, on one spot in the landscape at Çatalhöyük?

THE LIVED ENVIRONMENT

The notions of 'living in', 'dwelling' or 'inhabiting' have become of widespread interest in archaeology in recent years.[7] The most important component of these developments that is used here concerns the attempt to understand landscape and built space as lived or experienced. In practical terms, in what follows there will be a focus on understanding the ways in which use of the landscape for subsistence was embedded within, and indistinguishable from, cultural understanding and movement within that landscape. Use of the built environment at Çatalhöyük was pragmatic, socially constructed, and conceptually engaged. In what follows, the seamless web of culture and environment will be clear, as will the pragmatic entanglements of people within that web.

In an attempt to answer the questions 'why was it there?' and 'how did people live in it?', it is necessary to look at broad and local environmental and climatic changes.[8] The Konya Plain is part of the Central Anatolian Plateau, and is made up of Pleistocene lake marls. Located at about 1,000 m (3,300 ft) altitude, the central plateau today has a continental climate with a yearly precipitation (winter snow and spring rain) of <400 mm (16 in) (only <350 mm (14 in) in the Konya Plain itself). There is marked seasonal variation between very cold winters and dry, hot summers. Although the overall climatic conditions of the Konya Plain at the time of its occupation by the Neolithic population at Çatalhöyük were wetter than those of the present, the environment was still dominated by a semi-arid regime with moist winters and summer drought.[9]

In general terms, Anatolia experienced a rise in humidity in the early Holocene (the period around 10,000 BC after the Pleistocene or Ice Age), although this happened rather faster in neighbouring regions such as the Beyşehir lakes to the southwest and in Cappadocia to the north, than it did in the Konya Plain itself. Alluvial fans started to be formed by the increased flow of rivers into many parts of the plain, and there was soil development and vegetation growth in the period from 6100 to 4300 BC.[10] However, alluvial deposition had started by 7500 BC at Çatalhöyük itself. How vegetation changed through this period can be seen in sequences of pollen trapped in lake beds and other deposits. Pollen cores from the Konya region show that forest coverage reached its maximum around 4300 BC. Summarizing a core taken near the site and a series of other cores at various distances from Çatalhöyük, the pollen analyst Warren Eastwood[11] says of the pollen evidence that at the time of the earliest occupation of Çatalhöyük the landscape may be interpreted as a largely treeless grass steppe on the drier Anatolian plateau, giving way to open oak-grass parkland with some juniper, pistachio/terebinth and birch on the foothills, and to oak-pine-cedar woodland in the better-watered Taurus Mountains (Figure 32).

The first Neolithic people in the area would have lived in an increasingly complex mosaic of environments and types of vegetation. The Konya Basin contained some marshy areas and perhaps some small shallow seasonal lakes, as suggested by some of the bird bones at Çatalhöyük.[12] The vegetation across the plain would have included a complex patchwork of grassy steppe around the marsh lands, sedges and common reeds (*Phragmites*) within the marshy areas, shrubs on the better-drained soils, and trees along the river margins.[13] The first settlement at the site was likely to have been on a small rise in the uneven topography of the marl, above the damp ground of the alluvial deposits. At that time, the Çarşamba river would have run by the site. It spewed out into the plain and did not link into any other river system. The clayey nature of the alluvium deposited around the site suggests that the site would have been surrounded by wet marshy backswamps for much of the spring period of flooding of the river.

Thus, at the time of the start of Çatalhöyük, while the overall Central Anatolian Plateau was relatively dry (in comparison with neighbouring regions), alluvial fans had started to form as a result of the increased precipitation in the higher areas in the Taurus to the south and southwest. Many of the early sites in

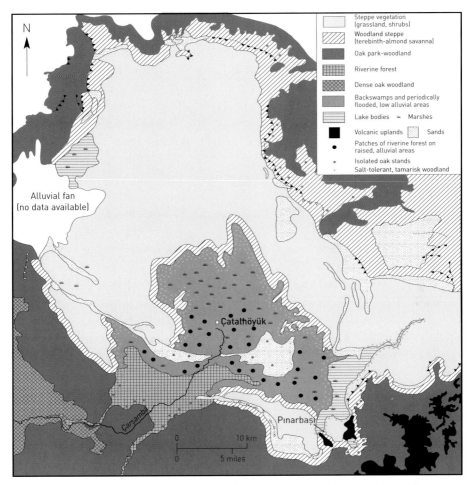

32 Map of regional vegetation in the Konya Plain at the time of Çatalhöyük. Çatalhöyük itself was founded on a small raised area in the wetlands – a low-lying marshy zone that would have been flooded during the spring. Alluvium was deposited by the Çarşamba river flowing in from the southwest. To the south lies better-drained higher ground, a valuable source of timber.

the region such as Suberde, Pınarbaşı and Can Hasan III are located near springs and river mouths. Çatalhöyük fits into this same pattern, with the particular location chosen subject to spring flooding (Plate 3). Despite, and perhaps because of, the overall dryness of the Plateau, Neolithic sites concentrate in locally wet areas.

The marls with steppe vegetation on the Konya Plain are not suitable for early agriculture. They are impermeable, nutrient-poor and become salty with heavy evaporation. However, bordering the lacustrine plain, the alluvial fans are much more suitable. Çatalhöyük is located in the centre of the largest of the fans on the south edge of the plain – the Çarşamba Fan, fed by the Çarşamba river from the southwest. The Çarşamba Fan was created in two phases from 7600 to 3000 BC and then from 2400 BC.[14] Associated with this fan formation, there was extensive spring flooding which created the backswamp clay around the site.

The data collected from the site in the 1995–99 excavations provide support for the view based on sedimentological studies that the site was located in a wetland environment. For example, grasses and plants from river edges are well represented in the carbonized seed assemblages.[15] The assemblage of bird bones has a predominance of wetland species, although there are few bird remains overall.[16]

In this particular part of the Konya Plain, environmental conditions will have been affected by a variety of local factors. It is important to identify how the larger regional changes relate to the specifics of the area around the site itself. Eleni Asouti's work on the charcoal recovered from the site shows a changing relationship with the environment during the early occupation of the site.[17] In particular a major change (at around 7050 BC) separates Levels Pre-XII.B–D from Pre-XII.A to VII (these levels are shown in Figure 18 and the overall sequence of levels is explained on p 43). In the lowest levels there are more riverine taxa (willow/poplar, elm) and hackberry. Asouti sees a gradual decline in precipitation after about 7000 BC as the juniper increases. It is of interest, therefore, that Emma Jenkins's study of the microfauna from a sample of the excavated deposits found a greater representation of amphibians in the lowest levels of the site.[18] In the KOPAL Area to the north of the East Mound, there are a series of Late Neolithic and Chalcolithic buried soil horizons above the early backswamp clay. These indicate a significant drying out towards the end of the occupation of the East Mound at the end of the 7th millennium BC.

So it seems that a partial answer to the question of why Çatalhöyük was located in this particular place was that, given a semi-arid environment, the site needed to be located in close proximity to lots of water. One might also have thought that, given the overall poor quality of the marl soils in the plain, that the alluvium and backswamp clays around the site would have been attractive to these early farmers.[19] These nutrient-rich deposits would have been annually regenerated by the spring floods.

However, the large-scale spring floods of the river by Çatalhöyük were probably unpredictable and could vary enormously in scale.[20] One response may have been to move at least some of the agricultural fields away to the higher and drier land to the south. One of the more fascinating and surprising aspects of recent research at the site is the demonstration that, indeed, at least some of the fields may have been located well away from the site. The first 'spanner in the works' came from the phytolith data.[21]

Phytoliths are the silica skeletons of grasses and plants – microscopic silt-sized particles that form inside the cells. When grasses are cultivated in clay-rich moist soils, they have more soluble silica available in the growing medium than those grown in well-drained dry-land soils. As a result, in moister soils large multicelled phytoliths form. Experimental data from the semi-arid region of southern Israel have shown that irrigated crops of emmer wheat (*Triticum dicoccum*, a form of early wheat) produce silica skeletons which commonly exceed 100 adjacent cells per phytolith and sometimes produce forms with as many as 300 cells. Conversely, wheat grown in dry-farming conditions depending primarily on rain-fed agriculture, produces many fewer multicelled silica skeletons.

Given the known conditions around Çatalhöyük we would expect to see large numbers of silicified cells from wheat phytoliths if they had been cultivated in the moist marshy soils around the site. A sample of wheat-husk phytoliths was studied by Arlene Rosen and these showed an interesting pattern. The numbers of phytoliths displaying greater than 10 cells constituted less than 15 per cent of the assemblage and there were no wheat-husk phytoliths with over 70 silicified adjacent cells. This suggests that the wheat was cultivated using dry-land farming in well-drained soils.

Other evidence has tended to support the claim that at least some of the fields were tended well away from the wet soils near the site. Andrew Fairbairn and other archaeobotanists working at the site have agreed, on the basis of the carbonized seed evidence (and especially the weed seeds, some of which are from dry-land contexts), that cereal farming may have used a variety of locations including the uplands 10 km (6 miles) to the south.[22] These uplands to the south would have been the nearest areas of extensive dry land at the time of Çatalhöyük. The charcoal data suggest that there were raised alluvial surfaces near the site supporting river edge vegetation, but Eleni Asouti does not think there was intense agricultural use of these hummocks.[23] Overall, there is a consensus amongst many project members that at least some cereal farming took place at some distance from the site. It has for some time been argued that early farming may often be associated with floodwater contexts,[24] and while initially it might be thought that Çatalhöyük fits into such a pattern, the palaeobotanical, phytolith and charcoal data suggest a rather different picture.

So the question 'why this location?' becomes even more stark. By being located out in the wet marshes, the inhabitants certainly had access to a wide range of resources, from fish and water-bird eggs (both of which have been found on the site) to the wild mammals attracted to the water and the fresh grazing on the annually renewed alluvium. One immediately local resource that we know was exploited on a large scale by the inhabitants was mud. In the KOPAL Area to the north of the East Mound there are many marl extraction pits.[25] These were cut down by the inhabitants of the site, through the (at the time) thin riverine alluvium and into the underlying lime-rich marls. We know that marl was used for a variety of purposes including the making of bricks and especially plaster. In the earliest levels of the site a fired lime plaster is used for constructing floors; in later levels, a softer lime-rich plaster is used to make floors and walls. There would have been a continual movement of material for plaster from the local environment onto the site. Analysis of the mud bricks also shows knowledge of a wide range of different types of local clays.[26] Clay was a hugely important resource involving a high level of energy expenditure. The marl extraction pits also extended down into the sands beneath the marl, providing another local source of material.

We shall see throughout this book that many of the social and ritual aspects of life at Çatalhöyük were centred on the modelling, painting, remodelling, repainting, retrieval and deposition of clay and plaster reliefs and sculptures. The spatial division of floors has great social significance, and is marked by the use of different types of plaster. The social and cultural factors involved in the need for different types of clay were part of a larger mix of factors leading to the particular location of Çatalhöyük. However, the economic, social and cultural need for mud was not the only factor in the location of the site by any means. A range of wild water resources were used, and wild cattle were locally available. Presumably some farming was carried out near the site, and perhaps there was use of hummocks and islands in the nearby wetlands, although the annual unpredictability of the scale of flooding must have made these unreliable field locations. But some fields, and perhaps some sheep and goat grazing (see below), occurred well away from the site.

Another response to the markedly seasonal environment and overall aridity could have been to undertake seasonal movements of settlement. The bird data from the site help to show that the site was permanently occupied.[27] Certainly there are species from all the seasons. Also, there is no evidence on site for breaks in occupation; indeed, the detailed studies of floors and other deposits indicate continual presence, even if groups of people were away from the site for periods of time through the annual cycle. Wendy Matthews[28] notes a seasonal cycle of activities visible on the wall plasters, with soot accumulating only in some (winter) months, and probably use of ovens on roofs in the summer. A reconstruction of a wide range of seasonal activities at the site has been provided by Andrew Fairbairn.[29] Figure 33 graphically illustrates the ways in which people were entangled in a complex landscape. Its seasonal workings caught humans up in a web of schedules, responses and movements – as people collaborated or dispersed to meet the changing needs.

A further way of dealing with a challenging semi-arid environment is to depend on other groups in a social network. Certainly there is much evidence for long-distance trade and exchange. There are many examples of such exchanges, such as the date palm phytoliths[30] perhaps indicating movement of storage baskets from Syria, Mesopotamia or the Levant, Red Sea and Mediterranean shells, Cappadocian obsidian, and the oak and other park woodland timber that had to come at least 10 km (6 miles) from the nearest uplands.[31] But it is of interest that the immediate social network seems to have been rather sparse. As already noted, a regional survey

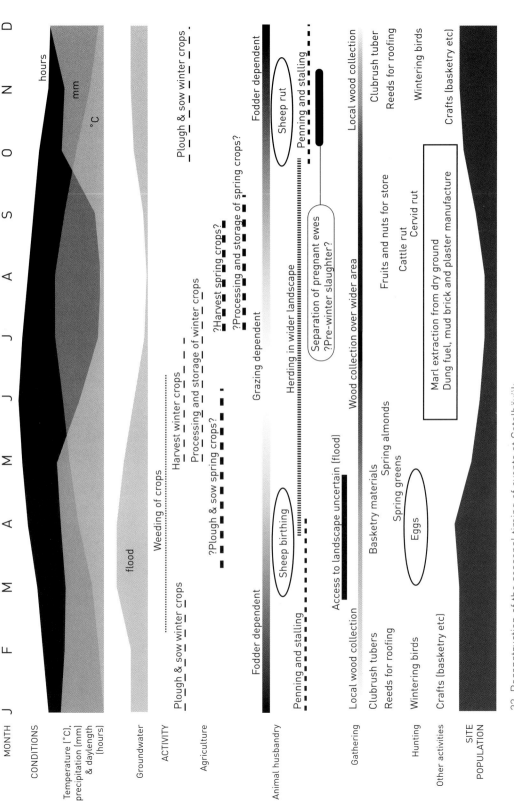

33 Reconstruction of the seasonal timing of events at Çatalhöyük.

carried out by Douglas Baird found no local sites that were clearly contemporary with Çatalhöyük. There was thus a dense network of support on the site, but the site was quite isolated locally.

The Role of Domesticated Plants and Animals

So what was the role of domesticated plants at Çatalhöyük? Already in central Anatolia, domesticated plants had come to be a resource at Aşıklı Höyük by around 8400 BC.[32] At Aşıklı Höyük, there was probably rain-fed agriculture on raised surfaces next to the Melendiz river and on hillsides and dry areas in the valley, close to the settlement. But in the millennium after Aşıklı Höyük, Çatalhöyük seems to have had a greater dependence on cultivated plants than did its predecessor. Andrew Fairbairn and other archaeobotanists who work on the project argue that domestic crops provided the dominant source of plant food at Çatalhöyük, with wild plants being present, but less important.[33] The main cereal is emmer wheat, but there is a wide variety of others. The importance of plants is also seen in the prevalence of storage bins in buildings (storage bins do occur at Aşıklı Höyük, but it is claimed that they are quite rare[34]). Hans Helbaek, during James Mellaart's excavations, had identified stores of domesticated emmer and einkorn (another early form of wheat) at Çatalhöyük, but also of pea and both domesticated and wild vetch.[35] The current project has found a store of lentils. All this suggests storage of a range of plants at a small, varied and non-intensive scale (contrast the huge stores of grain recorded by Nurcan Yalman in her ethnoarchaeological work in the modern villages around Çatalhöyük). Helbaek also noted concentrations of wild plants kept in houses such as almonds, acorns, hackberry and terebinth. The current excavations have demonstrated the intensive gathering of a small wild seed termed *Sisymbrium* which was probably collected as a food or seasoning. Quite a lot of the archaeobotanical samples contain plant tissue fragments, probably from the rhizomes of reeds collected for food. All this suggests the widespread use of a variety of plants, with a strong emphasis on domesticated plants. As we shall see below, there is also isotopic evidence[36] from human bones that confirms the importance of plants in what people were eating.

It is also possible that domesticated plants were grown as part of animal husbandry – at least in relation to the domesticated herbivores on the site, sheep and goat. But the archaeobotanical team found that dung used in lime-burning in the early levels contained wild grass stems and woody plant leaf phytoliths, suggesting that animals were grazing on wild plants rather than cereal stubble, and that they were not being fed cereal fodder. Perhaps this was not a well-integrated cereal/domestic animal system, or perhaps the samples analyzed were from times in the year when fodder was not available. If there was a major distance between the site and some of the agricultural fields, integration may have been impeded – indeed, as we shall see below, sheep and goat seem to have been grazed over diverse environments. In her study of phytoliths from the site, Arlene Rosen found a low correlation between wheat phytoliths and a variety of wild seed grasses. She sees the former as human food and the latter as dung fuel or animal fodder. Barley seems to be more associated with the wild seed grasses.

This tentative evidence of a partial separation or lack of integration between the main domesticated plants and animals may perhaps be glimpsed in on-site cultural behaviour. For example, we have seen in the art that there is much depiction of animals, either wild or domestic, but little depiction or symbolism associated with plants, wild and domestic. These distinctions are part of the puzzle that I outlined in Chapter 2. In addition, there is some preliminary evidence of a possible distinction between plants and animals in terms of the container types used for them. Analysis of lipid residues in potsherds from the site by Mark Copley, Kate Clark and Richard Evershed indicates that at least some of the pots were used to produce and keep animal fat (probably mainly sheep and goat fat), although they may also have been used for milk and to process plants such as cereals.[37] Arlene Rosen found a link between wheat phytoliths (and perhaps acorns) and particular 'bilobate' forms of phytolith probably from baskets – suggesting a particular link between a plant food and a basket container. It might be objected that baskets could not be used for cooking meat and keeping fat, but Sonya Atalay has provided many ethnographic examples of baskets being sealed and used in such ways.[38] However, the activities of both baskets/plants and pots/grease and fat processing are closely associated with oven areas. So any categorical distinction does not prevent the two types of food and activity from using the same space in buildings. In that space they come together.

But let us turn to the animal side of the subsistence economy. One clear result of the new project is that the more intensive excavation techniques used have shown that cattle are much less important in terms of food intake than had been thought in the 1960s by James Mellaart and his faunal analyst Dexter Perkins.[39] This pattern is seen in both the quantitative evidence of the animal bones and in the stable isotope evidence concerning human diet. Also the cattle are wild, again despite earlier claims to the contrary.

Amongst the cattle bones there is no evidence that only meaty parts of the carcass were brought back to the site.[40] This suggests cattle were hunted close to the site on the plain. This evidence fits very nicely with the evidence from stable isotope analyses of animal bones[41] that cattle have a much less wide range of diets than sheep and goat, again suggesting that they were not grazing over a great diversity of environments. Cattle were not the main subsistence resource but they played an important social-ritual role and so their local availability may have been of importance in site location.

Domesticated sheep and goat occurred in central Anatolia by the time of Çatalhöyük. At Aşıklı Höyük, there is evidence of sheep and goat herd management rather than full domestication.[42] Approximately contemporary with Çatalhöyük, Suberde has evidence of herd management of sheep. More widely in Anatolia there is evidence of sheep domestication at Nevalı Çori in the mid to late 9th millennium BC.[43] The evidence of domesticated sheep and goat at Çatalhöyük is thus not surprising. Stable isotope analysis of animal bones found that sheep had a very wide range of carbon and nitrogen isotope values, suggesting that they grazed over much wider areas than cattle or goat – or were traded/exchanged from afar unlike cattle. But the faunal data do show foetal/neonate bones of sheep in 'penning areas' in abandoned houses or in open areas close to the edge of the settlement (in Space 181) – suggesting on-site keeping of sheep and on-site birthing. At least some of the time some of the sheep were kept on or at the edge of the site.

From one perspective, wild and domesticated animals were recognized as very separate categories at Çatalhöyük. This claim rests on the lack of symbolic use of sheep and goats in the paintings, reliefs and to some extent in feasting. But while we can say that cattle were wild and sheep and goat were mostly domesticated at Çatalhöyük, from another perspective the distinctions between wild and domestic diverge from our own. For example, the discussion of the way in which cattle (the very large wild aurochs) may have been treated is complex. As we will see later in this volume, wild bulls had a special place in ritual and feasting, and their relationship with humans was undoubtedly very close.

There are other still more ambiguous and blurred categories. For example, the way that dogs were treated undermines any simple opposition between wild and domestic. They were domesticated, and they were not normally eaten,[44] but were used in special ritual or feasting contexts. They were not 'pets' but they may have been used in hunting (as suggested by some of the wall paintings). Mike Richards argues that the dog stable isotopes show a very similar pattern to the human bone, indicating a close connection to humans – probably the dogs were mostly eating human leftovers.[45] This closeness is supported by the paintings (which show humans accompanied by dogs) and by the special status of dog in the faunal data. Clearly dogs were on site, as seen in the amount of bone showing evidence of probable passage through the guts of dogs, and yet they do not get to gnaw bone. There is a relatively low level of gnawed bone on site, and there is especially little gnawed bone from floor and occupation deposits inside houses, suggesting that dogs were in the settlement but not in the houses. Detailed quantitative study of animal bone discard has found that there is more digested bone in some middens in abandoned buildings than in the external middens.[46] This may mean that the dogs were sometimes tethered there. Whatever the specifics of this complex pattern of dog-human relationships, dogs were clearly close to humans, but not too close. They were domesticated but used in rituals in special ways rather similar to wild animals.

Another ambiguous category may be birds.[47] There is a lot of eggshell at the site, from both hatched and unhatched eggs. This may suggest some degree of tending or raising of birds – goose and duck are the tentatively identified bird shells so far. But there is not enough bird bone at the site for birds to have provided a major resource.

Changes Through Time

There is much evidence for gradual change through time in the way that the landscape was 'lived' from Çatalhöyük. These changes were related to, and were perhaps causally related to, the environmental changes noted above. The decreasing wetness after the earliest levels parallels changes in the charcoal data as examined by Eleni Asouti.[48] In Levels Pre-XII.A to VII there is more oak and then an increase in juniper in Levels IX to VII. Through time there is also more intensive exploitation of firewood. Asouti sees the increase in oak in Level Pre-XII.A indicating people going further away for timber and firewood, as a result of clearance and degradation of nearby wetland vegetation.

Similarly, sheep and goat stable isotopes[49] are tightly clustered in Levels Pre-XII.C–D, but are much wider in Levels Pre-XII.A–B (after about 7100 BC), and are even more widely spread in levels above XII. This suggests a shift towards multiple feeding grounds, and parallels the charcoal evidence of a shift from local to extra-local fuel use. The evidence of on-site penning is also in the lower levels, so the notion of a local to a wider grazing of animals is strengthened.

The faunal data show that after Level Pre-XII.B usually only heads and hides of pigs and deer are brought onto the site. This could again be because people had to go farther and wider for resources. Perhaps the local drying out after the earliest levels is linked to this shift. But it should also be noted that many of these temporal trends could be explained as spatial differences. This is because our evidence for the earliest levels comes from contexts that are off the edge of the site, or close to it. Nevertheless, at present temporal change seems the most likely explanation.

And certainly, the changes continue through time. Oak and juniper were the main construction timbers, but the use of structural timbers declines, according to Mellaart, at the top of the site in Level II.[50] This could result from deforestation of the environment through extensive use, but there could be other factors involved such as changes in exchange patterns. There may also be a link to the sedimentological evidence for a drying out of the local soils right at the end of the occupancy of the East Mound (see page 78).

The theme of an initial local focus expanding outwards returns in other, more social guises. At first, as Douglas Baird's data suggest, Çatalhöyük seems to have sucked in population from the surrounding landscape. There may have been more of an emphasis on communities and on caring for the resources of the group as a whole (for example, there is some evidence of more use of party walls between houses in the lower levels). But through time, as we shall see in Chapter II, there is evidence of internal differentiation and specialization. Perhaps this internal differentiation led to a need to exploit a wider diversity of environments, and to compete more extensively for resources. As a result there was a shift from local to non-local resources, as noted above.

DIET AND EATING

Nitrogen isotope[51] values from human bones suggest people had a diet in which cattle protein was not a significant component. Rather, the diet was based mainly on plants and sheep and goat. This fits with the faunal data suggesting a predominance of sheep and goat. The sheep/goat mortality profiles[52] do not suggest a heavy dependence on milk, but pot residue analyses do show some evidence of milk use.[53] There is much evidence from the way in which the bones have been broken up of fat and marrow extraction from sheep and goat bones. This evidence correlates well with the residue results showing the predominance of small ruminant fats in pottery.[54] It is most likely, given the overall predominance of sheep and goat bones at the site and their intense processing in houses that these small ruminant fats are from sheep and goat.

Studies of wear and pitting on human teeth suggest that the diet was a mixed particulate one (i.e. without a lot of ground cereal) – consisting of, for example, whole grains, nuts, berries and meat. Theya Molleson and Başak Boz argue that Scanning Electron Microscope studies of the chewing surfaces of molar teeth indicate that food was often not cooked, had large particle size, and was not abrasive.[55] There is a considerable amount of wear probably resulting from regular consumption of hard things like tubers and uncooked grain. Other evidence does suggest cooking from the start. It seems clear, given the ethnographic, experimental and analytical data studied by Sonya Atalay,[56] that the clay balls which are found so commonly in the lower levels of the site were used in cooking, but there is a shift in cooking practices to the use of pots around Levels VI to VII. If the residue analysis is right in indicating the pots were frequently used for preparing and storing sheep and goat fats and grease, it may be that we should envisage in the upper levels a diet of meats and often uncooked and unground plants supplemented by or seasoned by fats and greases cooked and kept in pots. It may be that it was in cuisine that plant and animal, domesticated plant and animal fat, were brought together.

But as noted earlier, there seem to be restrictions on what was brought on to the site or consumed there. The lack of evidence of leopard is only one example. Pig are like deer in that meaty body parts are not brought on site very much, at least after the earliest levels of occupation. The data suggest the possibility of taboos and special treatment of different animals and plants. It could be argued that pig and deer became locally less available through time, and so less of the animal body parts were carried long distances back to the site after a kill. It seems odd, if such were the case, that it was not the meaty parts of animals that were brought back to the site. Rather, it was the cranial parts often used in symbolic and ritual contexts, and the feet, probably attached to skins, that were brought back.

It could be argued that the lack of leopard bones on the site could result from the fact that they were encountered more rarely and farther away from the site than many other animals. People may not have wanted to carry the bones and meat back long distances. Given the apparent depictions of animal skins being worn by people in the paintings, it seems likely that the skins were brought back, and we would have expected small feet bones to be included in the skins, as in the case of the pig and deer. Also, leopards may have come quite close to the site amongst the trees along the river and in the neighbouring wooded uplands. Presumably humans encountered leopards and big cats as they hunted cattle, equids, deer and pigs. They would have been competing for the same resources in similar locations. The fact that bones from these other animals are found on the site, but not leopard bones remains striking (see Epilogue).

CONCLUSION

The meat, marrow and fat from animals was brought together with plants in the cooking and cuisine around the oven in the house. As people ate in the house (Figure 34), the domestic unit was brought together and social relations were formed and reformed. Although it is clear that people stored their own food, and perhaps conducted many economic tasks in domestic groupings, the overall discussion of use of the environment in this chapter has also produced a picture of a great toing and froing as daily tasks were undertaken. As the seasonal round was followed, there must have been considerable organization at the scale of the community as a whole. It seems likely that households cooperated in the tending of fields away from the site. It would have made sense to share in the grazing of sheep and goats if they were taken well away from the site, as seems most likely. There must also have been cooperative decisions about who could extract marl from the nearby quarrying pits, and how to get construction timbers brought down from the uplands. The dispersed and extensive use of the environment from a dense central point implies a community scale of organization, at least to some degree.

It must, indeed, have been difficult to organize all these dispersed activities in such a large community. So why was Çatalhöyük located where it was and why did people cluster together in one place? I have argued in this chapter that a range of factors were probably involved in the choice of this particular location. On the Konya Plain there were many poor marl soils with steppe vegetation in a sub-arid environment. People therefore focused on areas with richer alluvial soils and easy access to water. Such soils, easily drained, would have been important for agriculturalists using digging sticks and simple technologies. People were also assessing the environment in terms of wild resources, from cattle to a wide range of water resources from reed tubers to water bird eggs. Early agriculture in this sub-arid environment, with seasonal but unpredictable floods, was probably risky and prone to failure. One response may have been to locate some of the fields and grazing areas well away from the site. Diverse wild resources may have facilitated the dependence on domesticated plants, sheep and goats, acting as a buffer in times of shortage.

Another factor in the location of the site may have been access to construction materials – we find large amounts of reeds in the middens on the site that were probably used in a variety of ways including matting and roofing. We find the impressions of reed mats on the floor – and in one building it was clear that different types of mat were placed on different platforms[57] (see Figure 81). But the site was also located within a wide variety of muds, marls and clay that were important in house construction. We have found extraction pits just at the edge of the site where people were digging down to obtain marl and the sands beneath it. This is the clearest evidence we have about site location. Mud and clay were the major resource that had to be carried on site, and they were used in everything from bricks and mortar, to platforms and installations, wall reliefs, pottery, clay balls, figurines, stamp seals and so on. Different types of mud plaster with different degrees of whiteness were used for the different platforms in the buildings. The environment was partly viewed from the perspective of the practices, rituals and symbolism of the house.

The environment was 'lived in' both practically and symbolically, and the location of the site shows these two components of living. There are undoubted economic factors involved in the location of the site within rich riverine and flood plain resources. But equally there were social, symbolic and ritual factors that affected all parts of life. Wild cattle were locally available, and they were central to social life, as seen in the bulls used for feasting, and their skulls and horns were a central part of the symbolic installations within houses. The suite of practical and symbolic factors was in the end more important than simple questions such as closeness to the agricultural fields.

But none of this really explains why so many people were drawn into Çatalhöyük. It might have been thought that by answering the question 'why here?'

34 Food preparation activities near the oven in the southern part of a building. Cooking and eating brought the domestic unit together, allowing social relations to be formed and reformed.

we would resolve the question of why the agglomeration and the attraction. For example, we might have found that agglomeration in one spot was the only way to survive in a difficult environment. This type of thinking lay behind Gordon Childe's 'oasis theory' about the adoption of agriculture and settled village life.[58] But in the Çatalhöyük case, it seems that the concentration of people in one place is not the obvious answer to environmental conditions. In fact people used the environment in a very dispersed way, particularly through time. So why didn't they just disperse and live nearer their fields or following the movements of the sheep and goats? Why did they, like their central Anatolian predecessors at Aşıklı Höyük, decide to concentrate in one place? In the chapter that follows we will examine some of the factors that created these 'towns'. But in order to answer the question why people agglomerated at all, we will need to understand the mystery of the site – its rituals and way of life. These will be explored in the rest of the book.

CHAPTER FOUR

The 'Town'

The leopards face each other in pairs. Those reliefs that most probably depict leopards (e.g. Plates 9 and 10) simply stand head to head. There are other pairings of possible leopards or felines (Figure 35) in which the front legs also face forward, as if the two are fighting. It is difficult to be confident about the interpretation of these pairings. James Mellaart saw them as male and female pairs,[1] but male and female leopards are often quite different in size[2] and the pairs at Çatalhöyük are closely similar in size. We cannot even be sure that two animals, rather than one, are involved. In the iconography of Pre-Columbian Central America, pairings of jaguars show the two sides of the same animal. But despite all this uncertainty about the meaning of the pairing of the Çatalhöyük examples, we can note an interesting tension in these images. The leopard is an intensely solitary animal. Males are usually found on their own, and females too are solitary unless they have

35 This pair of possible leopards face towards each other with their front legs also facing forward – apparently fighting. The leopard reliefs occur mainly as pairs at Çatalhöyük, perhaps indicating a social emphasis on balance and duality.

cubs with them. But in the reliefs, the leopard or leopards are paired and balanced.

There are other examples at Çatalhöyük of a similar tension surrounding pairing. For example, Figure 36 shows a white marble figurine from Level VI. The pair of women with breasts are joined at the hip and have one pair of arms. There is a tension here between unity and difference. We shall see that much of the life of the 'town' of Çatalhöyük was embedded in a tension between overall social balance and community, and individual difference. One sometimes seems to see this in the layout of buildings (Figure 37). For example in Mellaart's plan of Level VIB, what he called 'Shrine' 10 seems balanced by 'Shrine' 8 with storage or work areas in between. To the north of these 'shrines' is a row of lesser buildings covering an area which had earlier been used for midden as shown in Mellaart's and our excavations. To the north again there are two 'Shrines' 14 and 7, which seem to balance 'Shrines' 10 and 8. 'Shrines' 14 and 7 again have a work or storage area which balances that between 10 and 8. So there do seem to be two pairs of opposed buildings. Of course, it may be that this paired patterning is just an accident of the packing of houses and it may be wrong to pick out such patterning from within an overall distribution. But, nevertheless, as we have excavated in this area, the impression of some structure has been difficult to avoid.

36 A white marble figurine representing a pair of women joined at the hip as one, and with only one pair of arms – one of several examples of a tension surrounding pairings at Çatalhöyük.

There are undoubtedly other scales of corporate group at Çatalhöyük that can be recognized. For example, groups of houses are sometimes connected by access holes or by shared party walls. A number of houses seem to share the use of certain dominant houses for burial (see Chapter 5). There is also evidence of feasting involving large amounts of meat from cattle, at least enough for several households.[3] Some of the paintings in the upper levels show groups of people involved in teasing or baiting or hunting wild animals (Plate 15, a detail of which is shown in Figure 38). In some cases the human figures are all bearded (Figure 13). In Shrine F.V.1 there are 'crowds' of people, in rows, dancing, or agitated around the animals.[4] These activities, if they are any more than myth, could not have taken place on site. The paintings suggest collective action off site, although there is no way of telling how many households may have been involved in such group activities. It seems likely (see Chapter 3) that sheep were grazed widely and that there must have been some collaboration in herding. Flocks would have to be protected

37 The layout of Buildings in Level VIB as found by James Mellaart. 'S' represents what Mellaart identified as 'Shrines' and 'C' what he identified as 'Courtyards' – the present project has not found it possible to make such distinctions and terms all buildings houses at Çatalhöyük. However, it is still possible to pick out some patterning in what is otherwise an apparently random layout. For example, 'Shrines' 10 and 8, and 14 and 7, seem to represent two pairs of opposing buildings, laid out quite symmetrically. (For correlations between these 'shrines' and buildings excavated by the current projection in Level VII see Figure 45.)

38 This detail from a wall-painting in Level V shows a group of figures engaged in either the baiting or hunting of a large bull. The full painting is shown in Plate 15.

from predators – such as wolves and leopards. Leopards tend to prey on animals less that 70 kg in mass[5] and so are likely to have sought out sheep and goats. Collective action may also have occurred for planting and tending fields (especially as many of these were at some distance from the site – see Chapter 3), and obtaining trade goods, wood from the uplands, obsidian from Cappadocia, baskets from the Red Sea and so on.

On the other hand, there is a strong sense of the separate identity of each individual house. For example, while party walls occur, they are relatively rare. Overall, there is an evident desire not to share party walls. To have party walls would restrict a particular house's ability to rebuild or to change. Each house seems to have had its own suite of activities (hearths, ovens, obsidian cache, storage and work rooms and so on). Bricks with different composition or shape are used in the building of each house.[6] It is as if, despite the dense packing, each house retains its autonomy (see further in Chapter 5).

In this emphasis on the autonomy of the house, Çatalhöyük is similar to many contemporary sites in Anatolia and the Middle East. Yet the degree of packing of houses is only paralleled in other central Anatolian sites such as Aşıklı Höyük and Can Hasan III. Explanations of the degree of packing in terms of defence have little evidential basis. Whatever the reasons for this local tradition, the sense of the collective is both enhanced and contradicted by the daily problems of habitation that result (Figure 39). I refer here to problems of sanitation, water supply, movement, access to resources, and crowding that would both need collective action and create tensions between cohabitants. What then was the relationship between the individual house and the larger collective at Çatalhöyük?

THE SOCIAL GEOGRAPHY OF THE 'TOWN'

In the last chapter we saw that, in contrast to any sparse and perhaps fairly mobile settlement that may have existed on the open expanses of the plain, large numbers of people were concentrated in Çatalhöyük itself. Using a range of different techniques and using a range of different assumptions (about how many people tend to live ethnographically in roofed areas of a certain size, how many buildings might have been occupied at any one time, etc.), Craig Cessford[7] has worked out that the number of people occupying the site at any one time was between 3,500 and 8,000. There is good evidence that the levels of occupation varied considerably in extent and so at times the upper figures may have been reached. Our population estimates are based on the view that much of the site was covered in housing of the type excavated by Mellaart and by the current team. That much of the site was densely packed with housing was demonstrated by surface scraping and geophysical work.[8] Despite the many limitations of using geophysical prospection on uniformly compacted mud-brick sites, Clark Dobbs and Donald Johnson do detect some traces of possible Neolithic housing in unexcavated parts of the mound, suggesting a general extension of what we have found in the excavated areas.[9]

So in terms of size, we might call this settlement a 'town'. But it has few of the other characteristics that we might mean by that term. Despite careful sampling of the surface of the mound, we have not found public spaces, administrative buildings, elite quarters, or really any specialized functional spaces except those on the edge of the mound (such as lime burning) and animal penning. Indeed in 2004 we undertook excavation specifically to explore the idea that there might be some centralized functions at the site. We had earlier scraped the summit of the northern hill of the East Mound and found densely packed houses (Figure 40). But between

39 Reconstruction of life in the 'town' of Çatalhöyük. Many activities took place on roofs in warm and dry weather and there were areas for animal penning between the houses, as well as areas for refuse discard.

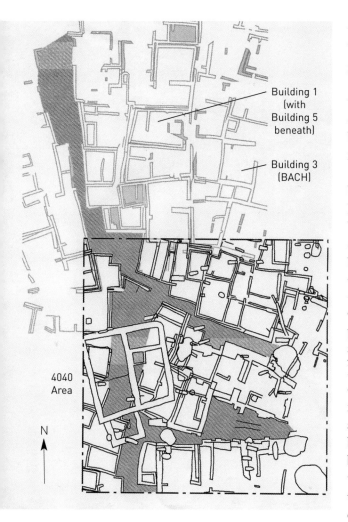

Building 1
(with
Building 5
beneath)

Building 3
(BACH)

4040
Area

N

40 Plan of houses on the north hill of the East Mound, showing zoning, with 'streets' (shaded) between zones. The 4040 Area is indicated by a dashed line in the south of the area. A later, historic, building occurs on a different alignment in the western part of the 4040 Area.

the houses there appeared to be 'streets' leading to a central triangular area of housing (see below). Some of these houses appeared on the plan to look different – for example with especially thick and buttressed walls, or with large internal entrances between rooms. So in 2004 we excavated these buildings to see if in some way they had some specialized function. What we found was more prosaic (Figure 41). We did find some thick buttressed walls, but they were just the result of reinforcing collapsing walls where they ran along the 'streets'. These were not special buildings in any way. They were just those at the edge of zones of houses (see below), and so more exposed to the weather and so more in need of strengthening of the outside walls. There was one unusual building (Building 47 – see below) but it was unusual mainly because it was later in date – and occurred at a time when houses had begun to change their internal organization.

So all there is at Çatalhöyük are houses and middens and pens. There is none of the functional differentiation that we normally associate with the term 'town'. Çatalhöyük is just a very very large village – it pushed the idea of an egalitarian village to its ultimate extreme. Of course, there must have been groups (such as a committee of elders) coordinating activities and possibly ascribing rules. But many activities, as will be discussed in Chapter 5, were carried out at the house level for most of the site's occupancy. Most production, even where there is some specialization of production, is carried out at the house level. And indeed, this is perhaps the greatest enigma of Çatalhöyük – that given the domestic scale of production and much social and economic life, why did people aggregate into such a major centre? The concentration of people into large settlements is found throughout the Middle East at this time and earlier. In many sites, however, there is more evidence of differentiation and specialization than is found at Çatalhöyük. As regional scholars such as Mehmet Özdoğan have argued, one of the distinctive characteristics of the central Anatolian Neolithic is the dense packing of apparently equivalent buildings.[10] At Çatalhöyük there is a particular tension between individual houses with their individual house walls, and the agglomerated, closely packed settlement of equivalent units as a whole. At Çatalhöyük it is difficult to identify central authorities or specialized groups or functions that could have produced the aggregation. In the uppermost levels of the site, however, there seems to be some change. For example, superimposed large ovens are found at one location in Levels IV and V and these are larger than the domestic ovens by far. They must have served a larger community than the individual house. But even here James Mellaart describes them as being in a domestic courtyard.[11]

In a modern town we would expect to identify different functional areas and buildings such as the industrial and residential zones, the church or mosque or temple, and the cemetery. At Çatalhöyük all these separate functions occur in one place, in the house. There is evidence, as we shall see, of production and of residence in the house. There is evidence of cultic use and of burial beneath floors of houses. Indeed, Çatalhöyük is as much a cemetery as a settlement. It is as much a ritual centre as a centre of production. These various functions are integrated in the house and, as a result, there is no larger-scale zoning of the town into functional areas.

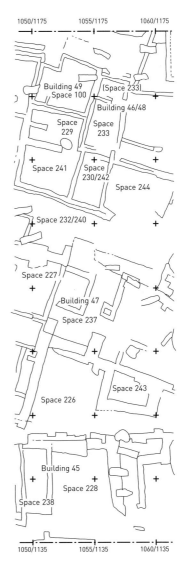

41 When, in 2004, we excavated part of the apparently 'special' triangular zone shown in Figure 40, we found that, in fact, these buildings had no special function or design. However, some collapsing walls had been heavily buttressed, and Building 47 was somewhat unusual because it was later in date than those surrounding it, coming from a time when the internal organization of houses had begun to change.

It is, however, possible that the East Mound was, through most of its occupation, divided into two equivalent paired halves. The contour survey of the East Mound shows a northern and a southern hill with a deep gully between them (see Figure 4). Mellaart concentrated his excavations in the southwestern part of the southern hill of the East Mound. But we have now (since 2004) uncovered a large number of houses on the northern hill, and have excavated about 10 of them to varying degrees. We are beginning to see possible trends that distinguish the layouts of the houses in the two areas. In the classic Mellaart house on the southern hill, there are important platforms in the northeast and central east part of the main room, with a prominent bench at the southern side of the central east platform. Burial is often concentrated under the central east and northeast platforms. Other platforms occur in the northwest and southwest quadrants, but it is these two eastern platforms which seem to dominate. On the north hill we have found some subtle differences, although a larger sample size may change the pattern. Here, while northeastern and central platforms occur (for example, a classic Mellaart plan was found in Space 227), it tends to be the northwestern platform which has most burial and most painting – for example in Buildings 1 and 3.

So we perhaps have here some difference between the two hills which corresponds with the spatial distinction. Douglas Baird[12] has made the case that Çatalhöyük was endogamous (people married within the 'town'). Baird's argument is that mating networks require populations in excess of 500 to avoid the ill effects of in-breeding.[13] Since Çatalhöyük is well above this threshold, it had the potential to be endogamous. Baird also notes the lack of evidence of other contemporary communities on the Çarşamba Fan of the Konya Plain. He suggests that endogamy would have enhanced close monitoring of social and economic interests, and could have been associated with the control of territory and resources. The maintaining of marriage ties within the bounded space of the 'town' could have enhanced control over dispersed resources. In fact it is difficult to provide good evidence one way or the other (for marriage within or between communities), but we can suggest that Çatalhöyük was a tightly knit community (given the high level of similarity between houses, and their close packing, and the need to walk over other people's houses to get to one's own). We have also seen that some balance between different parts of the community would have had to be maintained. One option is reciprocal marriage exchange between parts of the community. It might be hypothesized that the two halves of the East Mound acted as sections that married into the other half. It is also possible that the two balanced halves of the town took turns at providing such functions as leadership roles – maybe this was the main mechanism for retaining an egalitarian social structure at the site. But a range of other types of social distinctions and divisions are also possible as causes of the bipartite structure of the mound.

Can we identify other aspects of the social organization of the 'town' at a smaller scale than this bipartite division? And does the layout change through time? We have little evidence of the layout of the earliest levels of the occupation, although it seems possible that the earliest buildings were concentrated under the highest part of the southern eminence. What evidence we do have suggests some early use of party walls, although these are also found later. By Levels VII and VI (Figure 37) there is a very dense packing of houses over very extensive areas. This is probably the period of maximum occupation of the site, and both the north and south hills are covered well down their flanks, in cascading terraces. In the new areas that have been uncovered on the northern hill, there is evidence of zoning of the community in these levels and in Level V (Figure 40). The zones are bounded by what look like streets or alleyways converging on the hill top. However, at the time of writing, the first studies of the material in these 'streets' indicates that they were not walked or trampled on. There is no evidence of the type of wear and fragmentation of bone, lithics, carbonized seeds and pottery that would indicate traffic. Rather these lines seem to be just edges of zones – with refuse thrown from the roofs. The zones could have been organized in several ways – as clans, kinship groups, neighbourhoods, groups of people from particular areas or villages, and so on. Given the overall emphasis on lineage and ancestry at the site that will be discussed later in this book, I think that the most likely interpretation is one that is based in some way on kinship and descent.

In the uppermost levels of the site, Mellaart found streets which may have functioned as real access routes,[14] unlike the ones just described from earlier levels. There is more open space in the levels from VIA onwards,[15] and some evidence of multi-roomed, multifunctional houses (Chapter 5). At the same time the settlement seems to have gradually dispersed after Level V (that is, after about 6350 BC) and perhaps decreased in size – the strong sense of social unity and cohesion seems to have broken down to some degree. For example, there is less and less occupation on both the north and south hills in the upper levels, but a small eastern hill is formed. And it is also likely that sometime during the later occupation of Çatalhöyük East, the occupation over the river on the West Mound starts.[16]

LIVING IN THE 'TOWN'

Such dense habitation must have led to a large number of problems. There would have been logistical difficulties regarding sanitation, access, transport and so on. There would have been problems as structural instability in one house threatened the neighbouring structures against which it was built. There would have been difficulties as people walked across, or took animals across other peoples' roofs. Emma Jenkins's work on the microfauna provides an insight into how life was lived in these conditions.[17] The dominant presence of the house-mouse in most levels fits with possible evidence of infestation from some buildings[18] – and gives an impression of infestation in a densely occupied settlement. The thick floors in storage contexts may have been to act against rodents,[19] which probably lived in the less accessible parts of the site such as narrow gaps between buildings.[20] Presumably these examples provide just a glimpse into the many problems that would have been experienced as a result of the dense crowding. Living together in large agglomerations involved material entanglements that had to be dealt with socially.

Nurcan Yalman's ethnoarchaeological study of contemporary villages in the Konya Plain points to another problem - the difficulty of maintaining 'family' complexes of adjacent buildings.[21] As space becomes cluttered, it becomes difficult for individual families to expand into new space nearby, and long-distance moves have to be made. It becomes difficult to live near your ancestors, and perhaps this is why secondary burial (that is, movement of bodies from an earlier burial place into a new grave) occurs in some buildings.[22] As people have to live farther away from the ancestral house there may be a desire to bury the dead locally before return to the ancestral burial house. And perhaps through time this dislocation between space and ancestral affiliation undermines the coherence of local house-based groups.

As already noted, there must have been some degree of coordination to deal with all these issues. At times we can see traces of this, despite the strong egalitarian ethic. For example, in Figure 40 a line of house walls is visible running north–south on the alignment of the east wall of Building 1. This runs down the northern hill between adjacent houses which are all built to respect it. Such a line may well have functioned as a drain – to take rain and snow meltwater off the site. Such forms of cooperation must have been numerous and they imply some level of social negotiation that was coordinated. As faecal material was dumped into midden areas, it would have been in everyone's interest to have some control of how the dumping was carried out, to make sure that the faeces were burnt and covered in lime-rich soil.

MIDDENS

At Çatalhöyük, as far as we can tell so far, there are houses and pens and middens. Some of these middens may be in open areas which have long duration. Other middens occur in abandoned houses, or in sets of adjacent abandoned houses. Given the numbers of midden areas in relation to the numbers of houses, it seems that midden areas were shared between several houses. They contained refuse material from the oven areas in houses, but also other material. A preliminary quantitative analysis by Sarah Cross May of the densities of all the types of material excavated across the site concludes that there is most variation between categories such as midden, floor and fill (the latter is defined as the material placed in a building on abandonment).[23]

This supports the view that the organization of discard and other activities was highly rule-bound. One set of discard rules concerned the discarding of material into collective refuse areas or middens.

There is little evidence that the midden areas between inhabited buildings were used as courtyards. Mellaart's definition of courtyard[24] recognizes that these areas were mainly used for refuse disposal rather than activities. Indeed, there was little traffic or trampling in these areas. Deposition in middens is small-scale and relatively rapid. The term midden therefore seems appropriate. But how distinct is midden from other types of deposition and how much variability is there – are there different types of midden? Are there major differences between the midden material deposited in abandoned buildings, and that deposited in extensive open areas between buildings? Answering these questions will help us to understand how the 'town' was organized.

Sarah Cross May identifies middens as forming a distinct category in terms of the artifacts found in them. For example, they have a higher mean density of faunal and botanical material than other types of deposit. There is also a greater presence of small pieces of pottery, figurines, beads and clay balls in midden contexts.[25] The clearest pattern identified in the faunal remains is that external middens have a higher mass of animal bone and lower fragmentation (the latter perhaps due to faster deposition and less reworking) than fill and floors within buildings.[26] Also external middens have all the parts of the sheep-sized carcass, whereas other deposits have a more selective presence of animal parts. Detailed quantitative study of animal bone discard has found that there is more digested bone in some middens in abandoned buildings than in the external middens. As noted above, this may mean that dogs were tethered in abandoned buildings,[27] so these middens seem to have been used differently from those in larger open areas.

Ian Bull has worked with a large team to describe evidence of faecal deposition at the site.[28] They have studied the organic compounds, such as the bile acids from the digestive systems of animals and people, that are found in faecal material or coprolites. Their work shows that midden deposits at Çatalhöyük contain faecal material, most probably human in origin. In addition, middens were far denser in phytoliths than houses.[29] There is no evidence of burnt eggshell in floor deposits although it does occur in middens.[30] There are many quantitative differences in terms of wood charcoal[31] between middens and other types of deposit (the fill placed in abandoned rooms, the ashy rake-out from hearths and ovens, etc.). Whatever the specific explanations for all this patterning, elaborate processing and discard practices are suggested which separate inside from outside houses very clearly. We also see that middens are not just general dumping areas, but contain the results of specific discard activities.

Overall, it is clear that the buildings at Çatalhöyük were embedded within extensive areas of midden. Containing faecal and rotting organic material in a densely occupied agglomeration of buildings, these deposits must have been a health hazard, attracted lots of flies, and must at times have had a strong odour, although senses of smell vary very much from one cultural context to another. At Çatalhöyük much burnt material was placed on the middens and there are sometimes fire-spots in them where material was burnt.[32] These were deliberate and carefully regulated areas of discard, and the same areas were used over long periods of time. At Aşıklı Höyük, the same midden areas were used throughout the life of the settlement.[33] At Çatalhöyük there is evidence of change through time, so that areas of midden can be built upon,[34] and abandoned houses can be turned into middens. But there is also much continuity over many levels.

So the middens constitute a distinct use of space at Çatalhöyük that has a collective component in that there were clearly rules about how they should be used. The evidence of distinctive types of discard in middens, and the differences between midden types, as well as their long use and integral role in the functioning of the 'town', all suggest general rules of discard behaviour for the 'town' as a whole. Discard was carefully and collectively coordinated, although the tension with individual house behaviour again emerges in that individual houses could sometimes be built out onto midden areas. Further, the middens were made up of many small acts including individual fire spots and numerous spreads of material containing house sweepings, often including traces of wall and floor plaster. So, the middens as a whole have distinct characteristics, but they were made up of small individual dumps (perhaps basket-loads) of refuse from each house.

The 'Town' and its Borders

There are unities of Çatalhöyük as a whole which set it apart from other known sites of this period – such as the placing of obsidian caches in houses, and the use of specific styles of obsidian manufacture.[35] The overall corporate identity of the site could be seen in the degree of packing of houses at Çatalhöyük. And yet it is also notable that, given such packing, we have seen that there is such a strong preference to retain a house-based autonomy.

The degree of corporate identity is reinforced by the evidence of clear rules about what could and could not be done on the mound. It is possible to explore this question because as well as excavating houses and middens on the two hills of the East Mound, we have also sampled deposits off the hills. In particular, in 1997 and 1999 we excavated in the KOPAL Area to the north of the East Mound (Figure 4). This was clearly an off-site location. In 1999 we also excavated the deep sounding in Space 181. This area was again possibly off the mound at the time, or at least close to its edge.

As will be described in Chapter 5, a wide range of productive activities took place on site – from grease processing to bead manufacture, obsidian knapping and woodworking. The archaeobotanical evidence[36] shows that chaff is found on the site, suggesting on-site processing of cereals. This fits with the evidence (see below) from phytoliths of cereal processing in houses. The crops were then stored largely cleaned on site. On the other hand, the evidence from the KOPAL Area (such as awn remains), suggests that the earlier stages in the processing of cereals took place off site.

Tristan Carter and the team working on the obsidian and flint tools from the site[37] have noted a very close relationship between obsidian reduction, hearths/ovens, and the 'dirty areas' in the south or southeastern parts of main rooms in houses. There seems to be good evidence of an association between obsidian knapping and the domestic areas of houses. Obsidian caches also occur in such areas. And yet the off-site KOPAL Area has a very low density of obsidian in comparison to the contemporary deposition closer to habitation areas on the mound.[38] Certainly blanks and cores were prepared well away from the site, near the Cappadocian sources, but much daily knapping for use and re-use took place in the houses (being then discarded on middens) rather than off the site in the KOPAL Area.

The location of many activities at the edge of the site was presumably determined by very basic concerns about safety. For example, we have found evidence of lime burning towards the edge of the site in the South Area.[39] This process of producing lime for hard house floors and wall plasters in the earliest levels at the site involved extensive burning and the risks of fire. Wendy Matthews shows that outside lime burning areas used dung as fuel.[40] But there is little evidence that the lime-burning activity was corporate, and lime burning could have been undertaken at a household level even if it took place at the edge of the site.[41]

Another example of activities taking place at the edge of the site is animal penning. The identification of animal pen deposits provides a good example of the way in which different types of data can come together to suggest a robust interpretation. Certain deposits proved to have micromorphological evidence of compacted herbivore dung, thus allowing these deposits to be interpreted as penning areas. The faunal data showed foetal/neonate bones of sheep in these same deposits – suggesting site-edge keeping of sheep and birthing. Other penning areas seem to occur more centrally within the site,[42] but certainly it would have been easier to provide animal access to pens at the site edge. There is little evidence as to the scale of the penning activities but the penning areas are small and a household level of organization is again feasible.

A possible spatial difference between off-site, edge-of-site and full on-site locations has been noted by Nerissa Russell and Louise Martin[43] as regards sheep and goat bones. There is some evidence from the off-site KOPAL Area that sheep and goat feet and heads were sometimes discarded at slaughter locations on the edge of the site, and the meaty parts preferentially brought on site. Similarly, an edge-of-site location[44] has evidence of large-scale processing of sheep and goat bone for grease while the on-site locations have evidence of less homogeneous and more household-scale processing. The difficulty here is that this difference could also be temporal,[45] indicating a shift to more household-based meat and grease processing.

We do not yet have clear contemporary within-settlement domestic contexts with which to compare the KOPAL Area data.[46] But the KOPAL Area data do suggest other ways in which there is a clear difference between what can and cannot be brought on site. KOPAL is the only area where sheep and goat are in the minority. Cattle predominate, but also there are more deer and pigs than on the mound. Apart from equids, therefore, wild animals are much more common at the KOPAL Area. The difficulties resulting from a lack of contemporary domestic contexts on the mound inhibit discussion. In the early village settlements of Thessaly in Greece, Catherine Perlès argues that the lack of wild animals on sites results from a symbolic domestic/wild opposition.[47] It is possible that the same explanation will prove relevant at Çatalhöyük.

The KOPAL Area has a fairly even body-part representation of deer, whereas on the site it is mainly antler and perhaps skins that are found, especially after Level Pre-XII.B. After Level Pre-XII.B only heads and hides of pigs and deer are brought onto the site. Generally, cattle horns and scapulae are preferentially brought on site. Adnan Baysal and Karen Wright have studied the ground-stone artifacts from the site, and they note that there is a larger number of grinders in the KOPAL Area, suggesting that some (possibly group) grinding was done there.[48] As with the evidence from the sheep and goat faunal data, it seems that more collective action took place off the site. All these data suggest a strong set of rules about what could and could not be brought on site and while each house has its own walls, there is much evidence of corporate action and corporate identity.

It is also of interest that human remains were found in the KOPAL Area. In fact they seem to have been discarded in ways similar to the animal bones. It is possible that these human bones resulted from reworkings of bones from rebuildings and digging on site. But the bones looked fresh – and were predominantly adult in contrast to the large proportions of young people found buried in the buildings on site. Craig Cessford has calculated that there are insufficient burials found on site to account for the whole adult population at Çatalhöyük.[49] It is possible that the KOPAL evidence is somehow providing a trace of the off-site processing of the adult dead, and this may have been at a more corporate scale than the individual house burial on site or the small groups of houses that used the same ancestral house as discussed earlier. Certainly the human bones from different individuals in KOPAL are very jumbled and mixed together.

Despite our work at the edge of the site in various phases in Space 181 (South Area) and the KOPAL Area, we have found no walls or ditches that might have defined the site. Early village societies in the Middle East and in Cyprus and at Aşıklı Höyük were certainly able to build boundary walls around and in sites, although these are often described as non-defensive.[50] At Çatalhöyük, the sense of large-scale corporate identity was created not by encircling walls or by ritual centres or public monuments. Rather, it was constructed out of a dense communal huddling of houses and a set of habits dealing with what could and could not be brought on site, and what could and could not be done on site. This larger scale and more collective identity was at all times in tension with individual houses and their smaller-scale ancestral and exchange ties. There is some evidence of greater collective action off site and at its edges.

CONCLUSION

So the mystery of the attraction of Çatalhöyük only seems to grow. Given that the internal organization of the 'town' was so atomized and so small-scale, why did people aggregate at all? We have seen that there is plenty of evidence of collective action, but we have also seen, and will see further in Chapter 5, much evidence of a house-based organization of daily life. The site itself is hard to describe as a town, which is why I have generally left the word in quotation marks. There is little of the functional specialization and differentiation that one would expect in a large town.

We have seen the possible division of the site into moieties and zones or sectors which most probably have a social basis. We will see in Chapter 5 that there were probably small groupings of houses based on ancestry and descent. I have described how there may well have been collectives of people, such as elders, regulating the activities of the inhabitants. There must undoubtedly have been cooperation in economic tasks, but whenever we get a glimpse of how production was organized, it seems largely organized at the household level, as in the case of lime burning.

It does seem that social factors integrated with economic factors were important in the aggregation at Çatalhöyük. Douglas Baird provides a convincing model of how the aggregation occurred and what kept people together.[51] He argues that the use of the environment was very extensive. For example, as we saw in Chapter 3, the sheep grazed widely, and many resources were obtained from the Taurus Mountains (from timber to stone). There must have been people focusing on different resources in the different environments. Just in relation to the fields, it would have been helpful to be able to rely on others who could tend your crops. The same must have been true for herding and exchange and resource procurement. So the problem was how individual units could regulate and control access to far-flung resources. In these types of societies, one method was controlling the various and perhaps varied categories of relatedness that were constructed through such means as kinship, descent, affiliation and exchange. By creating a large settlement that was very closely knit, and perhaps endogamous, people created a network of relationships that could be used to control access to resources. These relationships could be continually maintained, watched, monitored. By being clustered into a large group, each individual unit also had more opportunity to promote its interests in terms of finding marriage partners, maintaining social and familial links, developing other exchange alliances, cementing links through ancestry and so on. Not only was there a larger potential pool of alliances, but the close contact meant that they could be monitored and maintained.

Evidence for the importance of a social dimension (in addition to economic factors) to aggregation has increased as a result of recent work in Turkey – especially in the southeast. Sites like Göbekli Tepe (which started 2,000 years before Çatalhöyük) seem to be to some degree social-ritual centres,[52] without traces of domesticated plants and animals, and occurring before or very early in the wider process of domestication. It used to be thought that large villages or 'towns' appeared at the same time as agriculture. But the decoupling of domestication and aggregation at sites like Göbekli has rather broken any idea of simple links between subsistence and aggregation, although such relationships remain important. We can begin to see an alternative where social factors play a bigger role. If at Göbekli people are coming together for rituals and ceremonies at certain times of the year, there are increased options for marriage exchange and other forms of exchange and alliance. By being settled there is more control of these social ties. One can be more sure of building long-term debts and obligations if the people one is dealing with are 'in place'. It seems likely that the social relations that were constructed in such 'places' were of various forms. Whatever their form, the social alliances and relationships built up over the long term, and allowed access, distribution and accumulation of resources to be monitored and maintained. As we shall see, at Çatalhöyük social relations had come to centre around kinship and descent. At such a site, social aggregation was an effective mechanism to monitor the alliances that allowed distant, varied and dispersed resources to be obtained, accumulated and exchanged. Aggregation allowed a social control of a dispersed economy. Both society and subsistence were involved.

But we can note too that this hypothesis about the reasons for agglomeration only works if people have become sufficiently entangled in social and material webs. In the case where people's entanglements are small-scale and short-term, it remains advantageous to organize the exploitation of the environment in small dispersed groups. Maintaining and controlling economic and social relationships remains small-scale. It is only when there are complex long-term dependencies between people and between people and things that large numbers of relationships need monitoring so that being close to related people in an agglomeration makes sense. There may be longer-term processes that lie behind the specific social and economic aspects of aggregation discussed here. I will return to this point towards the end of this book (Chapter 11).

CHAPTER FIVE

The House

I started this book with the puzzle of why there are no leopard bones in the faunal remains at Çatalhöyük. It seemed odd that while there was no physical evidence on site there were plenty of visual representations of leopards or large cats. The most striking depictions of leopards are as reliefs on the walls in houses. As we shall see, we now know that these buildings containing leopards and other reliefs and depictions are not shrines but everyday houses. So what was going on here? Why were leopards and other wild animals depicted in domestic houses? What was the nature of the house that made such imagery seem in place in the home?

This chapter discusses the house at Çatalhöyük in full and shows how it was central to all aspects of life – material, social and ritual. The chapter describes how people would have moved around within these spaces on a daily basis, how they buried their dead beneath floors, and painted walls and put plastered wild bulls' heads on pedestals. The chapter describes how social rules were learned as people conducted their daily tasks in these houses. These rules include how people moved, ate, swept up dirt, and defecated.

Right at the start it may be helpful to get away from the frame of our own experiences of houses by returning to Raymond Firth's account of the Tikopia in Polynesia. As discussed in Chapter 1, my aim in drawing attention to the similarities between Çatalhöyük and the Tikopia is neither to ignore the differences nor to strengthen my argument. I am not trying to say that this is exactly what it was like at Çatalhöyük. Rather, I want to try and get us prepared for something very different from our own world.

'The doorways, of which there are several, are openings large enough only to permit of entry on hands and knees. The interior, except on a very bright day, is dark and unprepossessing, the wooden rafters… are smoke-grimed…. The floor space is roughly rectangular, lacking in furniture, but covered with mats.'[1] In Firth's account, the floor space is divided into three sections (see Figure 11). A central area is common ground to all members of the household, a kind of neutral space for the performance of a range of activities. On one side of the central area are the house-hold fires and ovens, and in their vicinity sit the women and children. Opposite, on the other side of the central area, is the ceremonial area where only men may sit and on which food is laid out in a ritual manner. 'It is treated with respect, in that people do not turn their backs to it, and when they lie down to sleep they orient their heads in that direction – or at least refrain from pointing their feet thither. A crawling infant who strays that way is picked up.'[2] The explanation for this treatment of the ceremonial area is that the dead are buried there, beneath the mats on the floor. 'The visitor who enters a dwelling of any great age will see on one side of him a neat row of trapezoidal coconut-leaf mats, of the same type as those which cover the rest of the floor, only a trifle larger. They are arranged more carefully, and in some cases stand a little higher than the general level. Each marks the resting-place of a deceased member of the family, probably an ancestor of some note, and it is the presence of these dead forbears that is the basic reason for the respect paid to that side of the house.'[3] The Tikopia pay deference to the ceremonial side of the house and to the dead buried there, but they come to take the presence of their ancestors very much as a matter of course. For Firth too, living in one of these houses, avoid-ing this part of the house soon became second nature. 'After a few weeks the habit of avoiding this portion of the floor was so far ingrained that it was no longer a con-scious practice.'[4]

There are many other rules regarding how one moves around the space of the Tikopia house. The use of the various doorways depends on social position, and where you can eat and sit also depends on your gender, age and status. How you sit and whether you can sit leaning against a post depend on privilege.

We shall see that there are similarities between this description of a Tikopia house and those at Çatalhöyük. While James Mellaart conceived of some of the buildings at Çatalhöyük as 'shrines', the present project understands them all as houses with varying degrees of symbolic and ritual elaboration (Figure 42 and Plate 8). The house at Çatalhöyük consisted of one main room entered through the roof in which there was an oven and burial and other platforms, plus one or more side rooms used for storage, food preparation and other domestic tasks. These rooms incorporated into one building all the differentiated functions that we would expect to see in the different parts of a modern town – residential, industrial, religious, burial. There is some separation between these different functions within the Çatalhöyük house, as different platforms and areas or rooms are used for differ-ent purposes. But the house is where a wide variety of activities are brought together in relation to each other. The house is the focus of all forms of social life at Çatalhöyük. In the house, symbolic and practical aspects of daily life are

42, 43 The reconstruction above of daily life within a typical house is based on discoveries made during the excavation of Building 5 by the current project (a 3D representation of which is shown below; see also Plate 6). Compared to the more sterile drawings from the 1960s, an example of which is shown in Figure 57, these reconstructions give a much better sense of what living conditions at Çatalhöyük were actually like.

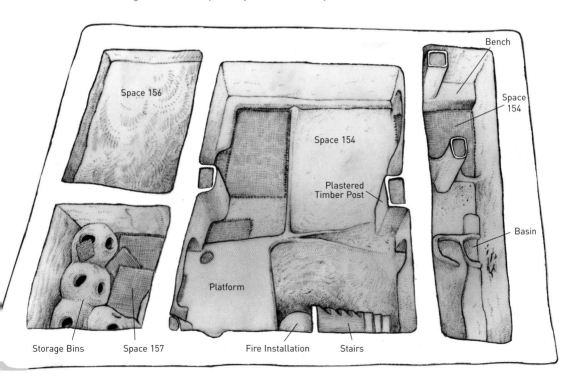

Space 156

Bench

Space 154

Space 154

Plastered
Timber Post

Space 154

Basin

Platform

Storage Bins

Space 157

Fire Installation

Stairs

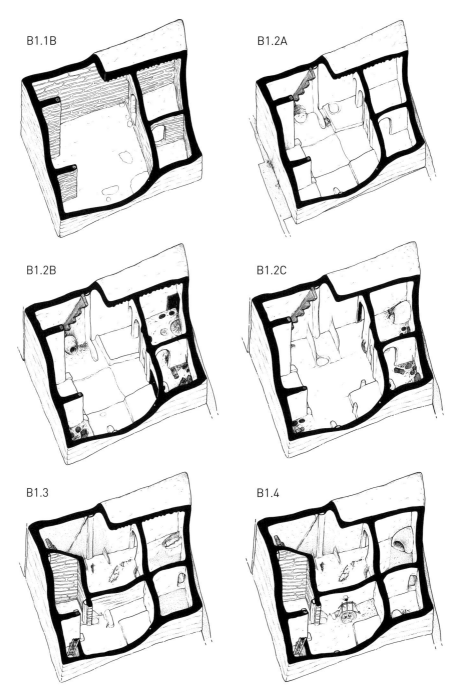

B1.1B

B1.2A

B1.2B

B1.2C

B1.3

B1.4

44 Sequence of phases of Building 1, from phase B1.1B (the earliest) to phase B1.4 (the latest). While the overall arrangement remains the same, with side rooms to the right (the west) and cleaner platforms for burial to the north of the main room, changes occur such as the move of the oven into a side room in B1.2C, and the halving of the building in B1.3 after a fire.

thoroughly integrated. This is one of the main themes in the account in this chapter.

I will discuss the organization of production in the house in Chapter 7. I will add there to the view that was already expressed in Chapter 4 that the house was the prime unit of craft or industrial production. Even when there is evidence for some degree of specialization of production (as in the case of bead production for example), this seems part-time and house-based. In this chapter I will refer to the evidence for productive activities inside the house, but show how they are integrated into other aspects of life. I will structure my account by considering the life-history of the house,[5] from its construction, through use, abandonment and reuse. I will concentrate on two buildings found in sequence on the north part of the East Mound – Building 5 found beneath Building 1 (Figures 43 and 44) – as well as referring to buildings in the South Area (Figure 45). So let us start at the beginning with construction – although, as we shall see, construction is often part of the same process as infilling and ending a house.

45 Map of the excavated buildings in Level VII in the South Area. The plan has Mellaart's building numbers in italics, while the numbering used by the current project (which has focused on the area indicated with a dashed line) is in larger roman script. The grid is at 5 m (16.5 ft) intervals.

CONSTRUCTION

There is clear evidence that, at least in the areas and levels currently under excavation, construction of new buildings was gradual and by accretion. We do not see evidence that whole 'levels' were constructed in one event. There are cases of construction events between the major 'levels' excavated by Mellaart. There is no evidence of an overall 'laying out' of the buildings in a level; rather, they seem to have been built gradually and continually. However, as we saw in the last chapter, there is sometimes evidence that houses were constructed so as to respect gaps between zones of buildings, or so as to allow water to run off the mound down aligned gaps between houses.

If buildings were on the whole constructed individually, there are exceptions. Spaces 112 and 109 in Level VII were jointly constructed, suggesting the involvement of a 'people unit' larger than one house (Figure 45). Similarly, Buildings 23 and 18 were built on a common foundation raft in Level X (Figure 48). In addition, these two buildings shared a party wall, and there was an opening between the buildings

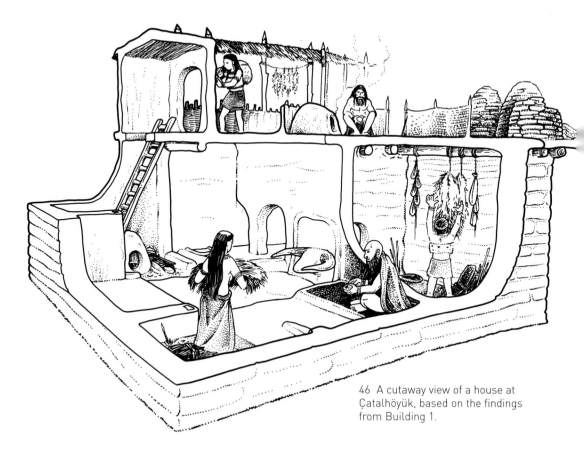

46 A cutaway view of a house at Çatalhöyük, based on the findings from Building 1.

which was closed off at some point during their occupation. It would, however, be inadequate to consider these two buildings as one,[6] as Buildings 18 and 23 replicate each other in terms of their internal fittings and functional arrangements. The use of party walls had been noted by Mellaart.[7]

The main outlines of the construction of the buildings are well known from Mellaart's[8] and our work (Figure 46). Walls were built of mud bricks that decrease in length through time (bricks are shorter in the upper levels of the site). In the lower levels the bricks are so long (sometimes well over 1 m (3.5 ft)) that it is possible that they were made *in situ* on the walls. The wet clay mixture could have been placed directly on the wall between wooden boards, although the mortar breaks between bricks perhaps argue against this. The walls were on average 0.4 m (1.3 ft) thick and originally 2.5–3.0 m (8–10 ft) high, often built directly on the partly dismantled walls of earlier buildings. We have found no evidence of windows, and entrance was usually down stairs set into the south wall above the oven of the main room, although other stair locations also occur. There was also a framework of major posts. These are only found in the main rooms, which perhaps suggests that the roof of the main room may have been higher or more substantial. The posts are often set in from the walls (e.g. Building 17, Figure 47), as if one of their functions was to create internal divisions of space. The interior walls, floors and posts were plastered. We have found that the surfaces of the wall plaster were originally rippled and uneven, even though the plastering was carefully carried out. This

47 Looking towards the west wall in Building 17 (Level IX) with the oven to the left. Two scars can be seen in the plaster with associated postholes. These are set away from the wall and in the example on the right there is evidence of a plaster partition extending into the room.

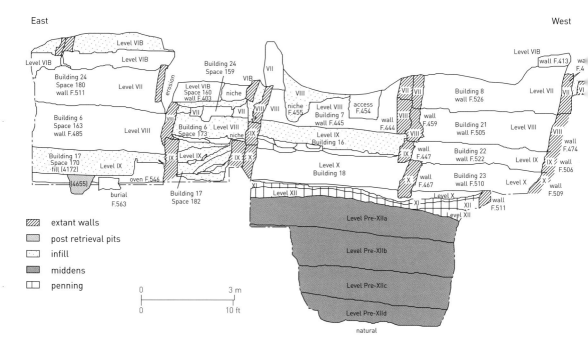

48 Composite section prepared by Shahina Farid and Duncan Lees for the sequence of levels in the South Area.

unevenness built up over time as small irregularities became exaggerated in the multiple layers of thin replasterings. While walls may have been covered with textiles to hide such unevenness, the frequent occurrence of painting rather suggests walls were not covered. It is not clear why the effect of uneven wall surfaces was desired or tolerated.

Construction had to deal with a whole series of practical issues. Dependence on specific materials had consequences that entailed further investments – this is the process of material entanglement that I described in Chapter 2. For example, nearly all north–south aligned walls in the South Area, through most levels, have a westward lean or slump, as is seen clearly in the composite section shown in Figure 48. This is presumably caused by the pressure of the weight of the higher central core of the mound pushing outwards. Specific solutions had to be found and repairs carried out. In a building in Level VIII, a wall was thickened to prevent slumping.[9] The walls of Space 112 had to be 'shored up' because of subsidence in the neighbouring building Space 113. Such slumping may have been part of the reason for the construction of double walls (the wall for each building built up against that for the adjacent building), and also for the provision of a frame of large wooden posts, which would have strengthened the overall mud-brick structure. Such problems and solutions provide a good example of material entanglement at Çatalhöyük. Living in a dense mud-brick 'town' produced a mound that caused pressure on walls and slumping. The best wood for such a purpose was the juniper and oak and some of this was obtained from more upland areas to the south (see Chapter 3). Obtaining the timbers (though many were reused) involved further social dependencies and cooperation (to gain access to the timber and bring it down river to the site). So materials and society became mutually entangled.

Despite this dealing with the consequences of construction, there is much evidence that initial construction of houses was carefully planned and ritually sanctioned. For example, in the pre-floor packing for Building 1 in the North Area, the overall layout of platforms in the building was already being prepared – the whole layout was conceived very early on.[10] The construction was also embedded in ritual. For example, there were three infant interments at the threshold into the main room,[11] placed there in the construction phase of Building 1. (The importance of thresholds is also indicated by the sprinkling of red ochre on the step between two rooms in Building 40, Level VIII.) There was another neonate in the construction deposits of Building 1, as well as some adults. The burial of four neonates during the construction of Building 1 is of particular interest, as no neonates were buried during its occupation. This role of neonate burial in founding structures also occurs in a Level XII building.[12] Here a neonate in a basket marked the end of a sequence of dumping and lime burning activities and the start of the use of the area for penning. It is possible that in all these examples, infants were buried opportunistically – they happened to die during construction and burial in construction deposits was seen as convenient. However, the focus on entrances and changes in use seems to imply a special significance for infant burial to do with foundation.

In Space 105, Level VII, there was a probable feasting deposit of animal bones beneath a wall. Such deposits are identified as having large amounts of relatively complete bones in a concentration. Building 40 Level VII has an equid scapula beneath a wall, which could be an intentional pre-wall foundation deposit although it could also be from the midden below the wall. There are several between-wall feasting deposits.[13]

In Building 1 in the south-central area of the main room in one subphase,[14] there was a complete split boar's tusk fishhook pendant, which was fresh and probably built into the makeup of the floor rather than lying on the floor. This could have been intentionally placed, as it is unlikely that it was not noticed when the fine plaster floors were laid. In Building 1 there was a strange hole dug into the south wall of the main room, then plastered inside and then covered over with wall plaster.[15] There is another cone-like insertion on the northern wall. The nature of these features is unclear, but they probably represent pre-existing objects deliberately placed in the walls of Building 1 that were almost immediately removed and the cavities rendered invisible by being plastered over. They are not necessarily of a ritual nature, but they are intriguing.

As well as placements in relation to overall house construction, there is evidence of similar acts in regard to features within buildings. An oven in the southwest corner of the side room in Building 1 included a small fragment of an animal horn figurine in its constructional material.[16] A plaster feature on the wall of the same building contained a substantial curved animal horn plaster figurine, which may have been deliberately included in the plaster.[17] These examples suggest a lack of separation between ritual and daily life. It is difficult to be sure of the specifics. Perhaps these deposits were symbolically protective (apotropaic). Perhaps they created memories and links. But in general terms we can say that the special deposits show that construction (as we shall see too of use and abandonment of houses) integrated ritual and daily practice. Thus even the 'simplest' of material acts in the house entailed entanglements with social and ritual knowledge. Rather than just building a wall, people had to have access to symbols and rituals that entailed further social ties.

REBUILDING

The need to shore up walls has already been mentioned. Entrances between rooms were frequently blocked up and plastered over. There is a continual process of rebuilding from level to level, from phase to phase, and within phases. Apart from the substantial restructuring of Building 1 after a major fire, the most frequent rebuildings and restructurings of internal space seem to be related to oven movement. Building 17 sees a major remodelling as the ovens in the northeast are switched to the southwest of the main room in one phase.[18] Some movement of ovens is found in most buildings. As ovens frequently seem to be related to stair entry, these shifts of location must often have involved changes to roofs (although there may have been more than one permanent hole in a roof). Thus, the amount of rebuilding in relation to ovens is very striking. There is much back and forth movement of ovens in the south part of Building 23 and in the southern end of Building 18. It is not clear why ovens get moved so much. In an experimental house that we have built by the site, we have found that the location of the oven beneath the roof entry hole produces puddling on floors (something we have also seen in the archaeological deposits beneath the stairs) and damage to the oven walls. It is also possible that the sooting caused by ovens in part of the house could be dealt with by a movement of the oven to another area.

As with major constructional events, the minor rebuildings often involve ritual acts. For example, in Building 17 there is a hearth in the southeast corner of the main room.[19] In the sealing deposit of one of the hearth layers there is a broken figurine with both head and torso present. The deliberation of this act is reinforced by the associated faunal remains in this unit that suggest the processing and eating of a young sheep. There is then a series of hearth replacements in this location until in a later phase a very similar broken figurine head was found in the 'dirty' occupation or rake-out associated with a later hearth.[20] Perhaps because even the smallest of acts, like rebuilding a hearth, would have had potential social and spiritual effects, it had to be hedged around by protective events.

USE – THE ORGANIZATION OF DAILY LIFE IN THE HOUSE

Many (if not all) daily acts seem to have been embedded in ritual. In Building 5 we see some evidence of these rituals within daily practice. Beneath a packing deposit against the wall in a side room,[21] a pair of sheep horncores with attached frontlet were found with a clay ball placed between them. The overall arrangement looked deliberately laid out to the excavators. The example of the broken figurine heads in Building 17 mentioned above suggests that mundane hearth use and replacement were interspersed with ritual events.

Daily practice within the buildings at Çatalhöyük was also formalized by divisions of space and activity. In Beidha, another Neolithic village in Jordan in the PPNB (see box on page 20 for the dating of the PPNB in relation to Çatalhöyük), there are discrete activities on different parts of floors.[22] Some areas of floor are devoid of artifacts or features.[23] Brian Byrd argues that in general, through time across the Levant, and in particular as one moves into the PPNB, the average interior area of buildings increases, as does the presence of internal features and divisions of internal space.[24] Byrd sees the increased size of buildings in the PPNB in the Levant as a function of the increased use of the insides of houses for activities, itself a function of more house-based and less communal forms of ownership.

By the time of Çatalhöyük, there is much evidence for internal divisions of space, much more so than at the earlier Aşıklı Höyük.[25] For example, Building 5 shows evidence for strong spatial divisions emphasized by aspects of the walls and floors. The main room has much more plastering on the walls than the side rooms. Another way in which divisions were represented in this building is in the platforms of different heights and the impressions of matting covering the floors (Figure 81). The matting appears to show a spatial hierarchy, which ranges from very fine matting, through fine matting and coarse matting to no matting, where baskets or coiled 'coasters' were placed.

As noted in Chapter 2, the main internal distinction identified in all main rooms so far excavated by the current project is between the areas near hearths and ovens which, to the naked eye, look charcoal-rich and 'dirty', and the lighter and sometimes white plaster floors and platforms in the rest of the main room where burials commonly occur. There are often ridges or platform edges separating the 'clean' and 'dirty' areas.

Some of the most obvious correlates of the difference in floor types are as follows. The 'dirty' area is normally in the south part of the main room, associated with ovens and hearths, and often entry stairs. These occupation floors seem to have ash and charcoal-rich material probably raked out from the hearths and ovens and from other activities. There are often obsidian caches below these occupation floors, and there is much evidence on the floors of 'industrial' activities ranging from obsidian knapping and bead manufacture to grease extraction. Pots or pot emplacements are sometimes found here (e.g. in Building 1, and there is a recent find of a pot embedded in the floor near an oven in the South Area[26]), as are scoops and small storage pits. The latter may have clay balls or collections of white and worn river pebbles. There is little or no visible art in this zone, and the only burials seem to be of neonates or infants. In the 'clean' area to the north there are often higher platforms, more painting, more burial, and whiter plaster floors with little visible debris on them.

We have so far identified two types of cooking fires in the buildings, although as more work is carried out a more detailed classification of fire installations may prove possible. So far it seems that there are 'ovens' which are fully domed and are usually set (often deeply set) into the southern wall and have a front entrance. 'Hearths' on the other hand are probably not domed and often occur away from the wall but usually still in the southern area. The ovens in particular are often associated with collections of clay balls (Figure 49) which, according to research carried out by Sonya Atalay,[27] were used as 'boilers'. As Atalay has shown, in many societies cooking is achieved by heating stones which are then put in a container to heat water or

49 Clay ball concentration near the oven on the south wall in Building 2 (Level IX). The balls were first heated in the fire, then put in containers to heat water or laid out to heat meat.

are laid out to heat meat. Indeed, such an example is provided by the Tikopia.[28] The Tikopia oven is used to heat stones. Then long sticks are used to push the stones out and spread them out into a layer. The spreading of the stones for special meals is a wildly exciting business and people gather round and take part in the spreading of the stones to make an open 'oven'. 'When the oven is spread satisfactorily – and the work is done with care – some leaves of the giant taro or the like are thrown on the glowing stones, and the food, including the packets of grated taro or banana, is packed on top.' More leaves are then placed over the food, and once the oven has been covered in this way, the food is left to cook entirely by its own moisture.

At Çatalhöyük stones were not plentiful, but a heating effect was achieved using clay balls. These were often kept by the oven, heated in the oven, and then probably placed in baskets or other containers or laid out to heat food. Fire-cracked clay balls occur frequently on the site in the earlier levels, until in Level VI pottery takes over this cooking function. So both clay balls and pottery are strongly associated with the ovens and hearths in the 'dirty' southern part of the main room of the house, and they are not closely associated with adult burial in the northern 'cleaner' parts of the main room. There are certainly exceptions, and I have already referred to an example of a building in which the oven moved between the south and north areas of the building. However, while ovens do frequently move around in buildings, this movement is normally (over 95 per cent of cases) confined to the southern parts of main rooms and to side rooms.

The terms 'clean' and 'dirty' are inadequate shorthands for a complex set of differences between floor types. Indeed, working out what this difference comprises has been a major focus of the recent research. A particular concern has been to determine whether residues in the oven zone result from *in situ* activities or from sweeping from adjacent zones. The densities of artifacts and micro-artifacts often differ on floors of different types.[29] Higher, whiter floors away from the ovens and hearths tend to have lower densities of material (see Figures 23 and 24). Floors near hearths and ovens are often termed 'occupation' floors or ashy rake-outs because of their high density of artifacts and charcoal. Sarah Cross May identifies higher densities of lithics on these occupation floors. An association between obsidian, ashy rake-out and hearths in the southern or southeastern parts of main rooms in buildings is repeatedly recognized.[30] The distinction between the better laid, whiter floors and occupation floors is also very striking in terms of faunal densities.[31] The archaeobotanical evidence has higher densities of botanical remains in occupation floors (mainly in terms of wood charcoal).[32] Chemical analysis of floor sediments has also identified clear differences between the floors and platforms in different parts of buildings.[33]

On the other hand, it is clear that much of the observed patterning in artifact densities in the floors at the site results from construction activities rather than use. Study of the micro-artifacts in wall plasters showed that even these had a good density of material (small animal bone, ceramics and lithics). Small worn objects became part of the matrix of the mound and are everywhere, and it is this 'background noise' of occupation material that gets incorporated into plaster.[34] Thus, it can be assumed that a proportion of the micro-artifacts in floor plasters too has not been trampled in through use, but has been incorporated during making and laying the plaster. However, even if part of the difference between 'clean' and 'dirty' floors is partly the result of construction activities (in the choice and forming of plasters) rather than use, the difference still remains as a significant distinction between different parts of a house floor.

At the micromorphological level, thin lenses of sweepings or occupation debris can be identified on the 'dirty' occupation floors.[35] But these lenses are rare on other floors. In excavation, the floor layers are so numerous and so fine that we are often forced to group together on-floor lenses, if any such are present, with the floor make-up, which itself contains redeposited occupation material. The nature of the material in the thin lenses of material on occupation floors has led to the assumption that the material here such as obsidian flakes is *in situ* activity residue.[36] This claim is based on the fact that different obsidian flakes in these areas can sometimes be fitted back together, suggesting that they had been knapped nearby. The close spatial association of obsidian flakes with the obsidian caches (usually found beneath occupation floors) from which the obsidian is assumed to have been taken to be worked also supports the notion that obsidian was worked in the areas near ovens and hearths. Certainly it remains highly likely that obsidian in ashy deposits (perhaps rake-out) near hearths and ovens is often *in situ*, or very close to being *in situ*. But it is also possible that it has been swept from a nearby location. *In situ* bead production and grease extraction are also possible on occupation floors in the South Area, although again, the material found on these floors could have been swept a short distance from other platforms in the building.[37] Whether the material in the thin lenses on occupation floors is the result of *in situ* activities or sweeping, the distinctions in the ways different parts of the floor in the same building were used remain clear.

Despite the overall pattern that I have described, nearly every building seems to have its own form of exception. Building 4 in Level VIII provides an example. There are clear edges to the 'dirty' occupation zone in this building, but because of the presence of a room in the southeastern corner of the building, the 'dirty' occupation area has been moved northwards – to what is still the southern end of the main room. Another distinctive arrangement is found in Building 17 in Level IX. Prior to Phase B the ovens were in the 'wrong' part of this house, in the north. But there was possibly a partition that separated the northern area from the main room (and similar partitions have been found elsewhere – as in Building 3). It is also of interest that the northern 'dirty' occupation deposits are not as rich as the typical 'dirty' area in the southeast corner of the room.

Cattle and other animal heads and horns tend to be installed away from the south walls of main rooms and away from hearths and ovens. This may have been partly for practical reasons, and the need to move around easily in this working area. An exception occurs in a building in Level VII.[38] Here a cattle horn was set within the oven structure in the southern part of the room. The archaeology is unclear – either the horn was sticking out into the room, or it was a hidden part of the oven structure (rather as small horn figurines are sometimes found in oven walls). But, whatever the specific interpretation, this example shows that the conventions regarding how different spaces could be used were sometimes changed or tinkered with to fit individual circumstances.

BURIAL

Other examples of shifts from the 'norm' are found in relation to burial location. Normally, all burial occurs away from ovens and hearths in the northern parts of main rooms under the higher whiter platforms. But exceptions often seem to be made for neonates and very young infants (such as in the burial shown in Figure 50).[39] This is not to say that neonates and infants are not also buried away from such areas, but so far no adult has been found buried in the southern 'dirty' occupation areas.

An association between the house and the dead occurs very early in the Middle East, and is certainly in evidence by Natufian times in the 12th to the 10th millennia BC in the Levant.[40] Burial occurs in open areas or in buildings without grave goods in an early phase at the village of Çayönü in southeast Turkey (10th to early 9th millennia BC), and a building with a room full of skulls occurs in the following phase. The basement floors in later buildings at this site were used as graves, although, as at Çatalhöyük a little later, in each sector of buildings there is one building with more burials.[41] Burial occurs beneath floors of houses at Nevalı Çori southeast Turkey in the late 9th millennium.[42] At Aşıklı Höyük in central Anatolia burials occur beneath house floors in the late 9th and early 8th millennia BC. There is, however, a greater emphasis on burial in houses at Çatalhöyük in the late 8th

50 A neonate burial in the southwest corner of the main room in Building 1 (skeleton 2197), in the 'dirty' occupation area. So far, no adult burials have been found in these areas, although neonates are found buried elsewhere in the house.

and 7th millennia BC than at Aşıklı Höyük or any other earlier site in Anatolia and perhaps also in the PPNB of the Middle East. It is true that there has been relatively little excavation below the house floors in the upper levels at Aşıklı Höyük, but the houses that have been excavated, including those in the deep sounding, have not produced the density of house burial seen at Çatalhöyük.[43] Indeed, Çatalhöyük could be described as a necropolis as much as a settlement.

In some ways, the tradition of burial at Çatalhöyük could be seen as conservative. For example, the special treatment of skulls is at its height in the PPNB (from the late 9th through the 8th millennia BC – for chronology see also box on page 20) of the Middle East, whereas at Çatalhöyük it remains a feature of the ceramic Neolithic. By the later phase[44] at Çayönü, there is an absence of burial evidence and burial may have become extramural. Mehmet Özdoğan[45] notes that after the PPN in eastern Anatolia and the Middle East burial generally becomes extramural. But intramural burial continues at Çatalhöyük into the ceramic Neolithic, throughout the 7th millennium BC. In central Anatolia there is a shift of burial away from houses at the later site of Hacılar[46] in the late 7th and early 6th millennia BC. In the 7th millennium in Greece, early Neolithic burial in Thessaly occurs between houses, but Catherine Perlès[47] argues that most people were cremated. Çatalhöyük would seem to be distinctive in terms of its retention of the importance of the ancestors

51 An example of single burial in Building 1 (skeleton 1495). More commonly, burials intersect with each other, or contain multiple discrete inhumations (see Plate 12).

within the house, even though other burial practices may have taken place off site (see discussion of the KOPAL Area data in Chapter 4).

One clear result of the current excavations at Çatalhöyük is that in contrast to the claims made by Mellaart, most of the burial at Çatalhöyük involves single, fully fleshed inhumation in graves dug beneath platforms in houses (Figure 51). Mellaart had found jumbled and disarticulated human bones beneath the platforms in the main rooms and his team interpreted the disarticulation in terms of secondary burial – that is, it was assumed that bodies were initially buried elsewhere and then reburied beneath the platform floors. This idea was supported by paintings of vultures apparently picking the flesh from headless human corpses (e.g. Figures 22 and 68). But the team of palaeoanthropologists working with the current project[48] is of the opinion that many (but not all[49]) burials were primary. Careful excavation shows that many bodies were placed in the grave intact – the joints are articulated and the smallest bones (often lost in reburial) are present. The jumbling that occurs beneath some platforms (e.g. Plate 12) results from the frequent practice of adding in later graves and bodies to the same platform. These later insertions often disturb earlier burials and careful excavation is needed to sort out the complex cuts and recuts as new graves are dug, new bodies added in, and earlier bodies disturbed. The new evidence challenges the evidence from wall paintings of the practice of excarnation (exposing the body to vultures before secondary burial in houses), at least for those buried within the settlement.

There appear to be some general rules about how the body is laid out at Çatalhöyük – for example, flexed beneath platforms and without pottery. But there is otherwise a lot of variability. There is remarkable lack of patterning in the specifics of how the body is laid out, which way it faces, and so on. Similar variability is found at Aşıklı Höyük.[50] Grave goods occur but they are not common (see Chapter 9). Mats or binding often survive as phytolith traces, and all the mats associated with adult burials were made from sedge (*Scirpus*), whereas neonate children were often buried in a particular type of basket. In her studies of the phytoliths from the site (see page 78), Arlene Rosen[51] found one unique type of multicelled phytolith, similar in appearance to those from a particular wild grass,[52] that may have only been used for neonatal burial baskets. Although not all neonate containers were made of this grass, when it did occur it was only in these infant burial baskets. Another significant aspect of these neonate baskets is the presence of phytoliths from the floral segments of the plant. Other baskets were composed of the stem and leaf portions. It is possible that the use of flowering grasses was intentional and related to the ideology surrounding the burial of infants, although more baskets will need to be analyzed in order to establish this as a true pattern. On the basis of the presence of the floral components, these basketry materials were most likely collected in the spring and/or constructed in that season. This might be indicative of the season of death for these infants.

USE – REPETITIVE PRACTICES

Conventions in the way in which internal space was organized may have been talked about, at least to some degree. The fact that burial and symbolic representations on walls respect the divisions of space (for example, adult burial and wall painting rarely occur near ovens and hearths in the southern areas of main rooms) suggests that at some level there was conscious recognition of the divisions. But the divisions were also born out of daily routines in the way that things were done. Repeated practices regarding how one moved around the buildings may have just been seen as 'obvious' and taken for granted. The degree of repetition of the internal divisions of space across years and generations at Çatalhöyük is one of the distinctive characteristics of the site.

It should be remembered, however, that repetitive practices were not only found in houses, although it is the house that was the main focus of socialization. Repetitive practices are also found in other spheres. For example, there is some continuity in the use of middens and other outside spaces. In general terms, the same areas of the site were often used for middens through many levels. At a smaller scale, however, middens sometimes do not show detailed continuity of practices – for example, fire spots occur sometimes in middens but their location is not repeated through time. In one midden there are repeated episodes of small-scale lime burning.[53] There are six stratigraphically distinct phases of lime burning in this one small excavation trench.

Returning to the house, it should be noted that seasonal and cyclical rhythms cut across the daily routines. For example, in Building 5 there is a cyclical nature to the sooting of the wall plasters – some minor plaster washes on the walls are not sooted and some are heavily sooted. It seems likely that at least during the summer, ovens and hearths were used on the roofs. During these times of the year there may have been little oven use inside buildings. There may have been other correlates of this seasonality. Perhaps it was only in the soot-free parts of the year that paintings were undertaken. The daily practices within the houses would have had a yearly round (Figure 33).

The repetition of practices in buildings found at Çatalhöyük is a characteristic of other and earlier sites in Anatolia and the Middle East.[54] Perhaps the clearest and most closely relevant example is Aşıklı Höyük, where the dated deep sounding sequence, which is over 6 m (20 ft) deep, covers somewhere between 200 and 600 years.[55] Through this time period there are six rebuildings of a house in exactly the same location and with the same location of hearths and midden.[56] This degree of continuity, also seen to a rather lesser degree at Çatalhöyük (see below), is not so commonly found in the early Neolithic in western Anatolia.[57] By the time of early

Neolithic Thessaly in Greece, there is much variability in houses, it is more difficult to see specific norms, and there is less evidence of continuity of houses.[58]
Variability in forms of house continuity has also been noted in the Balkans.[59] Later
in this chapter and in Chapter 11 I will discuss general explanations for changes
through time in the degree of continuity of practices.

As noted above, while buildings at Çatalhöyük could be built on midden or penning areas, they were more frequently – and as we shall see in Chapter 6 this is
especially true of the more elaborate buildings[60] – built directly on the walls of earlier buildings (see Figure 48). Building 5 and Building 1 built directly above it were
together occupied for perhaps 150 years. Both Mellaart's 'Shrines' 10 and 31 continued in use from Level IX to Level VIA which is a period of about 400 years. His
'Shrines' 1, 7, and 8 also continued across three to five levels. Mellaart did not excavate all levels in the same part of the mound and so only future excavation will be
able to show whether some buildings at Çatalhöyük were rebuilt for large parts of
the 1,400 years of Neolithic occupation at the site.

Clear evidence of repetitive practices at Çatalhöyük comes from the continual
replastering of the walls and floors. Study of these replasterings allows insight into
the repeated construction and use activities within buildings. Comparisons with
Neolithic sites in the Middle East, in this regard, are often difficult because of a
paucity of data. Generally in the Levant and eastern Anatolia, lime-plastered floors
are common in PPNB and related contexts. These floors are sometimes carefully
polished, and their thick, hard composition restricts the possibility for artifacts to
get lodged into floor matrices as a result of use. Such floors do not need to be
replaced on an annual basis and so there is less potential for artifacts to be trapped
between successive floors, and also less potential for studying repetitive practices in
floor construction. In addition, many well-known sites in the area were excavated
before detailed recovery of artifacts and detailed description of deposits became
standard practice.[61]

Fragments of hard lime floors are found at Çatalhöyük in the levels below Level
XI.[62] These required less frequent renewal than the later mud plaster floors, but the
production of quicklime involved large amounts of labour. Another reason for the
abandonment of these harder floors may have been the desire to dig through them
in order to insert burials, obsidian caches and other storage features.[63] For whatever
reason, the plastering of walls and floors became a frequent task after the abandonment of the hard lime flooring. The replastering with a lime-rich mud also
sometimes involved features such as basins and bins. In Building 4, a basin had multiple plaster applications that interleaved with the floor plasters.[64]

These multiple replasterings, especially in the middle part of the sequence at
Çatalhöyük where the plaster layers are more numerous, allow a unique insight
into repeated practices. Annual replasterings made up of foundation and surface
coatings occur routinely up to 50–100 times.[65] In Building 5, there are about 70 phases

52 A stair scar and oven on the south wall of Building 5. The large pit probably is the result of the retrieval of the wooden stairs (see Figure 53). The oven (or fire installation) was largely demolished prior to abandonment.

of major replastering, and as far as we can see, there is little major change in use of space in this building through that time.[66] For example, the oven and stair (Figure 52) seem to stay in the same place in this building through these phases (although further excavation may change the picture). However, despite this continuity of architecture and use, things do change. It appears that away from the oven in Building 5, more sooting is present throughout the first half of the plaster sequence than in the second half, which may relate to a change in the form of fire installation.

The plaster on some walls of main rooms can be up to 7.5 cm (3 in) thick, and in one case Wendy Matthews observed 450 layers of plastering on one wall.[67] But the degree of continuity between buildings, and the duration of occupation of levels, decrease in the uppermost parts of the site.[68] In the earlier and middle part of the sequence, the great emphasis on continuity of buildings and the degree of repetition of practices suggest that it was the house that was the main focus of socialization.[69] Social roles and rules were undoubtedly learned as children grew up carrying out daily practices within the ritually and symbolically charged spaces of the house. It was in the interests of dominant groups in society (perhaps these were the elders) to maintain the repetition of practices.[70] But also, the continuity involved a respect for the dead buried below the floors in the houses. There seems to be a relationship between buildings with most burials and those with well-maintained internal divisions of space. It also seems to be the case that buildings with most burials are more often rebuilt in the same location.

The particular historical moment that creates the multiple replasterings at
Çatalhöyük seems to involve the house-based construction of continuities and
links with the past (ancestors or the dead). It is part of a wider shift from community
to household-based organization.[71] As we will see below, there is a general trend
observable in Anatolia and the Middle East towards the increasing importance of
the house. This shift can be understood as a move towards house-based social
groups. Such groups competed in terms of their links to ancestors and in terms of
the handing down of rights and resources within the 'house'. The prime form of
socialization was the learning of daily practices within the house in the context of
respect for the ancestors. It was the continuity of the 'house', and adherence to its
rules, that guaranteed rights and resources.

ABANDONMENT

Perhaps a correlate of the focus on the continuity of the house at Çatalhöyük is a
concern with breaks in continuity – when the house has to be abandoned and
rebuilt. The reasons for abandonment vary. There is some evidence from Building 1
that the death of particular individuals could have triggered the 'death' of the
house, but the case is not clear.[72] The adding of new walls to shore up slumped walls,
and the internal divisions of space to accommodate new people and activities could
also have led to a lack of space and the desire to rebuild. Sometimes there are so
many plaster layers on a wall that the plaster must have started to fall off. Accidental
fires may have occurred causing destruction and rebuilding, as Mellaart claims for
many of the upper levels of the site, but in our work it seems that fires may also have
been set deliberately on occasions in order to end the life of a house.[73] Whatever the
reasons for abandonment, the moments of ending and starting anew had to be carefully managed and ritually sanctioned.

The general process of abandonment is clearly outlined in the results of the
excavations of Buildings 1 and 17. In Building 17, for example, there was first cleaning
and scouring of walls and plaster features, then the dismantling of the roof with the
resulting residues occurring on the floor. Then the main structural posts were pulled
out, leaving retrieval pits and scars in the plaster on the walls, and the walls were then
dismantled. The building was then filled with processed building materials.

One of the first events in the abandonment process involved cleaning. There
are different types of cleaning that need identification. First, there is the daily
sweeping of floors that led to deposits in middens, or perhaps in southern 'dirty'
oven areas of houses. This keeping of at least the white plastered raised floors with
burials clean was facilitated by the placement of mats. Second, there is the cleaning
that goes hand in hand with monthly, seasonal or yearly replasterings of the floors.
On the whole, at least on the white plaster floors with burials, the floors were

carefully cleaned before replastering, although it is difficult to distinguish such actions from daily cleaning. Finally, there is the cleaning of the last floors as part of final abandonment of a phase of use of a building. For example, relatively few artifacts and no substantial occupation type deposits were found sealed by the infilling deposits in Building 5.

Another act associated with abandonment was the placement of artifacts. Craig Cessford[74] discusses all the evidence for deliberate deposition of a wide range of artifacts from obsidian to axes to bone points in Buildings 5 and 1. But how much of this is 'ritual' placement as opposed just to pragmatic use and loss is unclear. There is some real repetition – like the placing of cattle scapulae in abandonment contexts – often near hearths.[75]

In Building 5, after the matting had been removed, a complete greenstone axe was placed lying on the latest surface in a doorway[76] (Figure 53). Given the presence of matting during the preceding phase the axe must have been placed during abandonment after the matting was removed. But the axe could have been used as part of the cutting down and removal of posts and other features – rather than as an offering. But in other cases, such as the placing of the famous seated female figurine with felines in a bin in Mellaart's building A.II.1, the intention seems to have been more symbolic.

The burning of the lentil bin[77] in the south part of the main room in Building 1[78] was slow; and over the lentils were layers of at least 13 wild goat horncores. As well as

53 Abandonment events in Building 5. The floors were carefully cleaned before abandonment, and a variety of artifacts were placed around the building, probably intentionally. The roof and upper parts of the wall were removed, and many other features were demolished or truncated.

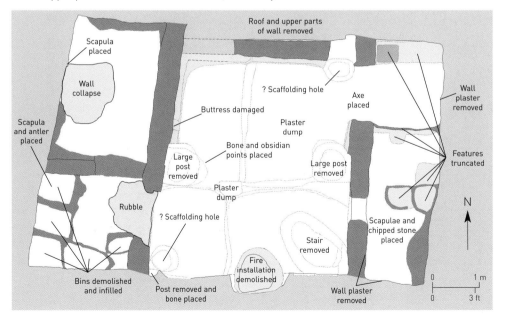

these burnt horncores, there was a cattle jaw, and a worked cattle scapula was placed nearby, perhaps after the fire as it is unburnt. It is difficult to interpret this evidence in terms of pragmatic dumping of rubbish into a lentil bin as some of the horncores were aligned with their tips facing forwards into the room, and cattle skull and scapula often had a special significance. The deposition seems deliberate, and occurred in relation to a large-scale burning of the building. At the same time a large fragment of a grinding stone with ochre on its surface was placed upside down in an adjacent basin, before the firing of the building.

As well as burning, another component of the abandonment process was truncation and scouring. In the last phase of occupation of Building 5[79] in the main room[80] in the southeastern quadrant, there is evidence of scouring or truncation of the floors at abandonment. The main oven was destroyed and the fragments left on the floor and in retrieval pits. Large extents of wall plaster were stripped from part of Building 5[81] during abandonment, indicating that they may have been painted or otherwise decorated. There were surviving traces of red paint including a single quatrefoil.[82] Also a plastered mud-brick pillar on a bench in Building 5 was truncated during abandonment.

Also in Building 5, the five bins in the southwest room[83] had their walls cut down to 20–30 cm (8–12 in) which represents a fairly thorough dismantling (Figure 54).[84] In discussions with members of the local community at Küçükköy, it was suggested that all this scouring and truncation occurred for practical reasons – the fine clays

54 Storage bins as they were found in Building 5 (see figures 42 and 43 for reconstructions). Their scouring and truncation may have been for practical reasons, but evidence from elsewhere in the site indicates that there was probably at least some symbolic aspect too.

used in the plastering are not easily available and abandoned plaster structures would have afforded a convenient source. While this may be part of the answer, some truncation and destruction seem more clearly social/symbolic. For example, the heads and hands/paws of the relief sculptures with upraised arms and feet are always removed (see for example Plate 18).[85] Mellaart[86] noted that large relief sculptures were often removed or destroyed on the west walls of main rooms, and we have found examples of such behaviour in Buildings 1, 2 and possibly 3. The reasons for these acts of destruction or retrieval will be discussed in Chapter 6.

In the main room[87] of Building 2 in Level IX, there were small 'pick' marks on the western wall and the plaster had been removed. On the floor by this disturbance was a large cattle horncore. This may have been part of a wall fixture that was removed on abandonment (there are some chop marks on the horncore which may result from the dismantling process). While some plaster reliefs were often removed, the leopard reliefs often seem to have been left with their heads and feet intact, further evidence of their special status. Ovens are sometimes truncated and dismantled, and sometimes (as in Buildings 2 & 4) carefully filled in. The villagers from Küçükköy suggested that these activities related to the abandonment of ovens may have been to ensure a firm base for future buildings located on the same spot. But either solution would have provided an equally firm base. Similarly, it was not necessary to knock down pillars in Building 5. Perhaps people needed the plaster and brick from the pillars, but the pillars would have acted as a good foundation for Building 1 which succeeded it.

In a number of cases in the current excavations (e.g. Building 2, but also in buildings in the 4040 Area), the dismantling of plaster features is associated with feasting remains. There are concentrations of the meat-bearing parts of large animals, especially wild bulls, at the first stage in the dismantling and infilling process. This suggests that the abandonment was often seen as a social and symbolic event, as well as having practical components.

INFILLING

The mixing of practical and symbolic motivation in the abandonment of houses is also seen in their infilling. Again, the practices of infilling are surrounded with social, ritual and symbolic concerns about continuity. Comparable activities are found at other sites. At the Neolithic village in southeast Anatolia called Çayönü some buildings, after several rebuilds, were 'buried' with a layer of small pebbles, and this 'burial' of buildings occurs right through the sequence.[88] Maybe like the dead that soon become ancestors the buildings are potent in themselves and require proper burial and maintenance. Aslı Özdoğan[89] notes that 'ritual' buildings in pre-pottery phases in eastern Anatolia and Syria are often carefully

cleaned, filled with virgin soil or 'sieved earth' before another building is constructed on top.[90]

There is some evidence that the fill deposits in Building 5 at Çatalhöyük were
carefully processed or even screened in the construction of a base for Building 1 that
was built directly above. The same processing is found in Building 4. But where did
the material come from? The amount of soil that went into filling the lower surviving part of Building 5 is about the same as the amount of mud-brick and earthen
material that could have been obtained from the destruction of the upper walls and
roof. But there are also cases of houses being filled with midden when they were not
to be rebuilt (such as Building 2). In other cases, Mellaart noted large amounts of
burnt material and construction debris in buildings. However, while a house could
be infilled in a number of different ways, much of our evidence of infilling is of a
carefully controlled process.

For example, there is some evidence at Çatalhöyük that different fills were
placed in different rooms. Sarah Cross May[91] has identified quantitative differences
between the fills in different rooms or parts of rooms across the site as a whole. In
Building 17, Level IX, an elaborate infilling process is suggested by the refitting of
obsidian flakes.[92] A hoard was scoured out here and deposited in fill material so that
part of it ended up in a pit that was dug to retrieve a post and part was thrown
through an access hole into an adjoining room.[93]

The last oven in use in a house, as in Buildings 1 and 4, was sometimes filled carefully and separately. In Building 4, Level VIII, the fill of one oven[94] is very complex.
The dome of the oven survived intact, so the soil to fill the oven was fed in through
the opening. It would have been easier to simply destroy the oven, or break the
dome and fill the oven from the top. But no, the oven was carefully filled through its
side entrance with clean soil. So both at the scale of the house and at the scale of
individual ovens, the infilling process was often carefully managed.

THE WIDER PICTURE

Inside all buildings at Çatalhöyük there was a wide range of functions and activities. The buildings were internally differentiated into rooms and platforms, and
there was much repetition of the same building form, within limited specialization
and hierarchy. But most buildings had their own separate walls and most production occurred at the domestic scale. What was the historical context that produced
this type of building? As already noted, Brian Byrd has discussed a general shift in
the southern Levant towards complex autonomous households by the time of the
PPNB.[95] The recent finds of very early and large elaborate ritual centres such as
Göbekli Tepe (Figure 55),[96] and the strong emphasis on ritual buildings at other
early Neolithic sites such as Jerf el Ahmar (a site in Syria with both domestic

55 Göbekli Tepe, Enclosure B. As early as the 10th millennium BC this site in southeastern Turkey had large ceremonial spaces marked out by monumental stone T-shaped pillars. These pillars often have elaborate carvings (see Figure 88).

houses and elaborate ritual buildings) and Çayönü have very much altered narratives of the development of village life.[97] It is clear that many sites in the 10th to 8th millennia BC were centred around communal rituals. The investment in public works, as at Jericho in the Levant, is sometimes remarkable.[98] Houses, on the other hand, are initially often relatively unelaborated with few internal divisions. House complexity increases through time. In the central Anatolian region one can see this shift very clearly. At Aşıklı Höyük in the late 9th and early 8th millennia BC, there are ceremonial buildings but houses are much less elaborate than at Çatalhöyük in the ensuing millennia, with a wide range of functions from burial, ritual and art to storage, manufacture and production more clearly drawn into the house.

In conceptualizing this overall set of changes, it may be helpful to return to Emile Durkheim's distinctions between mechanical and organic solidarity.[99] By mechanical solidarity Durkheim meant social cohesion based upon the likeness and similarities among individuals in society, and largely dependent on common rituals and routines. By organic solidarity he meant social cohesion based upon the dependence between individuals performing different tasks and with different values and interests. There is a greater division of labour. This distinction seems very similar to that between corporate-based and network-based pathways to social and cultural complexity as defined by Richard Blanton and Gary Feinman.[100] A corporate pathway has few overt differences between houses, little economic differentiation, an emphasis on kin affiliation, and an importance given to collective ritual and public spaces and constructions. The network route, on the other hand, has more emphasis on differences in wealth, craft production, and long-distance exchange.

It is not clear that all sites in Anatolia and the Middle East in the 10th to 7th millennia BC can be placed into a neat Durkheimian or related scheme, and there are dangers in suggesting an evolutionary sequence and a general typology. But new excavations identified above have certainly opened the possibility that village communities emerged within a primarily mechanical form of social cohesion, whereas through time individual houses became more important and there was more specialization and perhaps more organic solidarity emerges. Although Çatalhöyük is late in this sequence, there are intimations of both forms of solidarity. On the one hand, there are repetitive practices in houses which all seem very similar. This looks very much like mechanical solidarity despite the absence of common ceremonial buildings. On the other hand, practices which earlier might have been public and ceremonial (ritual, symbolism, burial of large numbers of skulls in the Skull Building at Çayönü) are placed in separate houses at Çatalhöyük. We shall also see that despite the occurrence of many productive activities (obsidian knapping, food preparation, storage) in all houses, there is some evidence of emergent functional differentiation as some houses focus on bead production, others on figurine production, and others on ritual links to the ancestors (see Chapter 7). This looks much more like organic solidarity. Through time in the Çatalhöyük sequence, there are intimations that it is the organic form of solidarity that increases as specialization increases and interactions between houses become more important (see Chapters 6, 7 and 11). There are dangers of using dualistic notions such as that suggested by Durkheim since most cases, as in the Çatalhöyük case, involve some complex mixture. But the scheme is perhaps useful in pointing to an overall shift from an emphasis on the collective to that on functional differentiation – a shift seen both at Çatalhöyük and more widely.

SUMMARY AND CONCLUSIONS

The orderliness of the 'town' as a whole – the careful regulation of activities and discard, the taboos about what could come into the settlement and be deposited there, the long-term repetition of midden areas and building areas – is repeated in microcosm in the house. In fact, I want to argue that the inside patterning is itself part of the larger structuring of the 'town' as a whole.

In order to explore this idea we need to consider what it meant to 'live' in these houses. How much time did people spend in them, and what was it like? It is often said that the houses were dark inside. But an experimental house built at the site by Mira Stevanovic has shown that during the day so much light comes in from the stair entry that the main rooms are quite bright. The white plastered walls were frequently renewed and often burnished and so they reflect light well. Even the side rooms receive some reflected light so that one's eyes get used to the relative dark in them and activities can be carried out there. We know that people knapped obsidian near the stair entries in the main rooms; indeed the location of the obsidian caches and the nearby working of obsidian may be related to the need for a light source. The oven, as a night-time source of light, is in the same part of the main room, near the stair entry.

But the rooms were certainly smoky. This is clear from the layers of soot that are found on the plaster walls. The frequent replastering of the walls may have been necessary to maintain the light reflection in the main rooms. We have also found several skeletons with carbon residues on their ribs probably derived from inhaling soot.[101] Most of the individuals with carbon residues are older people, and most old people have them. The carbon on the ribs has been interpreted in terms of the layers of soot identified on the plaster walls and the lack of architectural evidence for good air draughts in the houses – and in terms of the need to spend time in the houses over the harsh winters. The evidence can be interpreted in terms of the build up of residues of an indoor life, for both men and women. So certainly by their later years people spent a good amount of time indoors. On the other hand, some young people and children are buried in houses in significant locations, including special neonate foundation deposits by doors and burial by hearths. Perhaps both the old and the young, as we might expect, have an especially close relationship with the house.

So, as people lived their lives they spent at least part of it, when young and old, and especially in the winter, closely tied to the house. This immersing in the house provided an opportunity for socialization – that is, for the enforcing of society-wide rules through the daily practices of life in each house. The house was an important context in which social rules were taught and learnt – and much of this was a practical learning in the routines of domestic activities. It has long been recognized[102] that there was much repetition in the use of space inside houses at Çatalhöyük. We have seen that each house tends to have a main room, the internal walls of which have thicker layers of plaster, and a side room associated with storage and food preparation and with many fewer layers of plaster on the walls. While Wendy Matthews found that the main room in Building 5 had over 450 fine white silty clay plaster layers on the walls, adjacent side rooms were only plastered three or four times with orange and brown silt loam plasters. Hearths and stair entrances are normally found in the south of main rooms in buildings, and art and sculpture are not usually found on these south walls. In our excavations we have found a strong associated pattern – that somewhere near the hearth and stair entry there is at least one obsidian cache beneath the floors. Flint is rarely placed in these caches. We also see concentrations of basketry in southern parts of main rooms and in side rooms. These site-wide and society-wide conventions were maintained in the practices of daily life in each house.

We have already seen other repeated patterns. The floors of the main rooms are usually divided into platforms, or areas of different height, and the higher of these have a white plaster. The different floor areas are often demarcated by raised edges. These differences may also relate to floor covering – with different types of matting on the different platforms and floors. There is also a link to burial. The main burial platforms seem to be those with white laid plaster floors. Few burials occur beneath occupation floors, although neonates may be buried here.

There is a tendency for different categories of people to be buried under different platforms. For example, in Building 1 there are more young people buried beneath the northwest platform and more older individuals under the central-east platform. The distribution of 'art' and symbolism in the house also respects spatial divisions. Painting and sculpture are rarely found in the southern area of the house, and cattle heads with horns (bucrania – Figure 56) are most common on east and west walls. Vulture paintings only occur on north and east walls.[103] Burial is most

56 An example of a bucranium or plastered bull's skull. Traces of the horncores and a much smaller bucranium resting on the main bucranium can be seen. The horns and muzzle of each were painted red.

common beneath platforms against the north and east walls, and since the vulture paintings also show headless corpses a spatial link between vultures and death is suggested.

Examples such as this allow one to argue that despite all the changes that occur in the arrangement of activities in buildings, general tendencies tend to get repeated. The house was an important location for socialization into roles and behaviours at Çatalhöyük. As a child grew up in this domestic space, it learned that certain things could be done in certain places but not others. It learned the social rules about where to bury people or make beads, where to find the obsidian cache and where to place animal scapulae. In this way the rules of society were learned not through direct centralized control, but in the dispersed daily practices within individual social units. And all of these daily acts were set within the presence of the ancestors and within a symbolic world presented in the art and installations.

As Norbert Elias[104] has argued (see also Chapter 1), the social constraint that is produced by living in a large agglomeration of people is related to self-regulation and self-constraint. He suggests that as more people come together in larger communities, there is a need for more differentiation and regulation in order to be able to cope with the complexity of interactions. As he puts it, 'As more and more people must attune their conduct to that of others, the web of actions must be organized more and more strictly and accurately, if each individual action is to fulfil its social function. The individual is compelled to regulate his conduct in an increasingly differentiated, more even and more stable manner.'[105] At Çatalhöyük this regulation may have been compelled by differentiated groups such as elders or family or kin heads, but it was largely achieved in the daily repetitive practices within the house.

And yet, as we have seen, all these daily acts, and all the acts of construction, use, rebuilding, abandonment, infilling were set within a symbolic world. And they all took place in spaces framed by symbolism that had a strong social meaning – such as the pairs of balanced leopards. It may be no accident that Çatalhöyük is *both* a site with much domestic art *and* a site without strong centralized functions. Perhaps these two dominant characteristics of the site are closely linked – linked by the repetitive practices within houses. Social regulation was achieved by socialization within the house embedded within a strong belief system that was frequently referred to or made present within the house, surrounding the daily practices.

The social regulation within the house allows social cohesion without strong centralized functions (Chapter 4) as well as control over scattered resources (Chapter 3). The strong social control based on socialization of individuals within houses (as well as other processes such as collective feasting to be discussed in Chapter 8) allows far-flung resources to be coordinated and exploited. We can perhaps see this latter point directly in terms of the obsidian caches. Obsidian was obtained from sources in Cappadocia as we have seen. It came to the site as pre-forms which were further worked on site, largely within the domestic context. But why bother to cache the obsidian beneath the floors of the houses? I will explore this question more in Chapter 7, but at least one component of an answer is that the obsidian had to be brought from far afield into the house, to be embraced within the social rules and categories of the house, to be defined in relation to the social group by being placed spatially. It was through such social positioning that the far-flung exchanges could be integrated and exploited. Most (if not all) things had to be brought in and given meaning in relation to the house.

57 Reconstruction by James Mellaart of a building he called the 'Second Vulture Shrine'. Mellaart's reconstructions make the buildings seem rather sterile and static, whereas in fact they were lived-in and constantly being tinkered with and renewed.

Before the current project started excavating houses in 1995 I rather assumed that we would just dig down and find complete houses rather like those in Mellaart's reconstructions (e.g. Figure 57). But in fact what we found was very different. Rather than static things we found processes. The main result of the new excavations is to show the way in which the houses at Çatalhöyük have much internal detail which was always being tinkered with. Different parts of the floor have different heights, colours, plasters, mats and they are associated with different forms of construction and use. But there is also continual adjustment as the spaces are remade, reworked, moved or used for different functions. There is a tension between the focus on repetitive practices and the continual tinkering that went on in the details of daily life.

I have tried to argue in this chapter that this process of material detail is socially embedded. In Chapter 2, I gave examples of how plastering a wall or floor entangled people in all sorts of social and material dependencies, and of how burying the dead beneath floors had all sorts of material and social implications. But we now see how this point can be generalized to all the detail and change in the material life of the house. The movement of the oven changes the place of the stair and the entrance which affects movement patterns on the roof. The burial of someone beneath a platform means that special white plaster has to be obtained and used, implicating social relationships, dependencies, alliances and exchange. The placing of items in walls or during abandonment involves social knowledge, access to resources and so again social ties. The great density of material engagement in the house entails an enormously complex entanglement between people, society and things.

CHAPTER SIX

The Invention of 'History'

Images of leopards or big cats are found widely in the early Neolithic of Anatolia. For example, lions are shown at Göbekli Tepe in southeast Turkey in the 9th millennium BC.[1] And at Çatalhöyük big cats are found in several contexts – from the figurine of a woman sitting between cats to the widespread depictions of humans apparently wearing leopard skins. The pairs of leopards facing each other are also found in several houses. For example, James Mellaart found a pair of animals (Figure 35) with their heads and paws facing each other, as if fighting, on the west wall in a building he called VIII.27 (his building 27 in Level VIII). There are red spots only on the heads, but comparison with the other pairings suggests these may well be leopard depictions.[2] A pair of spotted leopards was also found in Mellaart's building VIB.44 (on the central part of the north wall – see Plate 9). But it is of special interest that another pair was found in the building directly below in building VII.44 in exactly the same position – in the centre of the north wall (Figure 58 and Plate 10).[3] A further single animal relief was found on the east wall of this building. Given that Mellaart excavated over 160 buildings, this seems an unlikely coincidence: that of the three buildings with leopard pairs, two should occur in direct sequence.

One finds similar continuities in other examples of art. In what Mellaart called 'Shrine' 8 for example, a bull occurs on the north wall across three levels. So the leopards and the other art immediately take us to an idea that I wish to explore in this chapter. This idea is that Çatalhöyük sees the emergence of history out of myth. So first, what do I mean by myth in the Neolithic of Anatolia and the Middle East? There are many symbolic themes at Çatalhöyük that occur widely across large swathes of Anatolia, the Levant and into the Zagros Mountains. These generalized themes such as the bull, the vulture and the big cat could just be seen as depictions

58 The top layer of painting on one of a pair of relief leopards, shown in full in Plate 10.

of real animals that had important symbolic significance. But I wish to argue that some symbolic themes were also often parts of myths. At least some of the symbolic images used in the Neolithic of Anatolia were fantastic. For example, some of the creatures represented at Göbekli are not real and include some sort of lizard or frog with bared teeth.[4] At Çatalhöyük itself, the splayed figure (e.g. Plate 18), is best interpreted as some sort of human-bear hybrid.[5] Some of Mellaart's interpretations of the wall paintings include fantastic animals. In addition, some of the art at Çatalhöyük has a narrative dimension suggesting a story or fable. For example, the baiting scenes show figures in rows dancing in an orderly fashion, and then there is a confusion of flailing bodies around aroused animals (e.g. Figures 13 and 84, and Plate 15). It is difficult not to read these in a story-like way. So when I suggest that there was a mythic component to the symbolism of Anatolia and the Middle East in the early Neolithic, I mean that the symbolism had both fantastic and narrative components.

A further reason for claiming a mythic component is that the symbolic themes circulated for a long time. Nigel Goring-Morris and Anna Belfer-Cohen[6] have argued that early Neolithic symbolism in the Levant continues from earlier traditions. Later at Çatalhöyük itself related ideas are used in a variety of contexts. The animal themes do not seem to have been used there in a totemic way (with each animal or totem indicating a particular family or clan) because we do not see some symbols confined to some areas of the site and not others. Rather what we see is a strategic choice from the range of available symbols. One way of explaining the longevity of these symbols is to argue that they were embedded in myths that were retold and passed down over millennia, with elaborations on the mythic themes in different contexts. Despite the overall conventions on where symbolism should be located (as discussed in Chapter 5), people were able to pick and choose the specifics of which symbols to use, very much on a household level. They also began to use the symbols to create specific histories that linked a specific past to a specific present.

I clearly do not mean by this that people at Çatalhöyük had a written history. But I do believe that one can talk about the constructions of history in non-literate societies. As an example of what I have in mind I would like to use an account of the Enga in Papua New Guinea.[7] The Enga, who are a highland agricultural people, traditionally have both myth and history. Myth (*tindi pii*) and history (*atome pii*) are intertwined in origin traditions, but otherwise they can be distinguished. Myths or tales do not claim to record actual historical events.[8] They disclose attitudes and worldviews and are not associated with particular tribes or times. They are continually updated and embellished by skilled storytellers. Historical accounts, on the other hand, are narratives that originated in eyewitness accounts and have been passed down over generations. They are intended to relay factual information about the past. They especially deal with tracing a genealogy of tribal members back to the founding ancestor through the male line. The earliest generations are fictive and involve birth from non-human ancestors like marsupials, snakes, birds and insects, but there is then a shift to the record of real people and events, dealing with the relations of people to land, major battles, migrations, and the divisions of society down to the individual family. The genealogies extend back 7 to 14 generations.

In material terms, the Enga are largely egalitarian and even 'big men' did not hold vastly more wealth (in pigs etc.) than others. But some people did come to be especially influential through the control of knowledge – especially historical knowledge. History underlies all public matters in Enga society. 'Land disputes cannot be resolved outside of their historical contexts, the settlement of wars hinges to a large degree on the history of relations between opposing groups, exchange often follows the paths of those who went before, and lessons of the past are recounted to those who threaten to make rash decisions. Historical knowledge is thus an important source of power and influence for Enga people.'[9]

In similar ways I want to argue that at Çatalhöyük people began to make specific connections between the present and the past that could be termed historical.[10] I will also argue that these connections were largely about individual family genealogies, that they concerned the handing down of rights and resources in the house, and that the manipulation of these histories led to some houses becoming dominant over others.

As people lived their daily lives on the mound they would have been ever aware of the past. They had to build the walls of new houses on earlier walls in order to prevent subsidence into fills or midden beneath. Building new houses would have involved a knowledge of the anatomy of the mound. For example, Shahina Farid notes that there were continual problems regarding the west wall of one room in the South Area – perhaps because the wall was free-standing it kept slumping.[11] The problems were addressed by the construction of a new wall on its eastern side bonded to a southern wall. Probably to avoid future collapse, the new wall was built in a large foundation trench cut through underlying middens and walls[12] reaching down to the top of a wall that had gone out of use three levels earlier.[13] Whether reaching down to the earlier wall was fortuitous or a deliberate act based on a long memory is not known, but the result was that a firm foundation was provided for the new wall.

Every time the inhabitants dug a pit or a trench they would have come across the potsherds and stone tools of earlier generations. People were entangled in a material past. Any rebuilding of a room would have potentially disturbed the bones of relatives. The plaster they placed on floors contained fragments of earlier plasters, bones and seeds. And so on. Of course, previous hunter-gatherers would have moved around a landscape in which earlier sites would have been known and recognized. In both cases, people lived in an environment of traces and memories. The intensity of these interactions with the past may have been greater in a mound such as Çatalhöyük, but this difference in degree is not itself what led to the shift towards a historical relationship with the past. It was social change that did that, as we shall see.

It is important to distinguish a conscious historical relationship with the past from habituated behaviour.[14] In the latter case, ritual and daily acts may become routinized and codified but there is no specific memory of events and histories. There may be community-wide memories embedded in daily practices and rules (everyone knows that the hearth is in the south of the house) without there being any specific memory of an individual house in which the hearth was in the south. There is an overall recognizable scheme from the bottom to the top of the mound which suggests the importance of habituated practices. In this scheme, as we saw in Chapter 5, higher, whiter and cleaner floors, often used for burial, are separated from lower, darker and dirtier floors. There are other continuities too. Ovens are usually placed in the south of the main room, and art rarely occurs near ovens. Pottery and clay figurines are never placed in burials. And so on. There is also a social dimension as there is some evidence that different types of people are associated with different platforms (for example, more younger people were buried beneath the northwest platform in Building 1). So it is important to try to tease apart the construction of history from habituated behaviour.

The first case in which I became alerted to the idea that historical links to the past may have been socially important at Çatalhöyük was in our excavations in Building 1 from 1995 to 1998. Against the west wall of Building 1 we found a large pit that had been dug down from higher levels through the building's infill (Figure 59).[15] This retrieval pit F.17 appeared to have been dug to remove or retrieve relief

59 This retrieval pit F.17 in Building 1 had been cut down from layers above, probably to remove a relief sculpture of which traces can be seen on the wall. A cattle horn inserted into the wall to the left was missed by the pit.

sculpture (only traces of which remained on the wall) from the east face of the west wall in the main room. This pit contained 'offerings' in the form of an assemblage of three bone points, a bird bone and eight assorted pieces of obsidian and flint placed in a group in its fill. And yet, whatever was on the west wall of this room had already been disturbed or even partially destroyed[16] by the construction of a wall termed F.18. Indeed, the sculpture on the west wall could only have been an integrated part of the room in an earlier phase of Building 1.[17] The period[18] between the last use of the sculpture and the digging of the pit was probably decades, based on the relative criteria of numbers of floors and oven bases and on radiocarbon dating. And so the retrieval pit F.17 implies a memory going back for some time. We can say with certainty that retrieval pit F.17 was dug down very carefully against the correct wall, in exactly the place where the sculpture was located. Given the amount of erosion off the top of the mound that occurred in the millennia after the Neolithic occupation, we cannot know how deep these Neolithic 'archaeologists' had to dig, but it was at least 0.7 m (2.3 ft) and probably substantially more.

In Building 5, there is a very large pit which had been dug down into the north-western corner of the main room just after it had been filled in, or just before the floors of Building 1 above were laid.[19] It is somewhat similar to F.17, but it is unclear what the digging down would have been to obtain. Similarly, a large pit was dug into a side room in Building 4.[20] The level from which this pit was dug is unknown as the relevant deposits were excavated in the 1960s. This pit could be another case of retrieval even though, again, we cannot identify what it might have been dug to retrieve.

These cases can be linked to others which show a concern with destruction and/or retrieval of sculpture from the west walls of main rooms. Mellaart records a frequent pattern of the destruction of the west walls of main rooms in order to remove sculpture.[21] Generally, when we excavate a house at Çatalhöyük we find that the sculptures, pillars and installations have been removed or destroyed. This may have occurred for many reasons, but in the case of retrieval pit F.17 it seems likely that the retrieval had the purpose of reuse or recycling. Craig Cessford[22] has shown on the basis of radiocarbon dating that a cattle skull and horncores which were deposited at the same time as lentils in a bin in Building 1 had a good chance of being earlier than them by up to 80–150 years.[23] Perhaps such retained items were kept simply because of a need for the materials. But it is also possible that such retentions and retrievals created links with past events. It is possible that animal heads commemorated events such as feasts or initiations or other rituals that were important in defining the house-based group. Even if sculptures and installations on the west walls of main rooms were often removed, most buildings did not have sculptures in such positions. Thus the people who dug pit F.17 cannot have assumed that Building 1 would have had installations on the west wall. Rather than this pit-digging being an example of habituated behaviour, there must have been a memory specific to this particular house that was retained over several phases of occupation. The retrieval indicates the construction of links to particular pasts.

Such a claim is clearer with another type of head – the retrieval and reuse of human heads. Certainly the skulls retrieved from human burials were reused. James Mellaart discusses the skulls found on the floor of a building he called E.VII.21 (Figure 57). Four skulls were found in this building in Level VII in contexts which we would now interpret as abandonment. 'One of these lay in a basket below the bull's head on the west wall; a second lay below the bull's head in the centre of the east wall and two others were perched on the corner platform below the vulture painting.'[24] In the recent excavations we have found individual examples – one in a pit associated with the main posts in Building 17 and two others in abandonment deposits in Building 3.

Some form of skull cult is widespread in Anatolia and the Middle East in Pre-Pottery Neolithic contexts. For example, at the PPNB village of 'Ain Ghazal there are examples of individuals being buried below hard lime plaster floors, then a little later their heads were removed.[25] The plastered skulls from Köşk Höyük in central Anatolia[26] and Çatalhöyük suggest links between central Anatolia and the plastered skulls of the Levant. At Çatalhöyük there are also links in the art between headless bodies and vultures. Symbolism and imagery surrounding vultures is again widespread. For example, there is a deposit of vulture, eagle and bustard wings at the site of Zawi Chemi Shanidar in northern Iraq dating to the 9th millennium BC.[27] There are stones engraved with an image very similar to the vultures at Çatalhöyük from Jerf el Ahmar in Syria.[28] So the ideas and myths surrounding death, vultures and skulls may have been very widespread and long term. But it is important to identify differences of content within these general similarities of form. In particular, it may be possible to see a difference between the skulls of generic ancestors and those of specific ancestors. In the Levant skulls are often grouped into threes, and at Çayönü skulls are collected into the Skull Building.[29] But at Çatalhöyük there seems to be more of an emphasis on individual and particular people and their skulls. One can perhaps argue that the face or head is the obvious locus of identity and individuality. Of the many burials excavated by the current project, only two have had their heads removed. In both cases there is evidence of cut marks and there is some evidence that the heads were cut off some time after initial burial.[30] It would thus have been necessary, at least in some cases, to remember the exact location of a specific burial or skull. Certainly we have seen that there were general rules about how and where people were buried, but these were not specific enough to locate a particular skull without specific memories of individual burials. There is also evidence that when bodies were buried it was known whether the head would later be removed. The very particular arrangement of the headless body in Building 6 (an unusual layout of the body and the placing of a cloth and plank over the torso – see Figures 60 and 61) shows that special treatment was given to this person prior to his burial. Once removed the skulls may well have circulated for some time before burial in specific abandonment or foundation contexts (such as the post pit in Building 17). All this suggests particular rather than generic links to ancestors.

60, 61 This burial from Building 6 was very specially treated with a plank and phytoliths (indicating a mat or cloth) over the body. The head was later removed.

In 2004 we made a discovery – one of the most exciting during my years of digging at Çatalhöyük – that bears on this issue of how dead relatives were treated and remembered. The find was of a skull, the facial features of which had been plastered and then painted red (Figure 7). The skull had been very badly damaged by an animal burrow, but still the features could be clearly seen. It put flesh on the distant past. It was like looking into the face of someone from 9,000 years ago.

The plastered skull was found held in the arms of a woman who had been placed in a pit as part of the foundation of a new building (Plates 13 and 14). This building (Building 42) was unusual in that it was built over a midden. The foundation deposit seemed to imply that if one could not erect a building over an ancestral building one could erect one over an ancestor. The way that the plastered skull occurred in a single pit/grave, and the way that it was held by a single individual, contrast strongly with similar rites in the Levant and southeast Turkey. As already noted, groups and caches of skulls are often found in those areas.[31] At Çatalhöyük the plastered skull is individualized. We cannot be sure that the features resembled a specific historical person, although the shape of the nose seems highly distinctive.

During excavation we lifted the plastered skull from its pit on the site and took it to the conservation laboratory so that the final stages of removing the soil could take place in a controlled environment. As the conservators cleared down under the lower side of the skull they found that the plaster over the right eye had been slightly displaced. But this patch of plaster told an interesting story. At least three layers of plaster and red paint could be seen. This provided evidence of the point I made above, that the skulls probably circulated for some time before being deposited. We do not know, of course, the interval between each plastering, but at least we can say that the plastered skull was kept and cared for long enough for three plasterings and paintings to occur.

Another category of material which suggests an emphasis on head circulation is figurines. These are often found with the heads missing, including the famous seated woman with felines (Plate 24). This pattern could easily be the result of normal breakage processes, since the neck is often the weakest part of a figurine. But in an example from Building 3, there is evidence of detachable heads, as have been found at Höyüçek, a site to the west of Çatalhöyük dated to the late 7th millennium BC.[32] In some cases at Çatalhöyük there is evidence of special deposition of broken figurine heads. In the southeast corner of the main room in Building 17, a hearth was found which had been rebuilt several times. In the sealing deposit of one of the hearths a broken figurine was placed (Figure 62) with both head and torso present, but separate. Two sub-phases of hearth reconstruction later, a broken figurine head

62 This broken figurine was found in the sealing deposit of a hearth in Building 17. The body and head were discovered separately.

(Figure 63) was again deposited – directly over the earlier example. This head was very similar in appearance and size to the earlier one, and both were quite different from other figurines found at the site. This evidence of activities that deliberately closed or ended the use of the hearths strongly suggests specific house-based memories based on the use of figurine heads.

So what I mean by the invention of 'history' is that people began to link themselves to specific pasts, especially the pasts of houses and genealogies. People did things in houses that referred to very specific and particular past events in the same house. But it was not enough simply to say 'I am a member of this or that group or house and we have our specific memories'. It was also important to provide objective evidence of affiliation and memory. Rather than just saying they belonged to a group, people dug down and brought up physical indices of their claim of belonging. The need to retrieve or reference past heads may have been the result of a wide range of factors that are difficult to disentangle. For example, the need to obtain or retain the physical objects may have concerned contested inheritance, or there may have been an idea that the physical object itself could protect, do harm, be of value in exchanges and so on. Whatever the reason behind the physical referencing of the past, some specific link seems implied by the evidence. This seems less a case of generic ancestors and more a case of building specific historical links backwards.

63 This broken figurine head was found in a slightly later deposit directly over the example shown in Figure 62.

The handing on of other types of artifact can also involve people in historical connections and entanglements.[33] Ground stone artifacts show much evidence of reuse and reworking, as a result of the lack of locally available raw materials. A long use-life for ground stone artifacts is found in many village societies today as discussed by Adnan Baysal and Karen Wright.[34] But, as well as the practical issues involved, social factors such as inheritance can play a role in the history of such artifacts. For example, in a number of village societies today, daughters inherit milling tools from their mothers. Matrilineal inheritance of stone milling tools can be documented in Akkadian documents from 2nd millennium BC Mesopotamia.[35] In 3rd millennium BC Mesopotamia, legal texts used the expression 'to transfer the pestle' (in this case made of wood) to indicate the transfer of property (land, gardens, slaves) from person to person. Whilst these examples are not directly relevant to Çatalhöyük, the ethnographic literature does suggest that we should be aware of the cultural as well as practical elements of artifact life-histories.

Many seals (objects used to stamp designs on cloth or skin) display signs of long and probably heavy use, and the same can be said for some of the figurines.[36] It is

VIA.10

VIB.10

VII.10

6.3

6.2

17B

17D

17E

Space 173
Space 163
hearth

Space 173
Space 163
hearth
hearth

ovens
Space 182
Space 170
oven
hearth

Space 182
Space 170
ovens
hearth

Space 182
Space 170
oven
oven
hearth

hearth
oven

64 Sequence of buildings in '10' – this house was excavated by James Mellaart in Levels VIA, VIB and VII as 'Shrine 10', and by the current project which called the house Building 24 in Level VII, Building 6 in Level VIII and Building 17 in Level IX. (For the stratigraphic sequence see Figure 48.)

possible that they were kept for longer than an individual human life span, although at present the specific length of time of use is difficult to determine. Bone tools also sometimes show traces of heavy wear, and there are examples of repair of bone ornaments.[37] It is possible that these items were handed down across generations, as part of the transfer of property that often constitutes an important component of house-based societies.[38]

DOMINANT HOUSES IN THE POLITICS OF HISTORY

Two specific examples of the replacements of buildings through time are provided in Figures 44 and 64. These sequences, which I have discussed in detail elsewhere,[39] show many repetitions through time, but also specific backward references and memories. While there are habituated practices in these cases, of the sort discussed in Chapter 5, there are also cases of repetition that are not site-wide patterns but are specific to these particular house sequences. In fact, most houses seem to show some evidence of both habituated practices on the house level, as well as backward references and memories. But are there also dominant houses at Çatalhöyük that at least in part base their position on the construction and control of histories (specific genealogies of people and houses)?

Some houses do seem more elaborate than others. These more elaborate houses were termed 'Shrines' by James Mellaart. More recently Tim Ritchey and Bleda Düring[40] have quantified the degree of elaboration of buildings in each level based on numbers of internal spaces, mouldings, basins, pillars, posts, benches and platforms (see Figure 65). Gradual clines of variation from less to more elaborate buildings can be seen at all levels, and the more elaborate buildings are interspersed spatially amongst the less elaborate. Despite the fact that all buildings are houses with a full range of domestic activity, storage and domestic production, there is a tendency for fine bifacially flaked obsidian points to be concentrated in the more

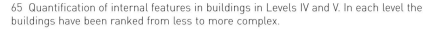
65 Quantification of internal features in buildings in Levels IV and V. In each level the buildings have been ranked from less to more complex.

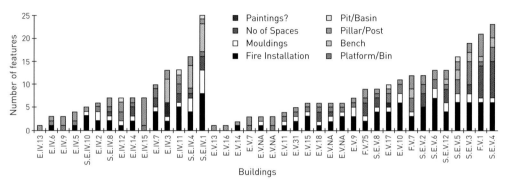

elaborate buildings.[41] The fact that obsidian cores too concentrate in the more elaborate buildings suggests some preferential access to or involvement with obsidian. Given the limited numbers of houses available for analysis, one could only tentatively say that the largest numbers of figurines come from very elaborate buildings. The degree of dominance is slight, and could even be reversed if one considered alternate criteria. Building 2 for instance had several caches of chipped stone deposited in its foundations, totalling over 50 pieces, although in architectural terms it is not elaborate.

But the notion that the more elaborate buildings were in some sense 'dominant' is best supported by the evidence of burial. In the case of Building 1, 62 individuals were interred in the structure during its construction and occupation. Of these at least 30 individuals must have been alive at the same point in time.[42] This is too many to have actually lived in the building on a day-to-day basis, as it is unlikely that more than 10 individuals did so, based on the size of the building and probable sleeping arrangements. This suggests that Building 1 acted as a focus for burial for a number of buildings. Building 1 could also be defined as elaborate in terms of its bucrania, paintings, posts, numbers of platforms, and mouldings.

Some elaborate buildings excavated by Mellaart in the 1960s also contained large numbers of burials, although the records are imprecise.[43] The two buildings he found with most burials are 'Shrine' 10 in Level VIB which had 32 skeletons, and 'Shrine' 31 in Level VII which had 58 skeletons. 'Shrine' 10 occurs second in terms of Tim Ritchey's ranking of 59 buildings in Level VIB,[44] and 'Shrine' 31 is also the second most elaborate building in his ranking of the 45 buildings in Level VII. At the other end of the scale, there are architecturally non-elaborate buildings such as Building 2 which have no burials. There are undoubtedly cases of elaborate buildings with few burials, but overall it seems probable that certain buildings became preferential sites for burial and these buildings were usually architecturally more elaborate. In this way they had a 'dominance' in relation to access to previous lineage members.

The dominant houses may have placed more emphasis on the repetition of bodily practices of the type noted in Chapter 5. The evidence for this is that the more elaborate buildings such as Building 17 (this is a renumbering of Mellaart's 'Shrine' 10 in Level IX) placed more emphasis on the maintenance of the internal floor scheme identified in Chapter 5. The distinctiveness of platforms and the degree of separation between floors with cleaner plasters and those with high densities of charcoal and hearth sweepings seem stronger in more elaborate buildings with burials, such as Buildings 1, 3 and 17, than in smaller buildings without burials such as Building 2 (and perhaps 18, 23 and 5). In Building 2, the ridges between the area near the oven and the more northerly whiter floors are ill-defined and there is overspill of charcoal-rich deposits across the ridges. This type of 'scuffing' is less common in the more elaborate houses.

9, 10 Two stylistically different leopard reliefs from Çatalhöyük. Both these pairs had been replastered and repainted on multiple occasions.

11 Burial from Building 6 of a child wearing bracelets and anklets.

12 (below) Skeletons from the northwest platform in Building 1. Most graves at Çatalhöyük contain multiple burials.

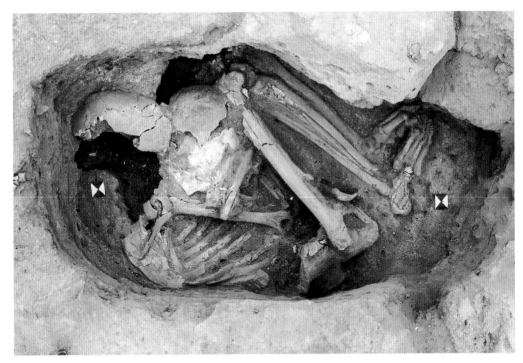

13 This grave in Building 42 contained a skeleton holding a plastered skull. The skull showed signs of a long life – it had been coated in several layers of plaster, each of which had been painted red.

14 The Building 42 grave reconstructed (the plastered skull itself is reconstructed in Figure 7).

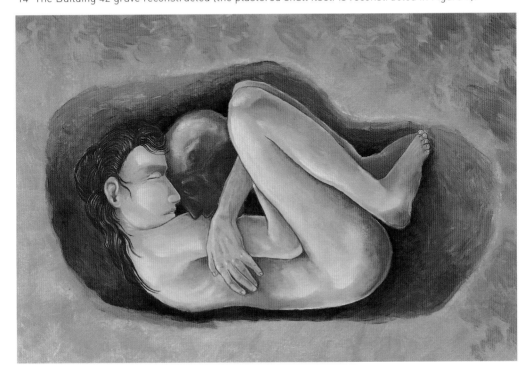

15 This large wall-painting from a building in Level V shows a group of figures, many of whom are wearing leopard skins, baiting or teasing a bull.

16 A detail from the painting above showing a possible equid and a headless human figure, one of the few human representations in the wall-painting that could be female.

17 The sequence of plastered bull heads or bucrania on the west wall of Mellaart's VI.10. The horncores would have originally appeared much larger when covered with horn (see also Figure 66).

18 Relief of a splayed figure from Mellaart's 'Shrine VII.23' (approximately 1 m (3.3 ft) high). Such reliefs were originally interpreted by some as representations of the Goddess.

19 (above) Three quadruped figurines from the current excavations. It is often difficult to discern the animals depicted, but many may be cattle.

21 (below right) Figurine from Building 42. This is an example of a type of figurine found in the upper levels. Made of limestone it is badly eroded and the face may have been scoured.

20 (above) Human form found in Level VI, shown wearing leopard skin and perhaps also standing alongside a leopard. It is made from blue limestone.

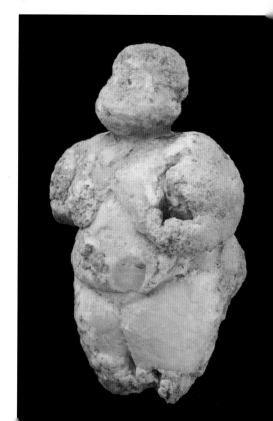

22 Clay figurine found in 2005 by a team from Istanbul University working to the south of the South shelter, in the upper layers of the site. There is a hole for the head and the back part of the figurine shows scapulae, ribs, vertebrae and pelvic bones.

23 This stamp found in the fill of a Level V building beneath the main South shelter on the East Mound sheds new light on past interpretations of the splayed-figure reliefs at Çatalhöyük (see Plate 18)

24 A clay figurine found by James Mellaart in a grain bin in a building called 'Shrine AII.1'. The head of the woman and the head of the animal by her left arm are not original.

What was the role of the dominant, more elaborate houses in the politics of commemorative memory? There is some evidence that these dominant houses were particular guardians of the archive of memories, alongside their particular investment in the regulation of daily practices. We have already seen that they have concentrations of burials, suggesting that the archive of lineal and/or affinal relations was constructed preferentially in the dominant house. There is also a clear link between houses with large numbers of burials and houses which are replaced through many levels. The current project has so far only excavated one building (Building 5 – the floors of which are yet to be excavated) below Building 1 which itself has 62 burials, but deeper sequences were excavated by Mellaart. From his data, the two buildings with most burials ('Shrines' 10 and 31, see above) in Levels VI and VII were both rebuilt through five levels (IX to VIA). Other buildings with many burials ('Shrines' 1, 7 and 8 in Level VI) also continued across three to five levels. Adjacent less elaborate buildings with few or no burials (such as Building 2 by 'Shrine' 10) are not replaced from level to level.

The floors of 'Shrine' 10 (Buildings 6 and 17) in Levels VIII and IX are lower than surrounding buildings, suggesting that this more elaborate building may have been modified and rebuilt at a slower rate than surrounding buildings (Figure 48). The way in which the bucrania on the west wall of 'Shrine' 10 in Level VI are stacked, with the lowest covered in floor plasters (Figure 66 and Plate 17), again could suggest a long use. Thus domestic houses used for large numbers of burials, and those houses which are more elaborate, may have been more closely tied to continuity and the preservation of a collective memory.

To understand one possible way that dominant houses may have used ancestral histories we can return to our example of the Tikopia as described by Raymond Firth.[45] 'Every individual family of father, mother and children is part of a larger group known as the "paito" and composed of similar families, tracing their

66 Bucranium series on the west wall of 'Shrine' VI.10 (see also Plate 17). The lowest example is half-covered with floor plaster, which suggests that these bucrania were in use for a long period.

relationship ultimately to a common male ancestor through male forbears in each case.' The cohesion of the 'house' depends on ties of descent from common ancestors. At different scales of ceremony, different numbers of people attend from the larger 'house'. The 'paito' is not a residential unit as its members may be scattered through several villages, but the existence of the group refers back to a common ancestral residential building. 'The house-name of the common ancestor frequently forms the name for his group of descendants, and his original dwelling commonly serves as a temple for ritual services to ancestors and gods. Other principal buildings of the group bear hereditary names carried also by men of the group…. In ordinary economic affairs the house does not bother to come together as a whole; the branches of it act as separate units.'

The evidence suggests that the politics of history at Çatalhöyük were primarily house based, and perhaps that dominant houses invested particularly in the construction and control of both repetitive practices and history. There were probably larger scales of construction of history, corresponding to the zones and sectors of the 'town' identified in Chapter 4. It is possible that some of the paintings, reliefs and installations in some houses played a role at this scale, but for the moment we have little archaeological evidence. At the broadly contemporary site of Musular there is evidence of large-scale feasting in open areas.[46] This site is very close to the main mound at Aşıklı Höyük and it was used towards the end of the occupation of that mound. It is possible that the large murals at Çatalhöyük record similar events

67 Mellaart's 'Shrine' 14 has a painting sometimes interpreted as showing a volcano exploding over a town like Çatalhöyük. We can tentatively identify this volcano as Hasan Dağ, a volcano that was active in the Neolithic and today can sometimes be seen from the site.

as they show large numbers of people in open areas. It may also be appropriate to mention the painting supposedly showing an exploding double-peaked volcano, which James Mellaart identified as Hasan Dağ, above what could be interpreted as rows of houses (Figure 67). Since Hasan Dağ was indeed active at the time of Çatalhöyük's occupation and is sometimes visible to the northeast of Çatalhöyük, it would be possible to suggest that the painting depicts a real historical event. There remain many uncertainties about the interpretation of both the volcano and the houses – an alternative interpretation is that this is a geometric pattern associated with a leopard skin. If the painting does have some historical component, it is of interest that it appears to be a one-off, and so may have catered to a larger group than that based round one house.

CHANGE THROUGH TIME

So far I have rather assumed that the emphasis on creating historical links in genealogies and houses was a constant feature of all the levels of occupation at Çatalhöyük. I will be discussing change through time in more general terms in Chapter II. But for the moment it may be helpful to point out that this emphasis on history, if indeed it can be described as such, emerges and changes through time.

As we have already seen, imagery, narrative, myth and habituated practices extend well back in time from Çatalhöyük. There are general similarities in forms of house construction, use of hard lime floors in the earliest levels, and in pottery forms and obsidian types that show influences from both the Middle East and from regional traditions in central Anatolia.[47] It is also possible now to say that many of the most important symbols at Çatalhöyük have a widespread and long-term ancestry. The continuities can be shown to be more specific than the general emphasis on the bull and the woman identified by Jacques Cauvin.[48] Thus, similar vulture images are found at Jerf el Ahmar in Syria[49] and parallels can be drawn with the concentration of raptor wings at Zawi Chemi Shanidar in the Zagros Mountains.[50] The supposed 'Mother Goddess' reliefs at Çatalhöyük (see Plate 18 and Figures 87 and 110) with upraised arms and legs are now most closely prefigured in a particular relief stone carving from Göbekli Tepe (Figure 88).[51] Indeed, there is a whole array of real and mythical 'dangerous animals' from Nevali Çori, Göbekli Tepe and Çayönü that parallel those from Çatalhöyük.[52] The plastered skull from Çatalhöyük recalls those from the Levant even if the specific way of using it differs (see above).

Whether these similarities can be put down to an expansion of people spreading out from Syria and the Levant and moving westwards into central Anatolia as claimed by Jacques Cauvin is not of immediate concern here.[53] Rather, it is important to note the enormous expanses of time (at least three millennia) over which such symbols seem to stay stable. Of course, archaeologists have long been aware of the slow rate of change of material culture in the Upper Palaeolithic of Europe, where types of stone tool, and even types of cave painting, stay relatively unchanged over many millennia. While the rate of change may speed up a little in the Neolithic of the Middle East and Anatolia, it remains very slow. In central Anatolia Aşıklı Höyük was occupied over long periods of time and there is remarkable continuity in its organization. The dated deep sounding sequence, which is over 6 m (20 ft) deep, covers between 200 and 600 years.[54] Through this time period there were six rebuildings of a house in exactly the same location and with the same location of hearths and middens.[55]

In my view, these remarkable degrees of continuity stem largely from two types of factor. First, there is the routinization or habituation of practices seen in small-scale societies where the transmission of cultural behaviour is embedded in small-scale, face-to-face, social interactions and dominance. Second, there is the role of myth. At the start of this chapter I argued that, despite many difficulties, a general and approximate distinction can be made between myth and history. There is a continuum from one to the other, but myth can be defined as more timeless (except for a distinction between 'then' and 'now'). There are of course 'origin myths' but these may not create a specific link into history and the present. History involves a more complex interconnection of events leading into the present. Myth is used politically in the present, but its 'otherness', the lack of historical connection between past and present, buffers it from change. Once myth becomes historical (or history emerges within myth), there is more potential for the manipulation of the past.

It seems possible to argue that the vulture, bull, upraised arm splayed figure and so on were all involved in various versions of generalized myths that circulated very widely in Anatolia and the Middle East prior to Çatalhöyük and later into historic times. At Çatalhöyük these same ideas and forms were taken up and retold and reset. They became appropriated into houses, whereas in sites like Nevali Çori, Göbekli Tepe and Çayönü they had been associated with special ritual buildings. What distinguishes Çatalhöyük in contrast to these sites and to Aşıklı Höyük is the concentration of symbolism in the house. Here the myths and symbolism were related to ancestors of that particular house, and thus to the histories of particular families and clans. At Çatalhöyük generalized myth was appropriated by the house and began to be transformed into history. As this happened, the rate of change of symbols and meanings began to increase as social groups competed with each other in their interpretation of history. It is, of course, true that burials occur in houses at Aşıklı Höyük, but probably not to the degree found at Çatalhöyük,[56] and in any case there is little evidence of symbolism in the Aşıklı Höyük houses. It was only at Çatalhöyük that symbolism and myth were so closely associated with the house and its ancestors.

CONCLUSION

One way of conceptualizing the importance of history in the house in the early and main levels at Çatalhöyük is in terms of 'house societies'. In anthropologist Claude Lévi-Strauss's definition of 'house societies' we see a move away from kinship classificatory models towards the 'house' as a corporate body holding an estate which reproduces itself through the transmission of its name, goods and rights.[57] Particularly in more recent research,[58] the materiality of the house, its practices and heirlooms are brought to the fore. The transmission of houses and of objects kept in houses forges social memory and constitutes social units.[59] In Polynesia, for example, an important component of the reproduction of the corporate group is the burial of ancestors and the transformation of houses into ritual temples.[60] Certainly at Çatalhöyük the embedding of ritual and daily practice in the construction, use, abandonment and reuse of houses shows the importance of the house in constructing continuities. Social units may have been established through their participation in the reproduction of the house. Objects are retrieved, and at least skulls are handed down. People become socialized into the 'house' unit by learning the ways to behave within its material walls. In these ways we could argue that it is the life of the house which constructs social lives as much as the other way round.

The politics of history[61] at Çatalhöyük are primarily house-based, although there are also supra-house, larger-scale constructions of history. At the house level, there are numerous events, from the most practical (like setting later walls on more secure earlier walls) to the most ritual (such as foundation and burial ceremonies) that lead to the construction of histories. People at Çatalhöyük used widespread myths, but they also appropriated these myths into individual house-based groups. A historical memory became more important in the sense that specific sets of links were made in the house from present occupants to past ancestors and to past houses and their contents. The length of these memories archived and institutionalized within the house is difficult to judge, but there is much evidence that people at Çatalhöyük remembered what had happened in houses in phases earlier than the immediately preceding one.

One function of the construction of histories may have been to create genealogical links to ancestors buried beneath floors. In this way a hierarchy of kin relations could be constructed. The histories could have been used to refer to debts and alliances, to refer to the ritual power of earlier elders, to awaken memories of great feasts or hunts. Whatever the specific function of the construction of a continuous historical memory, it could have had the effect of holding the house-based group together in the delay between investment of labour and its returns.[62] It also allowed dispersed resources to be managed and monitored as discussed in Chapter 3. But it also allowed social differentiation. More elaborate buildings invested more in the maintenance of

68 Conservation of a wall-painting from Building 2. This painting was found in a niche in the north wall of the main room.

memory in that they show more evidence of continuity and burial. This suggests that differences in power were closely related to the ability to construct histories.

But can we see contested histories, or is history at Çatalhöyük placed in the archive of material remains so effectively that any alternative to the dominant construction is made invisible? In terms of habituated practices we see some kicking and scuffing in some buildings, as the taken-for-granted ways of cleaning and doing things in the houses are transgressed – in however minor a way. In terms of history construction, perhaps the less accomplished wall-painting designs found in the smaller Building 2 adjacent to 'Shrine' 10 express a different voice (Figures 68 and 69). In our excavations of Building 44 there are traces in a bench of inserts, perhaps of bulls' horns. But the inserts had at one point been removed and the holes filled in and the bench replastered. So there is change and perhaps contention and forgetting.

69 Another wall-painting from Building 2, conserved and now on display in Konya Museum. The more accomplished wall-painting, recorded, recovered and conserved by Mellaart's team in the 1960s, is now on display in Ankara at the Museum of Anatolian Civilizations.

Perhaps the best examples of a challenge to the house-based control of history are seen in the upper levels of the site when forms of imagery appear in non-house contexts. By this I mean that symbols that had earlier only been used within the house come to be used in media that can be exchanged between houses. First, stamp seals take the wall designs into a new mobile context, and then, right at the end of the occupation of the East Mound and in the following Chalcolithic West Mound, the designs that had graced walls within houses are found on pottery. In fact these later walls seem not to be painted except perhaps in one-colour washes.[63] The pottery, however, becomes elaborately decorated. These changes suggest a gradual wresting of history away from the house. The symbols that refer to myth and history now come to be used to create alliances and exchange relationships between houses. These changes in the upper levels of the East Mound will be returned to in the following chapters, and particularly in Chapter II.

CHAPTER SEVEN

Revelation, Exchange and Production

The leopard is a secretive animal. It hunts by ambushing, from behind thickets or trees. It mainly hunts at night. Once it has caught its prey it drags it to a secure place such as up a tree, where it is less likely to be disturbed, while it devours the meat.

At Çatalhöyük the leopard reliefs on the walls of houses were continually being covered and revealed. They were multiply plastered. Of the pair of leopards in VIB.44 (Plate 9) James Mellaart[1] says 'in the latest phases these were whitewashed and bore no designs'. In earlier phases these reliefs had been repainted many times – about 40 times in all. The VII.44 (Plate 10) leopards had been repainted at least 7 times.[2] Given that walls in main rooms are usually replastered many more than 7 times, it is likely that for long periods the leopards remained unpainted, covered in white plaster. Similar sequences of use have been found for most wall paintings at Çatalhöyük. Most walls were covered in white plaster and soot most of the time – only rarely were they painted in geometric or figurative designs.

In a way, the whole of Çatalhöyük seems to be about hiding and revealing. As one approached the 'town' one would have seen a great mass of houses and roofs, animals and people. There may have been some bucrania on roofs (one was found possibly collapsed from a roof in Building 3[3]). But there would have been little indication of all the elaborate complexity inside the houses. As one descended the stairs into the smoky space of the main rooms in the houses, one would begin to see horns sticking out from walls, paintings emerging, platforms, benches, bins, ovens – all in familiar places, but in each house there are differences. There is always some surprise in the way that things are arranged or depicted.

Staying in the 'town' one might gradually learn the secrets hidden behind the walls; that a vulture skull was behind that protrusion on the wall, that a fox and a weasel skull were behind that lump of plaster, that there used to be a painting on that wall. And those that lived for long in a house would know in greater detail where individuals were buried, which head came from where, and exactly where the obsidian was hidden beneath the floor near the oven. The more that one was in the 'in group' the more one would know about what was hidden.

Indeed much of the status and prestige of individuals and families may have been linked to their ability to reveal what was hidden behind walls, or buried beneath floors, or visible in dark interiors.[4] Whether people such as 'shamans' were involved or not,[5] there would have been those that could intercede with the spirit world, the animal world, the world of the dead, and the ancestors. There would have been those that directed the performances of painting and uncovering, of digging up skulls and reusing them. Given the small size of the rooms, there would have been restricted access to view and participate as new sculptures were set in place and new paintings and burials made.

We saw in the last chapter that there is a great emphasis in Çatalhöyük on providing objective or material evidence of historical ties within house-based groups. Skulls and sculptures are dug up and recirculated. Skulls are kept over time. It is this material circulation that creates the fabric of the house-centred group. But there is always a revelatory component in the process. Things are hidden and then revealed. And often they are hidden in places where the ancestors or animal spirits are – beneath floors and behind walls. So when things return, revealed, they bring with them an aura from that other world. They have been magnified in their hidden journey.

This whole emphasis on the power of revelation occurs largely at the domestic scale – in each house. Learning the mysteries of the house, its histories and stories, would have been part of growing up. It would have formed the basis of house membership. One learnt from elders and ancestors, and so the established structures of a house-based society were engrained. But the notion of revelation was also intimately bound to larger scales of social relationship, as people brought others into the revelatory experiences of the house, as they built alliances and exchanged goods that had been hidden and revealed. Indeed, the whole process of hiding and revealing seems central to both social differentiation at Çatalhöyük and to exchange and alliance building.

The Tikopia again provide an example – this time of how secreted objects can come to influence the politics of kinship and exchange. The Tikopia traditionally used adzes made of clam shell and stone.[6] Some of these objects, and especially the larger shell adzes, were known as sacred. As Raymond Firth describes, 'these major adzes were treated as having great sanctity. They were kept each in the prime temple of the clan, hung up on a shelf at the side. As I myself saw, they were given the greatest respect and their very presence helped to contribute a great deal to the awe in which that section of the temple was held…. When the leading adze of Taumako was taken down for any special reason from its shelf, the whole clan brought food and valued property to the chief lest they die.' In general terms, the value or aura of objects can be created in a number of ways. Objects are often seen as of high value if they have travelled a great distance, been difficult to obtain, required a lot of labour to produce. They may have value and aura if they have a long and significant history. But another strategy that creates awe is to use the tension between availability and its lack, between revealing and hiding. Especially if the object has been kept in a secret or sacred place it has aura when it returns and is revealed. The strategy works by delaying access and so heightening desire, interest, expectation.

But what exactly was hidden and revealed at Çatalhöyük? We have seen that a major focus was ritual symbols, cattle skulls, human skulls. Obsidian too was treated in a like way. This was stored beneath the house floors and the cache was opened up from time to time (see below). But what of the daily acts of food storage? In Building 3[7] in some phases, bins, ovens and work areas were separated from the main room by a screen wall on which were installations of some form. In Building 2, the north wall had a deep niche, which could have been used for keeping or storing things, just below an upper painted niche. In Mellaart's 'Shrine' VIB.10 there were deep niches on either side of three bulls' heads on the west wall (Figure 66). In Building 1, a bin for storing lentils probably had a series of wild goat horns above, perhaps protecting it. Stored goods may thus at times have been seen as protected or concealed by non-human forces, from which they were then revealed. But most of the evidence for food storage is rather different. Mellaart[8] found a number of unelaborated screen walls separating off storage areas. In fact there seems to be a negative association between symbolic elaboration and storage or side rooms. Of the 28 most elaborate buildings excavated by Mellaart, there are 22 walls with doorways into side rooms. Of these, 15 walls are either plain or with only a single colour wash. Given that most walls (except the south walls) in this group of elaborate buildings are decorated, there is clear evidence of exclusion of symbolic elaboration from any association with side rooms and their storage. By way of contrast, we can return to my ethnographic work amongst the Nuba in Sudan described in Chapter 1. The Nuba grain bins and storage areas were often decorated, so it has always struck me as significant that storage bins are usually plain at Çatalhöyük. I will return to this evidence below and in Chapter 11. But for the moment we can say that the control of symbolic knowledge about hiding and revealing things only marginally involves stored food. It focuses on ritual and ancestral symbols and obsidian.

Storage, mainly of plants, occurs very early in the Middle East in the 11th and 10th millennia BC.[9] There are claims for very early communal storage, for example at the major Pre-Pottery Neolithic village at Jericho in the Levant,[10] but in many cases early storage occurs in or in relation to houses, and this is certainly true of Çatalhöyük. So for societies structured around communal sharing and reciprocity, or for societies engaged primarily in immediate exchanges, what can justify 'private' (house-based) storage? What happens when people start to keep and not give?

One response was to situate the keeping within a system of belief. The stories and myths may sanction keeping. But the accumulation may also have been understood as part of the process of giving. It is of interest in this regard that ritual feasting occurs at village sites in Syria such as Jerf el Ahmar and Mureybet in open areas in the PPNA.[11] And there are examples from the PPNB as at 'Ain Ghazal of pits in which statues were placed. These elaborate statues may have been very much part of a hiding and revealing nexus. In these ways people gave (in feasting and revealing) at the same time as they accumulated, both at the collective and individual house levels. Perhaps the revelatory experience was a necessary part of accumulation.

Also, and perhaps more importantly, the hiding and revealing could have sustained exchange relationships over longer periods. Archaeologists frequently talk as if exchanges of objects have to be repeated in order to cement alliances. But ethnographic accounts[12] of 'keeping while giving' describe ways in which the past associations of objects allow continued claims on those objects that have been 'given' away. I will describe similar processes at Çatalhöyük, and it may well be the case that the revelatory process created an aura and a history for objects that would be 'remembered'. But there is also a rather different process at work here. At Çatalhöyük a feast may be given and meat distributed, but the animal head may be kept and placed in the house. It may be dug up and revealed at later times so that the relationships established in the feast and meat giving can be reasserted. Similarly, there may be a set of kin and exchange relations centred around an elder, but after a person dies and is buried the skull may be dug up and revealed in order to recreate the kin and exchange relations.

EXCHANGE AND ACCUMULATION

The faunal data provide evidence of feasting in the form of concentrations of large, relatively unprocessed bones from large animals, especially wild bulls. This feasting may have been carried out at various scales, but at least in some cases sufficient quantities of meat seem to have been consumed for several houses to be involved, and in some cases numerous houses were involved. Presumably prestige would have been gained from such feasting events.[13] Indeed, the killing and processing of a wild bull is itself a feat of considerable proportions that is revealed in the feasting event.

The materials used in feasting could have been used to extend the feast's social efficacy through time. Some of the feasting seems associated with the foundation and abandonment of houses, in which case the houses themselves commemorate the feasting largesse. It may also be the case that the wild bulls that were particularly associated with feasting[14] were commemorated in quadruped figurines

70 In 2005 the first bucrania to be discovered by the current project were found in Building 52 in the 4040 Area. One is set into the west wall, while to the left can be seen the remains of a bench with cattle horns set into its side.

(although identification of species is usually difficult – see Plate 19) or in the bucrania placed in houses (Figure 70). But there were also artifacts used in feasting that could have extended the social effects of the events in material form. For example, Ana Spasojevic[15] notes that the obsidian associated with one possible feasting deposit has a large ratio of used and retouched pieces, while a number of the bones show cut marks. Some of the obsidian used in such events may have been retained and caused the events to be 'stretched out' over time.

The clearest example of accumulation at Çatalhöyük is the hoarding of obsidian below floors (Figure 71). In every house there is at least one shallow scoop, somewhere near the oven/hearth and stair entry. In these scoops are found up to 77 pieces of obsidian. As shown by James Conolly and Tristan Carter,[16] these obsidian pieces are blanks or pre-forms for making a variety of tools. Associated with these caches there is evidence of *in situ* obsidian working, and in one case at least, the flakes can be refitted onto a pre-form that is like those found in the caches. Some scoops are empty or have only a few pieces in. It seems clear that obsidian came as pre-forms from the sources in Cappadocia 170 km (105 miles) away, and was taken into the house where it was buried. People then dug down and excavated pieces when they needed them and worked them nearby inside the house.

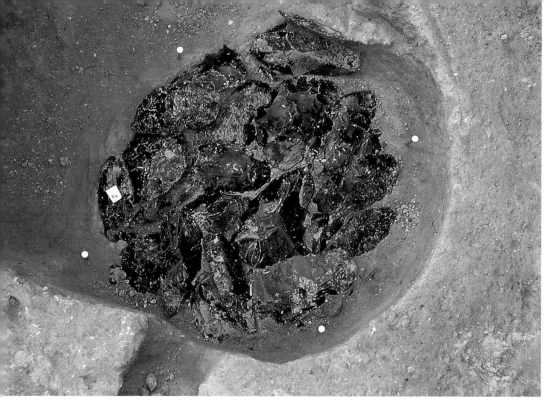

71 Obsidian cache found in a building in the South Area of the site.

This all seems straightforward – except the burying. Why bother to bury the pre-forms? Why not just keep them in a bag or a niche or in the rafters or in a basket or a wooden box? We know all these containers existed. So why bury the obsidian, when it would then have to be dug up when needed? Perhaps these valued objects needed to be hidden to prevent theft, but there are other ways of hiding.[17] Part of the answer has to do with the social importance of the house as discussed at the end of Chapter 5. But another part of the answer may be suggested by the hoard in Building 1.[18] In this scoop there were 12 blades (probably blanks for projectile points), six positives and six negatives from opposed platform cores (Figure 72). But

72 Twelve blades, six positives and six negatives, from the obsidian cache beneath the floor in Building 1.

the pieces do not fit together. They are very regular and must have been chosen from a variety of different cores. In this case too, a basin was soon built over the cache, suggesting it was not intended to be retrieved. Together with the symmetry of the blades, this suggests that this deposition was a ritualized event (see reconstruction in Figure 74). The same may be true of other obsidian caches. The same parts of the floors, near the ovens and the house entrance, were also where neonates and very young people were buried (and as we have seen other people are buried away from the ovens, usually in the more northerly parts of houses). Is it possible that the caching of obsidian beneath the floors was connected in some way with the web of meanings associated with the people and things buried beneath floors?

If such indeed was the case, the obsidian when it returned from its cache would have had added aura. The removal and distancing of things often creates aura,[19] and the crossing of people and things into liminal or ritualized space can allow a renewal or rebirth.[20] So when the obsidian returned it may have had special meanings, which may have added to the authority of those that hid and revealed it. Those that knew where the cache was, and were empowered to open it up again, had a special position as a result of this knowledge and power. The gifts of projectile points or other tools made from the cached obsidian would have had special memories and associations and would thus have created longer-term relationships and indebtedness.

The same process is not found for other artifact types. There is shell and there are baskets from the Red Sea, and shells from the Mediterranean.[21] Some of the beads found at the site, especially in association with burials, are made of exotic stones (and shells) – such as apatite and carnelian. Most, however, are made from marble and other stones available within 40 km (25 miles) of the site.[22] It could be argued that the beads were 'stored' as necklaces, mainly on children and female adults found in graves – but there is no evidence that the beads in graves were ever retrieved. As a further example, the basalt and andesite materials that were used to make a majority of the ground stone tools come from volcanic outcrops 40 km (25 miles) or so away. But there is no evidence that these were hoarded. The special status of obsidian is also indicated by the flint. In comparison with the obsidian, it too came from long distances, but it is very rare in hoards.[23] A particular set of meanings was created for obsidian and one indication of this is suggested by the spatial association with neonate burials.[24]

73 It is not certain what stamp seals were actually used for, but designs could have been made on cloth or skin with them.

Long-term dependencies in exchange, the idea of keeping while giving, can be created by marking or stamping objects in distinctive ways. The stamp seals (Figures 73 and 75) found at Çatalhöyük may have had

74 The caching of obsidian blades seems at times to have been a highly ritualized event.

something to do with ownership.[25] They occur mainly in the upper levels of the site – from Levels VII to II, but with a concentration in Levels IV to II. There may, then, be more of a concern with ownership and property in upper levels of the site, although this argument is perhaps undermined by the two cases of inscribed designs on obsidian in the Pre-XII levels.[26] There is also depositional evidence that the stamp seals are closely associated with houses. They again emphasize the domestic scale of keeping and giving. But also they begin to do something else. They extend the designs seen in the art in the houses out onto other, more movable objects (such as cloth or skins) and perhaps bodies. Through time, things may become involved in a shift away from the centrality of the house to the importance of exchange between houses (Chapter 11). As one moves into the Late Neolithic and Chalcolithic at sites such as Çatalhöyük West and Hacılar, the designs that had been found on walls and in houses at Çatalhöyük East are now found on pottery.[27] With the seals, and the objects stamped, these things can be moved around and exchanged between houses. The designs used in the art shift from being inward and house-focused to being about outward interaction between houses.

75 Stamp seals (and the designs made with them) occur mainly in the upper levels of the site and may reflect an increasing concern with ideas of property and ownership.

STATUS DIFFERENTIATION

Evidence that exchange was used to set up specific sets of relationships over the social landscape is provided by the obsidian sourcing results.[28] Tristan Carter notes that the two Cappadocian sources, Göllü Dağ-East and Nenezi Dağ, used for the Çatalhöyük obsidian are the same distance away, and the obsidian has equivalent technical qualities. At Çatalhöyük a preference emerges through time for Nenezi Dağ obsidian. This must be partly cultural-social as there are no technical or distance advantages of the one type of obsidian over the other. It is perhaps linked to changes that we cannot observe in specific networks of people and exchange in their relations to workshops and quarries. Very specific exchange networks have been noted in relation to the use of the Cappadocian quarries by the inhabitants of Aşıklı Höyük.[29] Overall it seems likely that obsidian and perhaps other forms of exchanged object carried a history that influenced their further use and exchange. As yet, however, we have not been able to demonstrate that different sources were used by different status groups at Çatalhöyük.

While a primarily domestic mode of production seems prevalent throughout the 10th to 7th millennia BC in Anatolia and the Middle East, there are some indications of status differentiation seen in burial and house construction. There is little agreed evidence of social stratification in Natufian burials,[30] but for the PPNA and PPNB there is perhaps wider acceptance of some degree of ranking in the Middle East, if often cross-cut by processes that lead to levelling of social distinctions.[31] Danny Naveh[32] has recently argued for major social differentiation at PPNA Jericho on the basis of the tower and burial variation, but in my view the evidence is not convincing. In Anatolia, as early as the late 11th and early 10th millennia BC at Hallan Çemi, Michael Rosenberg claims that some buildings have public functions.[33] These buildings are partly identified because they are more elaborate and one has a complete auroch's skull hung on the wall. Public buildings already occur in the early Aceramic Neolithic at Göbekli Tepe, as part of a wider emergence of public structures at for example Jerf el Ahmar, Jericho, Çayönü and Nevali Çori.[34] There is often a lack of evidence regarding whether these public buildings were associated with elites – and on the whole, many of these early societies seem fairly egalitarian in most areas of behaviour. At Aşıklı Höyük, there are elaborate buildings that presumably had public functions and there is little evidence of social differentiation.[35] But by the mid to late 8th millennium BC at Çayönü in southeast Turkey, the Skull Building shows social differences in grave goods, and in each sector of buildings at this site there is one building with more burials than others.[36]

At Çatalhöyük the current project has shown that there is a less clear-cut distinction between 'shrines' and 'houses' than Mellaart suggested.[37] The argument is both theoretical and empirical. On the theoretical side, Nurcan Yalman has harnessed local ethnoarchaeological data to show how complex and dynamic can be the links between architectural layout and social structure.[38] On the empirical side, we have found no evidence of public buildings, despite intensive surface sampling. All buildings appear to have been lived in, and most if not all buildings have some use of painting, red ochre or other 'special' activities.

There are clearly disparities in the architectural elaboration of houses as defined by numbers of benches, platforms, sculptures and so on. These have been quantified by a number of authors as shown in Chapter 6. Despite the fact that all buildings are houses with a full range of domestic activity, storage and domestic production, there is some indication that fine bifacially flaked obsidian points are concentrated in the more elaborate buildings.[39] The fact that obsidian cores too concentrate in the more elaborate buildings suggests some preferential access to or involvement in obsidian. The largest numbers of figurines come from very elaborate buildings.[40] The notion that the more elaborate buildings were in some sense 'dominant' is best supported by the evidence of burial, including the burial and recovery of human heads, as was discussed in Chapter 6. But the degree of dominance is slight, and could even be reversed if one considered alternate criteria.

There seem to be cross-cutting dimensions of differentiation, and the same build-ings are not placed equally on each dimension. So again, a relative lack of status differentiation is suggested. Mehmet Özdoğan sees much more evidence for social differentiation in eastern as opposed to central Anatolia.[41]

A similar lack of social differentiation, but with some inkling of status differen-tiation, is seen in the burial data. As already noted, there is much variability in the way that bodies are laid out in graves, and this variation does not seem to link to any variation that could be ascribed to status (such as platform height or make-up). And burials do not show a large degree of related variation in terms of grave goods.[42] There are some subtle differences though. For example, a greater proportion of those buried under the central-east platform in Building 1 had burial goods. But dif-ferences are slight and it is often children that have the most artifacts.

The best suggestion of some degree of social dominance in terms of burial comes from the special treatment of bodies from which heads had been removed. As noted above, the Çatalhöyük evidence regarding head removal seems to deal more with individuals than collectives. The special nature of head removal is indicated by its rarity, and by the depictions of an associated myth in the art, and by the special treatment of bodies from which heads have been removed (Chapter 6). All this sug-gests that head removal was reserved for particular people who may have had some form of social dominance.

Despite such examples, the overall pattern at Çatalhöyük is that the degree of social differentiation is slight. This is true of both architectural and burial data. In addition there remains little evidence for public buildings and centralized ceremo-nial functions. Even if these are found in future work, it remains the case that we are dealing with a largely domestic mode of production. Undoubtedly, some special-ization of production does occur, but in most such cases, such as bead or bone tool production, or obsidian mirror manufacture, the specialization seems at best part-time, and fully embedded within a domestic mode. As noted by Mehmet Özdoğan, this relative lack of social differentiation sets the site and central Anatolia apart from the east.[43] There is a related larger pattern, that centralized ceremonial does not occur on many sites to the west. Perhaps the clearest example is early Neolithic Thessaly, where Catherine Perlès[44] argues that most ritual/symbolic acts seem to have taken place in and around houses rather than in specially dedicated ceremo-nial buildings. Only at Nea Nikomedia has a possible 'shrine' been identified. Thus Çatalhöyük may have a significance in setting a different tone to social structure. As the Neolithic spreads to the west, the status differentiation and public ceremonial that are so prevalent in eastern Anatolia and the Middle East become less apparent.

What differentiation there is at Çatalhöyük seems to concern the symbolic and ritual elaboration of the house. It is this variation that produces the cline in Figure 65, and it seems only loosely associated with other variables. One interpre-tation of the data is that the minimal degrees of differentiation at Çatalhöyük concern the control of knowledge about symbolism and beliefs, about the right ways of doing things, about how to perform rituals, and how to depict scenes, myths and histories. In the end, it may have been the revelation of such knowledge that lay at the basis of much social difference. The persuasive performance of revelatory experience, the provision of objective evidence for belief – these may have been the main struts of social difference, closely linked to such factors as the exchange of obsidian.

SPECIALIZATION OF PRODUCTION

The small-scale and often house-based scale of production is shown in a number of types of data. The lime burning found in the lowest levels at Çatalhöyük[45] seems to have been small scale, perhaps at the household level, despite the fact that large amounts of lime-rich material would have been needed to make one of the hard lime floors in the earliest levels. Adnan Baysal and Karen Wright conclude that the activities associated with ground stone – food processing or ochre grinding for example – were done at a small scale given the size of the artifacts.[46] The existence of ovens in all houses, and the faunal evidence for intensive bone processing in houses suggest a domestic scale of food preparation.

There is house-based brick production, and obsidian production (at least for some obsidian industries found at the site[47]). Nerissa Russell and Louise Martin have suggested that the existence of covered animal pens near houses suggests domestic ownership of livestock (sheep) rather than large-scale communal herding.[48] As already noted above and in Chapter 6, there is some evidence for a degree of specialization of production in the more elaborate buildings, particularly in the upper levels of the site, but the degree of variation is slight.

A telling matter is the organization of storage (see Chapter 2). All houses seem to have had their own storage capability, and the variation in storage capacity seems limited. Bins occur widely, in small numbers, and usually in side rooms. Crops are stored largely fully cleaned.[49] There is possible evidence from phytoliths that different bins were used to store different material (and this is also known from Mellaart's data). Perhaps we could see the northwest room[50] in Building 5 as for larger-scale storage. But in fact in this and adjacent rooms, activities seem small scale, with individual 'coasters' which may be basket bottoms.[51] Phytolith evidence suggests a general link between baskets and wheat, perhaps in terms of storage.[52] There are also small stores of bones.[53] It is difficult to interpret the data in terms of large-scale and/or centralized storage (at least not on the ground floors of buildings).

As regards the clay balls found at the site and used for cooking, petrographic analysis (identification of the stone 'filler' placed in the clay) conducted on a small number of balls, mini balls and shaped clay objects illustrates that there actually is not one recipe for making clay balls, but instead, ball fabric can vary considerably within buildings and from level to level. Sonya Atalay attributes this variability to the choices in mineral inclusions made by individual clay ball crafters during production, and to variability in clay sources and the use of different sources by different crafters. Given that different clay fabrics and tempers were used for different types of object (balls, figurines, pots, bricks, plasters) even within the same house, Atalay argues for a small-scale part-time craft specialization.[54]

A similar claim can be made for the beads (see Figure 76). These were made at the domestic scale, probably near the hearth or oven.[55] It is of interest that evidence of bead production in Building 18 occurs through several phases. Different houses

76 These beads were found in a burial in the 4040 Area. Bead production took place in the oven locale, and there is some evidence of small-scale craft specialization at Çatalhöyük.

focused on different types of object and this specialization was passed on through time. Thus while Building 18 had a focus on beads, Mellaart noted that his 'Shrine' VIA.10 had 14 stone figurines and VIA.44, the 'Leopard Shrine', had eight. Adnan Baysal and Karen Wright interpret the VIA.10 example as including unfinished objects, and thus *in situ* production.[56] Another example is 'Shrine' A.III.2, which 'produced a large number of stone tools as well as raw material and might have been a stoneworker's shop.'[57] Mellaart found nine figurines in AII.1. Five of these were very similar to each other and were found around the hearth. Naomi Hamilton suggests domestic or house-based traditions in figurine production because of their diversity and the sometimes clustering of groups and types in buildings.[58] The concentration of stone figurines in particular buildings could suggest some

77 Bone artifacts from Çatalhöyük. A range of types are found including rings (sometimes with protrusions as in the top left example) and points.

house-based part-time specialization of production, although in some cases we may be dealing with house-based differences in use or discard habits.

The presence of substantial amounts of preforms and waste from bone tool (Figure 77) manufacture in the South Area has been noted by Nerissa Russell.[59] The distribution of this manufacturing debris suggests household-level rather than specialized production. There are some indications, however, that there may have been limited, part-time specialization in bone tool production. People who were particularly skilled at such a craft may have supplied their neighbours. It might have been thought that the obsidian mirrors involved a high degree of specialized knowledge and skill, but experiments undertaken by Jim Vedder show that the total amount of time involved is limited (3–4 hours of fine polishing) and that the work could have been carried out part-time between other tasks.[60] All this supports the notion of predominantly house-based or small-scale production.

There may also have been some larger-scale centralization of production. Several of the examples mentioned above as having evidence of some degree of specialized production are more elaborate buildings (e.g. Mellaart's 'Shrine' 10), and we have seen that James Conolly and Naomi Hamilton have argued that more elaborate buildings were associated with obsidian cores and figurine production. Specialization of production may have increased through time. For example, large ovens in open areas that could have served several houses were found by James

Mellaart in Levels V and IV.[61] Thus some houses in the later levels of the site may have become dominant over others partly through an ability to provide more food, or through the production of valued objects. However, the evidence for this larger-scale of production remains restricted to certain artifact types and suggests differences in degree rather than qualitative differences between distinct social levels. It seems most likely that much of the variation in elaboration of buildings, and in the numbers of burials, relates to the ability of household members (perhaps especially elders) to mobilize ritual, symbolism, revelation and their performance, even though exchange and production played their part. It was largely through the control of knowledge that ancestral ties were constructed. And it was through the revelation of such ties and associated mysteries that some degree of status was maintained and some degree of keeping and accumulation (of obsidian and cattle for example) was justified.

CONCLUSION

So we have come across a perhaps rather surprising pattern. One might have thought that social power within and between houses was based on the control of agricultural and other subsistence products in these early farming societies. But in fact there is little evidence of much social focus on the storage of foods. And there is little evidence of significant variation in the productive capacities of different houses. Larger and smaller houses seem to have had similar amounts of storage capacity and seem to have been involved in similar productive activities, even though some differentiation exists. We have not found larger caches of obsidian in the more elaborate houses. Storage areas for food are not strongly differentiated, and they are neither symbolically elaborated nor surrounded in ritual. Of course, domesticated plants and animals were probably the basis on which settled life and a relative degree of economic self-sufficiency of houses depended, but this economic dependence was not matched by a social elaboration of these areas.

Instead, we have seen that the main symbolic and ritual elaboration surrounds the hiding and revealing of certain items. I have tried to capture a tension which I see as prevalent at Çatalhöyük between hiding and revealing. This productive tension underlay the main discourse of power at Çatalhöyük. It was the way that ancestry and identity were defined, life cycles lived and exchange conducted. It was this set of relationships, rather than those dealing with the storage and production of daily food, that were the mainstays of social life. But at the same time this same set of relationships may have justified the storage of food and the preliminary control of production (and exchange of obsidian) both within and between houses. By revealing and giving, it was possible to keep and to begin to accumulate in some areas of life.

Going into Çatalhöyük one would begin to have its mysteries revealed. This sense of aura, secret knowledge and revelatory experience must have been part of the attraction of the site to its visitors. Its inhabitants too would not have been able to see the details of the art and symbolism in each house unless they entered in. There was always thus a sense of exclusion and inclusion – just in the architecture of the settlement. Growing up in a house, one would have known how things were laid out, but even amongst those living in the house there may have been those that knew more than others what was cached or buried where, and what had been painted on what wall. It was the continued re-enactment of the rites and revelations of the house that imbued a way of life and sustained a social order through daily practice, as I argued in Chapter 5. The symbolic, mythical and historical sets of knowledge underpinned a social order, but they retained their social force at least partly from the processes of hiding, retrieval and revelation. As things are secreted away they can gain a special status or aura. When they are revealed again, they have added power, and those that control the revelatory experience benefit.

The mysteries were revealed at a number of scales, at public events, feasts and burial ceremonies, but mostly they were revealed at the scale of the house. It was again through the house that the larger social whole was constructed, and it was through the performances of revelation in the house that social groups were able to exchange, affiliate and produce in order to sustain some degree of dominance. In a largely egalitarian society, relative dominance was embedded within giving and revealing.

CHAPTER EIGHT

Materiality, 'Art' and Agency

The leopard reliefs are distinctive in that they are left in abandoned houses with the heads on. We saw in Chapter 6 that there are many examples of head removal at Çatalhöyük and I have interpreted this as part of attempts to make ancestral links. People, bulls, figurines and the relief splayed figures (probably bears as we shall see below) all often have their heads removed. One of the felines on which the naked lady sits in Plate 24 is headless, but if we focus tightly on the reliefs of pairs of leopards it is notable that they retain their heads through the life histories of houses.

Since leopard bones were not brought on site, we do not see circulation of leopard skulls as part of ties to ancestors, although it is possible that leopard skins functioned in this way and have simply not survived in the material record. It is difficult to make a case that leopards were centrally involved in the types of process discussed in Chapter 6 – that is the construction of descent and lineal ties. But they do seem more involved in some of the aspects of life that I wish to discuss in this chapter. There are several cases of humans in positions of control of leopards or big cats. There is of course the famous figurine of a woman seated on or between big cats (Plate 24), with her hands resting on their heads and their tails reaching up over her shoulders, and there are other depictions of women and men standing by or sitting on leopards or big cats or other large animals (Figure 78 and Plate 20). Unlike the cheetah or lion, the leopard is a very solitary, unso-cial animal – and very difficult to tame (although there are reports

78 Brown limestone carving of figure possibly standing by or sitting on a leopard, one of several similar examples found by James Mellaart.

of taming of leopards for social display[1]). And yet it is possible that in some of the Çatalhöyük imagery it is shown tamed by people. The people actively ride or tend the leopard and other animals (and perhaps too their spirit powers). This theme, of human agency, will emerge as a central one in this chapter, as we look more closely at materiality and 'art' at Çatalhöyük.

MATERIAL ENTANGLEMENT

In Chapter 2, I made the point that life at Çatalhöyük involved a complex series of material-social entanglements. I used the example of plastering a room and showed that this involved a complex series of requirements – such as particular tools and knowledge, rights of access to land, the ability to mobilize labour, access to cattle, and so on. I used the example of how shifting from clay balls to pottery for cooking changed the way that one could work in the house and so had an impact on social relations within the house group. I used the example of how a shift in the location of the oven would have an impact on relations between houses. In the large agglomerated 'town' of Çatalhöyük people became increasingly entangled in a social, material, conceptual web of dependencies and relations. People, society and things became increasingly codependent. I assume that similar entangled webs occurred in other early villages, but the rich information from Çatalhöyük allows a particular and detailed view.

As we have progressed through this book we have seen many other examples of such entanglement – how at the regional level, for example, the exploitation of dispersed resources depended on close social ties within the community. At the 'town' level we saw many of the material-social problems of living in a large agglomeration: the problems of dealing with mouse infestations and human faecal material; the issues of overcrowding and access to space; the problems of bringing animals into penning areas on site. In Chapters 5 and 6 we saw how the social fabric of domestic life was embedded within the material fabric of the house, and how the construction of house histories involved people, their bodies and the circulation of the material furnishings of the house. In Chapter 7 we saw how social position and authority may have been closely related to the hiding and revealing of materials and knowledge. In all these examples, people and things become entangled in economic, social, symbolic and conceptual dependencies.

As a further example, I have been very struck by the numbers of different categories of containers which people lived with at Çatalhöyük. There are different pot types (Figure 25 shows an example) although they are not highly diverse.[2] There are several different basket types[3] (Figure 79) and we know that different types of basket were used for young and old people in burial. James Mellaart also discovered a wide range of types of wooden containers (Figure 80). In some buildings we have

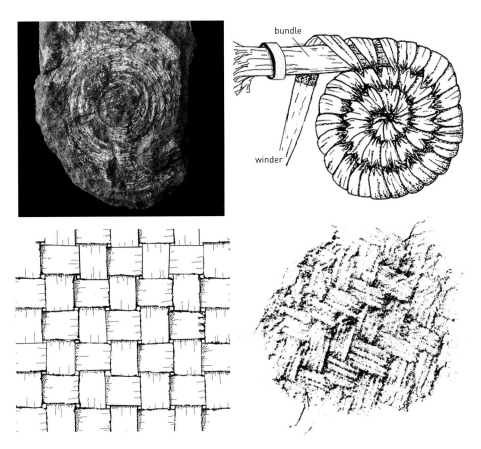

79 Different types of matting and basketry. These traces are usually seen at Çatalhöyük as impressions in plaster floors or as phytoliths (as in the top left example).

pots *in situ* on floors, especially near hearths and ovens, and we have frequently found the traces (as phytoliths) of where the baskets were placed in the southern and western parts of buildings (e.g. Figure 81). The containers seem all to have had their place in the buildings. It is also the case that different types of matting (see Figure 79) were used on different platforms and floor areas. So as you walked around a house at Çatalhöyük, you would have walked through a social map laid out on the floor. This map was made up of baskets, pots, wooden containers, mats all in their places and some or all of them would have been associated with different categories of people, or different individuals. The social order is here sedimented in the material world. As a child grew up in such a space it would have learned the social world at least partly in terms of this material-social-spatial map.

We can make a similar point by looking at how objects 'stretch' social relations over time. Once again, in this case in relation to temporality, social life at Çatalhöyük came to depend on materials, and materials acted as agents in social life. As crafted material objects were exchanged, their 'thingness' had social effects.

80 Different types of wooden container. These and other forms, such as lidded boxes, were preserved in cases where high-temperature burning of houses carbonized the wood in buried layers beneath.

81 Phytolith traces of 'coasters' (basket bases or mats) and the different types of floor matting used in Building 5. Each type of 'coaster' and mat, along with the other types of container found at Çatalhöyük, seems to have had its place in the building.

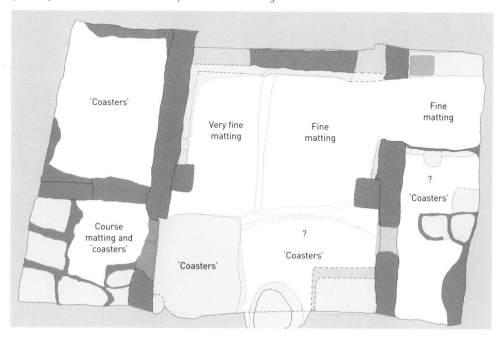

The objects endured, and they were often associated with specific memories. Thus objects create extensions of events and become involved in longer-term social dependencies. We saw this in relation to the construction of histories in Chapter 6 as well as in the exchange of objects in Chapter 7. As a further example of the latter, we can consider the effect of the early introduction of pottery. In the extreme case where I give you a piece of meat in exchange for a handful of gruel or berries, there is an immediacy to the exchange. There may be memories and associations of the event, but the event can be relatively transient. But if I give you the meat in a pot, then the gift is 'stretched out' over time. If I keep the fat of sheep and goats in a pot,[4] the processing of the animals is 'remembered' in the pot and its contents – the products stretch out over time. The pot refers to the memories, exchanges and events as it is kept and reused.

In this chapter I wish to extend this discussion of materiality (the way that social life and materials became codependent) by looking at some of the ways that materials were involved in human agency in the world. There has been increased interest in recent years in 'magic' and ritual in the Neolithic of the Middle East[5] and much of this deals with the way that objects intervene in social processes. The objects act as material agents or delegates for humans.[6] Control of 'magic' and ritual is often associated with dominant groups. At Çatalhöyük, it may be that elders, or the elders in dominant lineages or houses, had a special relationship with ritual and material agency. We have seen that the houses, and especially the dominant houses, were involved in links to the ancestors, and we shall see that those in the houses were also involved in interceding with animal gods or spirits. It is possible that elders within houses protected people with their knowledge of spiritual and material effects.

Many people have recently pointed to the ways in which material objects in the early societies of the Middle East get used to protect against spiritual and social harm. For example, Hans Georg Gebel has looked at deposits in, under and between walls at two late PPNB sites in the Levant – Ba'ja and Basta.[7] He suggests that these objects and practices are involved in hiding materials and meanings. He gives examples of caches of stone axes, paintings, baby burials, pottery in walls. He sees these in terms of wanting to 'strengthen' the wall. The caches act as a 'medicine', placed during the construction of the wall to act as a delegate of humans against threatening external forces.

Similarly, Michael Morsch discusses the clay figurines from Nevali Çori.[8] Some 665 figurines were found, including both male and female representations, and some zoomorphic. Many are very small, like those from Çatalhöyük, and some look quite like the schematic anthropomorphic examples from Çatalhöyük (Figure 82). There is a lot of modelling waste and clay lumps. At Nevali Çori, the clay figurines have to be considered in relation to the monumental limestone sculpture, in comparison to which the clay figurines seem very secondary. Unlike the sculptures they are not found in the cult buildings but rather in discard locations, usually broken and mainly in spaces between houses and in the round 'houses', but not in the rectangular house rooms. They probably do not represent a goddess, and are more likely to have some sort of 'wish-vehicle' function.[9]

Returning to Çatalhöyük, James Mellaart discussed the uses of red paint and red ochre in the houses – in fact they occur in some way in almost every house[10]. In our excavations we have found red ochre sprinkled on burials, and on thresholds between rooms especially. Mellaart noted the use of red paint on wall panels above floors, on benches, platforms and animal heads in plaster, and on baskets and boxes. All this use of red, he argued, 'wards off evil spirits and protects the object so decorated, be it the body of the dead, the wall of the house or shrine near which he slept, the bench or platform on which he sat or slept, the posts which support his roof and which might fall down, the boxes in which precious possessions were kept or the baskets in which his food was stored.'

The present project has found evidence of similar functions for geometric painting, at least in one case. The paintings in the houses at Çatalhöyük must have played a very different role to the installations and reliefs. The latter existed over many years, and we have seen how they were often involved in creating links through time and across generations. But the paintings were only visible intermittently. Through most of the life of any particular house, the walls were white or sooty. But for short periods of time they became transformed into a blaze of colour and activity, either as figurative or geometric paintings. The paintings were then plastered over and the walls reverted to their plain form. It seems that the plaster in the main room was redone as often as every month or season.[11] This suggests that the paintings may have been associated with intermittent events in the life cycle of the building and its inhabitants – perhaps initiation, birth, death etc. All buildings that we have excavated have some traces of painting. Building 2, for example, a relatively unelaborated and small building with no burial and minimal platform differentiation, has lozenges in the northeast corner (Figure 69), and a red geometric painting in a niche on the north wall (Figure 68). The lozenges are not well executed and look quite casual. But in all buildings there is red wash or some other painting at some point in their life.

In Building 1, a clue as to a function of the geometric paintings has been found (Figure 83). Here there is a possible spatial and temporal link between geometric painting and the burial of mainly young people.[12] It is the northwest platform in the main room that is surrounded by painting during part of the occupation of this house. It is this platform under which young people were preferentially buried. But there is also a temporal link. It is always difficult to assess which wall plaster goes with which floor plaster, and only approximate correlations could be made in Building 1. But in general terms the phases of painting corresponded to the phases of burial under this platform. One possible interpretation of this link is that the geometric painting acted in some way to protect or to communicate with the dead below the platform. A comparable association has been found in the adjacent Building 3,[13] where again the northwest platform contained most burial in the main room, with an adjacent concentration of burials of young people, and red paint concentrated (or was best preserved) on the walls around this same northwest platform.

The need to protect in relation to death is seen in a number of other possible ways. The use of red ochre in graves has already been remarked upon. When we dig burials we often come across great concentrations of beads made in a great variety of materials from shell and bone to stone of various types. In particular, we find concentrations of beads on juveniles and infants. One of the best-preserved cases is shown in Plate II, from Building 6. This baby was furnished with beads around its wrists and ankles. The care and richness lavished on these young individuals cannot be read in terms simply of status. Adults do not show clear status differentiation in terms of burial, and it seems more likely that the objects placed with young individuals have more to do with some form of protection – that is with an apotropaic function. The occurrence of shells with ochre and spatulae (small 'spoons') in childrens' graves may have had a similar function. So in both the provision of painting (decoration) around a burial platform that focuses on young people, and in terms of the provision of ochre and beads (decoration) in the graves of young people, some protective agency seems the most likely explanation.

A similar case can perhaps be made for some of the most bizarre and inexplicable burial practices we have seen at Çatalhöyük – the placing of carnivore scat around the body. The two examples of this discovered by the present project have been studied extensively by Emma Jenkins[14] and have been compared with an example found by Mellaart. Alternative explanations have been considered, such as that the grave was left open and used as a lair by a carnivore, but these hypotheses have been rejected. The most likely, if strange, explanation is that the scat of a carnivore such as a weasel was collected and put in the graves. Why might such a practice have been followed? It is helpful to refer to some broad ethnographic knowledge here. Mary Douglas[15] argued that dirt and danger often have great ritual power. Carnivore scat combines both the danger of the carnivore – as well as the teeth and bones of the mice it has eaten and digested – with the dirt of the faecal material. It thus ideally links danger, death and dirt. To place such material in graves may have had great ritual and protective power.

Many of the figurines found at Çatalhöyük may have had protective functions. They are largely found in domestic refuse contexts.[16] Many are extremely small and often seem quickly and simply made[17] (Figure 82). They are often low fired, or partially fired, and there are many clay lumps and even unfired clay balls that could have been

82 A small roughly made human-like figurine found in the current excavations.

83 The burial of young people below the northwest platform in Building 1 was closely associated with geometric painting.

involved in figurine manufacture. They were probably made often, quickly, as part of daily practices. But they are sometimes deposited in contexts which suggest they had some practical use in protecting people and things. We have found them placed in oven walls, in house walls, in the make-up beneath floors or in abandonment contexts. Naomi Hamilton argues that some of the small clay horns that are found in wall plasters and oven walls may have got there accidentally, and certainly, the inclusion of artifacts in plasters and clays as background noise may be a factor.[18] However, in some cases the horns and figurines seemed so out of place in an otherwise clean deposit that a votive or protective role seemed more likely to the excavators. In other cases, the specifics of the deposition are very deliberate. In one building a group of animal figurines was placed beneath the floors of storage bins,[19] and Mellaart discovered the large female figurine on felines (Plate 24) in a grain bin. In the southeast corner of Building 17 a crudely made figurine was broken by removing the head, and the body and head were placed in a sealing layer over a hearth. A few hearths later in the same location, a sealing deposit contained a very similar broken head (Figures 62 and 63). So it seems that in this corner of this house there was a particular custom of depositing a particular, unique figurine form, broken, over a hearth when abandoned and remade. I agree with Mary Voigt that these figurines are primarily mechanisms for achieving or effecting wishes,[20] with various types of practical functions. They are so small because they are only needed as brief 'acts', then discarded. These are daily life, everyday events, which is why there are so many in middens.

A number of the quadruped figurines have been stabbed with sharp objects while still unbaked. These stabbed figurines seem to provide a clear instance of material agency in that presumably the stabbing of the clay material was thought to have effects in the world. Another possible example of material agency with regard to figurines is a deposit which contains five figurines, three of uncertain type. Occurring at the interface of two buildings, this may have been a foundation deposit.[21]

Tristan Carter and his colleagues working on the obsidian from the site argue that there are cases of intentional depositions of obsidian. For example, in Building 1 there are deposits of obsidian placed at the base of a moulded wall feature.[22] In 2004 we found obsidian placed around the edge of a platform as part of a floor make-up in Building 44. The large obsidian pieces were crammed into the join between the platform wall and the floor. In other buildings there are cases of individual obsidian pieces being placed in special locations as part of construction events.[23] There are also examples of obsidian projectiles being placed in retrieval pits in the centre of the west walls of houses as part of abandonment practices.[24] These obsidian examples may involve placing objects with a special value or aura in contexts where they may have had a protective role, or may have been given as gifts or sacrifices or offerings to the spirits or deities.

So it can be suggested that many material objects at Çatalhöyük, from small figurines and geometric art and red ochre to obsidian and beads, had apotropaic functions. In Chapter 5 I provided many examples of objects and deposits that were placed in construction contexts, probably to 'protect' the house and its features. As we shall see, much of the figurative art and installations suggests that people lived in a spirit world that was thought to be able to have negative effects. These could be warded off by using charms, protective symbols and so on. The reasons for this use of materials as agents are probably varied. There may have been an increased concern regarding the death of young people as the society became more sedentary, and as people had larger numbers of children because of increased needs for labour, exchange and inheritance. There may have been increased conflict over inheritance and rights as densities increased and families expanded in size. In the most general terms, there would have been increased potential for social conflict in a dense settlement in which people had to deal with movement, access, resources, rights. There may have been more fears and suspicions of social stigma, gossip, cursing. People may have increasingly become involved in a cycle of blaming, cursing, and protection against such actions. Objects acted as delegates and intercessors in this process. As people, society and crafted materials increasingly became entangled and codependent, so the codependent material agents were further enlisted and engaged in a social world in which spirits were involved. This does not need to be seen as a descent into irrational sorcery – but as a practical attempt to deal with real problems.

ART AS PRACTICAL SCIENCE

In a number of ways, then, from figurines to geometric art to the reliefs that were dismantled and handed down to succeeding generations, art is involved practically. In these cases, the 'art' is not 'art' in the sense of something simply to be contemplated with aesthetic sensibilities. The art at Çatalhöyük does something. This is not to say that the objects do not have an aesthetic dimension. The attractiveness of the designs, and the beauty of the form of things may have been a central part in attracting or repelling the spirits.

In this emphasis on having a practical role, the art at Çatalhöyük might be thought to contrast with some of the products of the modern artists inspired by the site (Chapter 1). Some of the contemporary jewelry, painting and music have a central aesthetic focus. But other work, especially the installation art, is designed to do something. It can be argued that the 9,000-year-old 'art' at Çatalhöyük is closer to science than it is to some contemporary art, in the sense that it aims to intervene in the world, to understand how it works, to change it. Dialogue between ancient and contemporary artists can lead to changes of perspective both for artists and archaeologists. The dialogue challenges the tendency among contemporary artists to appropriate the ancient art into their own perspective. The archaeological evidence can contribute to an understanding of the 'otherness' of prehistoric art. Equally, interactions with modern artists draw the archaeologist back to the tensions between the practical and aesthetic qualities of the prehistoric art.

I wish to turn now to the forms of art at Çatalhöyük which most directly confront our sensibilities. I refer to the figurative art which often has a clear narrative content. In order to understand this we shall see that it is necessary also to refer frequently to the reliefs and installations. But it is the figurative art which is the greatest wonder of Çatalhöyük, and the greatest challenge to interpretation. It is this which requires particular sensitivity in understanding 'otherness' and which requires greatest awareness of our own assumptions.

To help us move forward in this process, I wish to refer again to ethnographic examples. This time, rather than looking to farmers like the Tikopia, we can draw inspiration from hunter-gatherer belief systems. The art at Çatalhöyük has been interpreted by David Lewis-Williams from the perspective of the San peoples of southern Africa, and from an understanding of the shamanistic practices found in hunter-gatherer societies throughout the world.[25] The term 'shaman' is problematic as it often conjures up specialist practitioners, but we can use the term loosely to refer to people who perform tasks such as healing, divination, control of animals and control of the weather, often by entering an altered state of consciousness.[26] Lewis-Williams argues that throughout the world shamanistic peoples believe in a tiered cosmos, which often has three levels. There is a subterranean level inhabited by spirits and spirit-animals such as frogs or monsters. There is an upper level in or above the sky with its own spirits and creatures. Humans live in the intermediate level. He argues that the architecture of Çatalhöyük embodies this type of tiered cosmos – especially in that humans move around on the surface of the site (the roofs) and then descend into the dark and lower interiors. Verticality is suggested by the stairs and by the upright posts set in the walls, and by pillars and platforms. Lewis-Williams notes that bull heads are often associated with the posts and pillars and he suggests that bulls were probably the pre-eminent spirit animals that made travel to the subterranean world possible. It is of special interest in this regard that in Mellaart's 'Shrine' 10 in Level VI, the tiered bulls' heads were set in the floor, at least in some phases, as if rising out of it (Figure 66). In Building 1, whatever sculpture was on the west wall of the main room seemed to start from below floor level.[27] There are also scenes in the art in which vultures have human legs – so perhaps ritual leaders 'became' vultures as they flew (interceded) between the intermediate level and the upper, sky level of spirits.

Lewis-Williams also suggests that the walls of the buildings may have been seen as permeable. He refers to the many cases in which vulture beaks, boar tusks and fox and weasel teeth were set into walls and then repeatedly plastered over.

He sees these wild animal parts, along with the bulls' heads and wild rams' heads set on the walls, as 'coming through' the walls. He notes the niches, sometimes painted red, that go deep into the walls. He suggests that the repeated replastering over of teeth and bulls and leopards and wild boar tusks in the walls may have been a re-enactment of the letting through of the animal or animal spirit in shamanistic performance and then the sealing off to stop intrusion from the lower spirit world.

Taking his cue from the fact that most animals in the art at Çatalhöyük were hunted and were not domesticated, Lewis-Williams points out that in many hunter-gatherer societies the hunting of meat-producing animals is often inextricably bound up with the acquisition of the animals' supernatural power. Some animals are richly imbued with supernatural power – a power that the ritual practitioners need in order to reach the spirit world. There are what seem to be hunting scenes in the figurative art at Çatalhöyük. But in many cases, what is going on is the teasing or baiting of wild animals. In these latter scenes, wild boar have their hackles raised, stags have erect penises, people pull the tongues and tails of wild dangerous animals and scratch their backs and perhaps make noise around them (Figure 84). According to Lewis Williams, these hunting and baiting scenes can be seen as the acquisition of special powers, and the taking into the house of horns, teeth and beaks was an appropriation of spiritual power. Lewis-Williams even goes on to say that ritual leaders may have competed with each other in their abilities to master the power of important spiritual animals such as

84 In this transcription of a wall-painting found in Level V, a group of figures bait or tease a stag and wild boar; both animals are aroused, the wild boar with its hackles raised, and the stag with an erect penis.

the bull. In many hunter-gatherer societies, shamans are believed to have the ability to guide the movements of animals into the hunters' ambush – and so by their ritual observances they can ensure a successful hunt. We have seen that at Çatalhöyük there is a preference for the use of wild bulls in feasting. Thus any ability of a ritual leader to ensure a successful hunt would have had enormous social significance.

According to this view, shamans need to derive their power from 'out there', beyond society. Domestic animals such as sheep and goat are part of society. So the ritual leaders focused on the physically more powerful and dangerous animals, such as the aurochs and leopard, as well as the vulture, the ram, the stag, the wild boar, the weasel, the fox, the bear. Indeed different ritual leaders may have claimed relationships with different wild animals – some with felines, some with bulls, some with vultures and so on.

Lewis-Williams's ideas are also relevant to the emphasis on death at Çatalhöyük. 'Death' in shamanistic communities often means 'transition to the spirit world by whatever means'. For example, when a San shaman falls in a deep trance he is said to have 'died' – the spirit leaves the body and journeys to the spirit world. The ability of the shaman or ritual leader to go beyond death and return gives a special status, and would be especially important in a society in which the ancestors had so much social importance. By going down into a deep room in which the dead were buried, the ritual leaders could travel to the ancestors through the walls, niches and floors.

PROWESS, ANIMAL SPIRITS, HUNTING AND FEASTING

I want to take some of these insights offered by Lewis-Williams and add a more social and Çatalhöyük-specific dimension to them. A central clue is the discovery by Nerissa Russell and Louise Martin that wild bulls are used preferentially in feasting.[28] Their claim is based on the association between the bones of male cattle and concentrations of large numbers of relatively complete large animal bones, often in contexts such as house foundations, house abandonment, or discard between house walls.

As we saw in the Prologue and in Table 1, the art of Çatalhöyük provides few representations of domesticated animals and even fewer of domesticated and wild plants. The art is dominated by wild animals. This emphasis on the social importance of wild animals is seen clearly with sheep and goat. Not only do domesticated sheep and goat rarely occur in the art and symbolism. There is also some evidence that wild horncores of sheep and goat were kept intact and used symbolically (for example being arrayed above the lentil bin in Building 1), while domestic ones were more often treated as butchery waste. Some of the scenes concerning animals appear to show hunting while others show the baiting or teasing of wild bulls, deer, boar and bear. The same scenes could be interpreted as human figures obtaining the spirits of the animals by touching their tongues, nostrils and tails. Large numbers of people are involved (in some scenes all the figures are bearded – in others sex is not shown). These scenes may be largely mythical or they may relate in some way to real activities involving baiting, hunting and gaining spirit power.

It is thus of interest that these human interactions with wild animals have a representation in the activities identified on site. For example, as already noted, certain deposits identified as derived from feasting deposits have higher frequencies of bull bones. The special importance of the bull in the art has often been claimed, and the association between wild bulls and feasting gives some foundation to that symbolic importance. It has long been claimed that social competition through feasting was a central part of the process of domestication of plants and animals.[29] Certainly there is now good evidence in the Middle East from at least as early as the PPNA for roasting pits in open areas that can best be interpreted in terms of feasting, and in Anatolia public feasting has been claimed in the early to mid 10th millennium BC.[30] Roasting pits in open (public) areas have been identified at several Neolithic sites in eastern Anatolia,[31] and large-scale processing of animals occurred close to Aşıklı Höyük in central Anatolia.[32] The public nature of the feasting at Çatalhöyük is partly indicated by the size of some of the deposits, and partly by their nature. For example, feasting deposits have been found in the fill between walls.[33] In one such case the remains of at least five cattle were found, suggesting the consumption of a huge amount of meat. The extensive gnawing (by dogs) on these bones, in contrast to the bones found within buildings, suggested that the feasting had occurred outside buildings.

So feasting was a public event, involving social exchange, as well as ritual. Wild, male cattle played a central role. The special nature of these events is perhaps related to the fact that cattle were not a major part of the diet, despite their prevalence in social and ritual settings. But there were other animals too that had special roles. I have already noted that after the lowest levels, post-cranial deer elements become rare on the site. Pig are like deer in that meaty body parts are not brought on to the site very much. This pattern may have occurred because pig and deer were increasingly difficult to find near the site, so that only trophies could be bought back. But there is no evidence that only the meaty parts of cattle were brought onto the site. Cattle may have been more available locally, but it seems possible that taboos developed about bringing certain animals and animal parts onto the site, as in the case of the leopard.

Often it seems that it was the sharp, pointed, dangerous parts of wild animals that were brought on to the site and used in the art and installations. A bear paw was found with plaster attached to it in a side room to Mellaart's 'Shrine' 10,[34] so it had perhaps been attached to a wall. There are other sharp parts of wild animals attached

85 This figurine from Göbekli Tepe is one of many representations of male sexuality and the phallus at the site.
86 An engraving from Göbekli showing female sexuality.

to walls – wild boar tusks, the teeth of fox and weasel, cattle horns, vulture beaks. This concentration on dangerous animal parts follows on from the earlier sculpture at Göbekli Tepe in eastern Turkey (Figures 88 and 89).[35] At that site there is a clear association between the art and phallic imagery (Figure 85), and many of the animals shown in the art are male with erect penises.[36] There is also an engraving at Göbekli Tepe which shows female sexuality (Figure 86). Some of the animals shown in the Çatalhöyük paintings have erect penises and have their hackles raised. There seems to be an association with sexuality. Perhaps the Çatalhöyük paintings are related to initiation, or to feasts at which young men and/or women had to show prowess. Certain parts of animal bodies, including heads, are perhaps then brought to houses as memories of the large-scale events. These heads may then become passed down so that links to great hunters/teasers and feast providers can be maintained.

87 Since the head and hands of splayed figure reliefs were always removed when a building was abandoned, interpretation has always been problematic. New finds, however, suggest that they represented wild animals, and in the case of Çatalhöyük, probably bears.

The case of the equids is interesting with regard to the above argument. The equids at the site are wild, but they are not included in houses as part of installations. There are some equids in marginal positions in paintings in one room, but there do not seem to be special deposits associated with equid, except for a few equid scapulae. So it seems that it is mainly dangerous wild animals and animal parts that are treated in special ways when brought on site. In fact they may have a special power when brought on site. As many as eight pairs of wild goat horn-cores were placed over the lentil bin in Building 1.[37] This may be seen as the wild 'protecting' the domestic, and animals 'protecting' plants. Again, there seems to be a pattern according to which dangerous wild animals are given a special social and symbolic status.

Another interesting case is provided by the large 'splayed figures' of the type shown in Figures 87, 110 and Plate 18. These have human-like bodies, and some have visible 'belly buttons'. The heads and 'hands' are always broken off in abandonment, and James Mellaart initially interpreted the heads as feline, on the basis of the shape of the scars left on the wall. Later he saw them as goddess figures.[38] Recent finds from Nevali Çori and Göbekli Tepe include sculptures which are splayed figures with tails and bared teeth, but which have tails (Figure 89).[39] In my view, the Çatalhöyük examples are best interpreted as some sort of wild animal or animal-human hybrid, and a stamp seal found in 2004 seems to support this (Plate 23). Here the head and the hind paws remain. They clearly show that the figure is an animal, probably a bear.

88, 89 The many stone pillars at Göbekli are engraved with a range of animals, birds and creatures – here (at left) five birds against a net-like background are depicted above a wild boar with an erect penis and a still partly buried fox. The splayed figure from Göbekli (at right) bears a resemblance, apart from the long tail, to those found at Çatalhöyük.

As I noted in Chapter 6, much of this imagery was widely found in Anatolia and the Middle East in the period leading up to settled village life. I argued there that these widespread motifs probably circulated as myth. In the Levant, wild cattle skulls associated with either human graves or possible communal structures have been found from the PPNA into the Pottery Neolithic.[40] As in the art at Çatalhöyük, at 'Ain Ghazal in the Levant bulls are much more prevalent amongst the animal figurines than they are in the faunal assemblage.[41] Wild boar are represented in the painting and installations at Çatalhöyük, and the same animal is depicted at Göbekli Tepe in eastern Turkey (Figure 88).[42] Wild boar teeth and tusks are found in the PPNB in the Levant.[43] Vultures are an important part of the symbolism at Çatalhöyük, and there is widespread evidence of an emphasis on birds of prey in the Middle East. Nigel Goring-Morris and Anna Belfer-Cohen refer to a marked rise in the numbers of raptor talons in the Natufian, as well as to stylized statues of birds of prey at sites in eastern Anatolia.[44] Vultures are depicted at Jerf el Ahmar in northern Syria and in the wall paintings at the Pre-Pottery Neolithic site of Bouqras in Syria. Weasel and fox teeth are placed in the walls at Çatalhöyük. Fox teeth are used as pendants in some Natufian sites, and the fox is shown in the art at Göbekli Tepe. At Middle PPNB Kfar HaHoresh in Israel there are several examples of fox mandibles in graves.[45]

Çatalhöyük, then, takes a widely available emphasis on dangerous parts of animals and birds and gives them a special focus. I suggested in Chapter 1 that it may be helpful in making sense of this imagery at Çatalhöyük to refer to general anthropological discussions about the ritual importance of death and violence. We can talk about the violence, sex and death of the imagery at Çatalhöyük simply in terms of male prowess. But for philosopher Georges Bataille, as discussed in Chapter 1, violence, sex and death in ritual create moments of transcendence.[46] One returns from this 'other' world transformed and more able to cope with restraint in society. The anthropologist Maurice Bloch also discusses how in ritual, things are turned inside out in some 'other' world 'beyond'. For him, the violence and symbolic killing take the initiate beyond the transience of daily life into permanent entities such as descent groups. By leaving this life, it is possible to see oneself and others as part of something permanent and life-transcending.[47]

As noted in Chapter 1, these ideas seem to fit Çatalhöyük very well. We have seen how the sphere of ancestry and the passing on of rites in houses is closely tied to many of the key components in a prowess-animal spirit-hunting-feasting nexus. In particular, continuities through time are created by the handing on and circulation of bull and other heads. And the sharp animal parts are placed in walls, uncovered and covered over again, as part of the hiding and revealing processes discussed in Chapter 7, and themselves linked to both exchange and ancestry.

But lest we become too taken in by abstract theories, we can perhaps return to some very basic material considerations. At one level, bulls and other wild animals may simply be central to the art and symbolism at Çatalhöyük because they are big or powerful or dangerous. By having these qualities they can be used in a variety of ways to create social effects. It seems also fairly straightforward that at least some of such animals are central to feasts. Wild bulls provided the largest amount of meat on one animal in the area. Even leopards would have had trouble bringing one down. So the fact that a feast-giver could provide such an animal would itself have given prestige. And it seems likely that the hunter/teaser/killer of the large or dangerous animals would also have been celebrated, and that the heads and other animal parts would have had histories that made them valuable in social life. Those who had killed such wild animals may also have gained supernatural powers from them.

The specifics of this interpretation of the figurative art and associated installations in terms of a prowess-animal spirit-hunting-feasting nexus may be wrong. For example, perhaps the animals shown in the teasing scenes are already dead and people are just taking the power from them by touching the tongue or tail and so on. Also, it is clear that the focus on the dangerous parts of carnivorous animals does not fit all the symbolism at Çatalhöyük or at sites like Göbekli Tepe since there are also depictions at the former of wading birds, and at the latter of ducks.[48] In such cases it may be more fruitful to focus on the role of these birds as having more meat than smaller birds and thus being useful in feasts. But at Çatalhöyük the large birds do not

90 A figurine with a seed in its back from a midden in the upper levels of the site in the South Area.

show up in feasting remains. Nerissa Russell has suggested to me that the birds may have been seen as messengers to the sky. However incorrect the specifics, and however much variation on a theme, there seems to be good evidence for an overall social focus in much of the art on feasts, wild animals, sexual and other prowess, and hunting.

As if to confirm this set of associations, we can turn to the minimal evidence for special uses of and symbolic roles for plants at Çatalhöyük. The reasons for the lack of such evidence may be partly taphonomic.[49] The seeds from the site survive through accidents of charring, and the seed assemblages are very mixed. James Mellaart found 'numerous offerings of grain and crucifer seeds' on a platform beneath the 'Leopard Shrine' of EVI.44.[50] And there are possible depictions of plant gathering. I will elsewhere (page 213) discuss a figurine which had a wild seed placed in its back (Figure 90).[51] But the list of possible symbolic associations that the archaeobotany team is able to muster is short, especially for domestic plants.[52] As one of many examples, there is no evidence for significantly different plant remains in burial fills.

So why are plants and domestic animals not more prevalent in art, ritual and social feasting? Again, the answer may be taphonomic in relation to plants, and sheep and goat do constitute a part of the feasting deposits. So we should be careful not to exaggerate the contrasts. But it is also possible that dominant groups in society (such as the elders in each house, or those in the dominant houses) partly based their power on interceding in relation to wild animals and ancestors. Perhaps these forms of domination attempted to deny new forms of power based on domestic production, even if they themselves were partly based on that production. In upper levels in the site, and on the later West Mound, there are signs that it became possible to assert the significance of domestic production more openly (see Chapter 11).

THE HUMAN PRESENCE

It is clear that the materialization of the social structure at Çatalhöyük did not lead to fixity and lack of change. Indeed the rate of cultural change seems to increase through the sequence and the rate of house rebuilding also increases (see Chapter 11). One can argue, in fact, that material entanglement produced a representation in the object world of the social structure such that it could be contested and changed. There is much emphasis on constructing continuities through time, and links to ancestors were a central part of claims to membership of 'houses'. There was much bodily repetition of routines and people were thoroughly entangled in a material world. But at the same time, there were moves to transform traditional modes of life as we shall see in Chapter II. There is a continual tension between continuity and change, with the latter beginning to get the upper hand in the upper levels of the site.

The inverse of objectification is greater awareness of the self as will be discussed more fully in Chapter 10.[53] After the Ice Age, as material entanglement increased, the human as agent becomes more apparent. Human representations do occur of course throughout the Upper Palaeolithic, but active humans, running and hunting and interacting with animals become especially common in early Holocene art and symbolism. In Anatolia and the Middle East, it often seems as if, while human representations occur early on, they come to have a clearer and more central role through time. The Natufian in the Levant has an animal rather than a human art.[54] There are probable human representations at Göbekli Tepe in southeastern Anatolia, and they are clear as statues slightly later at Nevali Çori. At Çatalhöyük, despite some recent finds in the lower levels, there seems to be an increase of the large rounded female figurines in the upper levels. In Greece, Catherine Perlès notes that in the earliest Neolithic in Thessaly figurines are indistinctly human, and highly schematic. In later Neolithic phases, figurines are more clearly human and sexual features are more clearly marked.[55]

These human figures in Anatolia take us straight into the prowess-animal spirit-hunting-feasting nexus. The monumental architectural stelae at Göbekli may be representations of humans, and they are covered with elaborate symbols of large animals, large birds, frogs, spiders and erect penises. At Nevali Çori the standing stones are still more clearly human. Harald Hauptmann also discusses a stele showing hands holding an erect penis.[56] Such large human images may represent ancestors, but whatever they are they are human. The distinctive move here is to put human-like figures as central in interceding with animal spirits and perhaps with ancestral beings and other worlds.

The picture is complex, but in the most general of terms I think it is possible to see an increase in the representation of humans, especially active humans, gradually emerging after the Ice Age. Mary Helms argues that a shift from animal gods, to ancestors, to human gods may accompany the development of farming and settled village life.[57] I would argue that this shift towards a centring of human agency came about as the inverse of the entanglement process. People became more invested in a web of material relations so that their social relations were 'objectified'. Thus the 'made-ness' of social, ritual and mythic life would have become clearer. The social world became more malleable and susceptible to transformation. Humans lived increasingly in a material world which they had constructed and which they could change. Humans came to see themselves more clearly as agents able to transform social lives by transforming material objects, artifacts, monuments and environments. People crafted their own worlds by crafting the gods.[58] They began to use things to effect change – economically and socially, but also spiritually. They became invested in materiality as part of trying to make sense of and control the world.

CONCLUSION

There is a great expansion of material culture associated with the first settled 'towns' and the first farmers. By the end of the Neolithic there is a lot more 'stuff' in social life. We see the emergence of ceramics, polished stone, permanent houses, more frequent burial and so on. People and made things became codependent to a degree that had not been seen in earlier hunter-gatherer societies. This sedimentation of social life in a complex and 'heavy' material world, with all its dependencies and investments, all its networks and ties, might have been expected to slow down rates of change. But in fact what we see is a speeding up of rates of change, and increasing variability through time.

Many of the symbolic themes I have been discussing have roots in much earlier hunter-gatherer societies. Many of the themes are widely found at the start of the Holocene and probably had a great ancestry as myth. There are certainly some new features (such as the centrality of human agency). But many of the symbolic themes are widely found. So the question is not so much 'why was a new symbolic world created?', but rather 'why were symbolic worlds materialized at this time?'.

As people became more materially entangled in their social lives, they crafted community. The material and social entanglements were intimately related. But the intense social networks that were created also involved fears, conflicts, attempts to establish authority and responses against authority. All the material intervention can be seen as a way of affecting the world – even an early form of science. By intervening people tried to understand, make sense of, control the world around them. In the art of this period across Europe people are shown intervening as agents. Rather than being dominated by ideas of reciprocity (with other people and with nature), people intervened in the world. The domestication of plants and animals (this all-important intervention) can be seen as just an offshoot of this changed way of interacting with the world.

I will argue in Chapter 11 that the domestication of plants and animals can well be seen as an unintended by-product of this new materiality. We have seen that in fact people's social lives centred on a series of related traits involving prowess, animal spirits, hunting and feasting, and that these traits were often linked to ancestry. Little social focus was placed on domestic animals, domestic plants, food preparation, storage and pots.

CHAPTER NINE

Women and Men, the Old and the Young

Perhaps it was an ambiguity of the leopard that made it so appropriate for the symbolic world of Çatalhöyük. We have seen that on the one hand it is a solitary animal with individual markings, and yet it was used in the symbolism to suggest balance (the opposed pairs) and even collectivity (the scenes of large numbers of people wearing leopard skins). In the last chapter I argued that the leopard was also part of the symbolic focus on hunting, teasing, prowess and feasting. It fits into this scheme as a large dangerous animal that also hunts and is hunted. But there is another very different characteristic of leopards. Amongst leopards 'the maternal bond is strong and enduring. Mother and offspring often have reunions after separating, and the mother may continue to share kills until her offspring become fully self-sufficient.'[1] For example, a two-and-a-half-year-old male was recorded as often joining and hunting with his presumed mother at night.

91 Figurine of a woman wearing a dotted, possibly leopard skin top (found in Level II).

These ambiguities and contradictions meant that the leopard could be a potent symbol in a complex social world in which there were tensions between the individual and the collectivity and between the prowess-animal spirit-hunting and feasting nexus linked to ancestry and domestic production. Another important tension concerned gender. In some ways the leopard skins are associated with men. In at least one of the teasing and baiting scenes, the individuals wearing

leopard skins (or imitations of leopard skins) are bearded. But there are also figurines or statuettes showing women wearing tops that are dotted and could be
interpreted as leopard skins (Figure 91). The people standing by or sitting on leopards are both men and women (Figure 78 and Plate 20). In more general terms, the
leopard is sexually dimorphic in terms of size. James Mellaart interpreted the pairs
of leopards as male and female.[2] But in fact the two leopards in the pairings are very
similar in size.

GENDER

As noted in Chapter 1, groups on Goddess tours regularly visit the site from the
USA, Germany, Istanbul and elsewhere. They come to pray, hold circle dances, feel
the power of the Goddess. There is a great diversity of such groups from Gaia
groups, to Ecofeminists, to Goddess New Age travellers. Individuals are often visibly moved by the experience of visiting and it is undoubtedly the case that for many
the existence of the Goddess at Çatalhöyük is important for their personal sense of
identity. The project has entered into dialogue with some members of the varied
Goddess groups on its website, and some of the research directions being taken
result from these interactions.

The varied Goddess groups with an interest in Çatalhöyük ask different questions of the site. In fact, the focus on gender issues at early agricultural sites has a
long history. Before the 18th century, scholars in Europe had believed, based on
Aristotle and interpretations of the Bible, that the political development of society
began with patriarchy.[3] During the 18th century, however, reports from North
America told of societies that traced heritage through the female line, and in the
early 19th century a Swiss jurist named Johann Bachofen argued that a phase of
women's social power had preceded the patriarchal family. These ideas influenced
many scholars in the second half of the 19th century and throughout the 20th century, including Sigmund Freud and archaeologists such as Gordon Childe and
Jacques Cauvin.

James Mellaart too was steeped in the scholarship of this European tradition, so
it is not surprising that when he discovered opulent female imagery, such as that
shown in Plate 24, he presumed that it represented the 'Mother Goddess'. The
powerful naked woman sitting on a seat of felines, with her hands resting on their
heads, seems to conjure up precisely the tamer of nature so well known from historical mythologies in the Mediterranean, the Middle East and Egypt. But it was
another archaeologist who most effectively took up the 'Mother Goddess' view of
Çatalhöyük. Marija Gimbutas in a number of publications including her 1974 book
Goddesses and Gods of Old Europe argued forcefully for an early phase of matriarchal
society, evident at Çatalhöyük but also found across Europe with the advance of

agriculture. Patriarchal societies came later, she contended, in conjunction with metallurgy, horse riding and warring.

More recently, cultural anthropologists have withdrawn from making such sweeping generalizations, because human groups living today or in the recent past offer a diverse picture when it comes to the roles of the two sexes. Furthermore, anthropology provides no substantive evidence for true matriarchies. The record does show, however, that in most recent and contemporary societies women have some form of authority or that women at certain stages in their lives, or in certain contexts, have power. Rather than talking simplistically about matriarchies and patriarchies, we should expect, according to the ethnographic evidence, a more complicated picture, which is just what we find at Çatalhöyük.

We cannot assume that clear gender differences occurred in all or any areas of life at Çatalhöyük. To get some sense of the subtle and varied relations that can exist, we can turn again to Raymond Firth's account. He describes[4] a Tikopia work party that has gone out to the fields: 'The work is of a very simple nature: the turmeric plants are dug out of their little shelves in the hillside with a digging stick, the clusters of roots are examined and broken up into separate nodules, most of which are set aside to be taken home, and a few having been exposed to the sun and rejected for technical reasons are dibbled in again to provide a crop for next year. Some cleaning of the roots also takes place. Pa Nukunefu and the women share the work fairly among them, he doing most of the clearing of vegetation and the digging, they some of the digging and replanting, and nearly all the cleaning and sorting. There is no strict division of labour, and the tempo of the work is an easy one.'

Similarly, 'men and women of the household share in the work of getting food ready, most of the processes, as the kindling of the oven fire, the preliminary scraping of tubers or peeling of bananas being done by either. In ordinary households there is a tendency for the actual cooking to be left to the women, but as if in compensation certain arduous details in the preparation, as grating taro and expressing coconut cream, are specifically the charge of the men. The physical strain involved is the most potent reason why these are not normally performed by women. But nothing is more common on public occasions than to see men and women together around the oven.'

What new light can the evidence from the current excavations throw on the question of gender relations at Çatalhöyük? It should be noted that all the burial evidence from the current project deals with the lower levels of the site – up to Level V. We have not, at the time of writing this book, had a chance to study human bones from upper levels. So, in relation to the lower levels, given the argument in Chapter 6 about the social significance of headless bodies and detached skulls, a good place to start is with the sex of these 'important persons'. The two skeletons that we have found with their heads removed are male, but there is a cranium of a female recovered from a post-removal pit in Building 17.[5] Two examples of crania deposited at abandonment in Building 3 are a female and a juvenile.[6] Thus it seems that ancestry could be claimed through both male and female lines at Çatalhöyük (and similar numbers of male, female and immature heads have been found in the PPNB in the Middle East[7]).

The plastered skull found in 2004 in Building 42 provides another example from Çatalhöyük (see Figure 7 and Plates 13 and 14). The skull itself is male but it was held by a female. As discussed in Chapter 1, we have to be careful and not jump to conclusions about what this association between skull and skeleton might indicate. But given all the evidence arrayed in Chapter 6 about the ways in which people at Çatalhöyük made specific links between the present and past ancestors, it seems reasonable to interpret this association of skull and body as in some way showing ancestry and links through time. What is of interest for the present discussion, then, is that the plastered skull is held by an adult female. The association can be used to support the idea that a central female presence is possible in lines of affiliation stretching through time. Other interpretations are undoubtedly possible, but the plastered skull and its associated burial at least do not contradict the claim that both males and females were important in ancestry and lineage.

Another way of assessing the importance of individuals in burial may be the timing of the burial in relation to the ending of use of buildings or parts of buildings. The probable last burials in Building 1, that seem to end a phase of burial and/or occupancy, are mainly adults but also juveniles. All the adults are male.[8]

Some of our strongest scientific evidence about the relative status of men and women in the early and middle levels of Çatalhöyük concerns diet. If women and men lived notably different lives, and if one or the other was dominant, then we might expect to uncover disparities in diet, with the dominant group having more access to certain foods, such as meat or better joints of meat. So we have searched hard for such evidence as I will now outline, but we have not uncovered clear differences.

Several lines of evidence suggest very similar diets and lifestyles for men and women. There is some slight indication that women were fatter in relation to their height than men.[9] Women tend to have more teeth with caries than men, but in terms of wear on the teeth Başak Boz found no difference.[10] Analysis of the bones shows little evidence of specialized tasks for men and women and little evidence of radically different lifestyles. Sexual dimorphism is low for the sample as a whole although the reasons for this are complex and possibly multiple. The stable isotope evidence for human bones[11] does not show statistically significant differences in diet for men and women (Figure 92). Carbon residues on ribs occur on older individuals whether they are male or female.[12] Thus both men and women were associated with smoke-filled houses in the later parts of their lives, and there is no evidence that it was particularly women that were associated with the house.

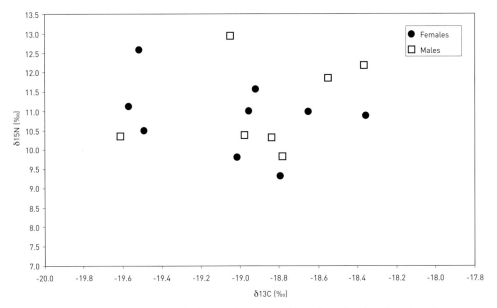

92 Plot of the chemical variation in bones of males and females, showing the values for nitrogen (vertical axis) and carbon (horizontal axis) stable isotopes. The data seem to indicate that there is no relationship between sex and diet.

None of this suggests a strongly codified set of social rules regarding sex. Overall, there is little evidence that gender was very significant in the allocation of roles at Çatalhöyük. There must have been differences of lifestyle in relation to childbirth, but these differences do not seem to be related to major social distinctions. There may, however, be changes through time. There is some indication that gender demarcation becomes more evident in imagery and representation in the upper levels of the site. It is in these upper levels that figurines become more clearly gendered, and one of the wall paintings shows a large group of bearded men engaged in baiting wild animals. The increased independence of houses, and the increased specialization of production in the upper levels (after Level VIA) of the site, may be linked to an increasing separation of male and female work and identity as will be discussed in Chapter II.

What can we say about the ways in which male and female bodies were treated in burial? Archaeologists are accustomed to studying the layout of graves and of the artifacts in them to assess social distinctions. We have looked carefully to see whether men are always buried in one part of the room and women in another, whether men are buried on their left side and women on their right, whether men face one direction and women another and so on. James Mellaart thought he could see such differences but when the data from the earlier and modern excavations were examined by Naomi Hamilton,[13] no clear patterning could be identified. Men and women seem to have been laid out in similar ways. Certainly there were some differences in the artifacts associated with the bodies. In 2004 we

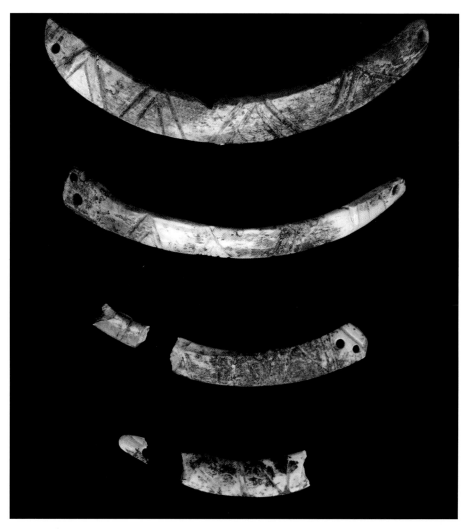

93 Boar's tusk necklace found during the current excavations in the South Area.

found a decorated boars' tusk necklace buried with a woman (Figure 93). Mellaart[14] had noted some gendered differences in grave goods such as boars' tusk necklaces and mirrors with women, as well as what he called 'cosmetic sets' (e.g. shells with ochre and small bone spatulae – though in the current excavations we have found these mainly with children). Mellaart saw men as having fewer necklaces, and instead having maces, belt-hook fasteners, obsidian points and flint knives/daggers. Other items such as stamp seals he saw as occurring in both male and female graves. In fact because the numbers of graves with any sort of artifact association are slight, and because the most common artifacts such as beads can occur in both male and female graves, it is difficult to argue for a strongly differentiated pattern. While some differences do exist, they seem relatively slight compared to many societies in which males and females are treated and laid out very differently during burial.

These arguments, that women may not have had clearly gendered roles in practice, have angered many in the Goddess communities, but it would be unethical to carry on supporting arguments for which there appears to be little evidence. Many followers of the Goddess have engaged in dialogue and have been able to see that the new evidence can be incorporated into a revised perspective – for example, one in which some equality existed in practice. Thus it is possible to ask questions that are of interest to particular groups, and then to enter into a dialogue that can contribute to changed perspectives.

It would seem that the evidence I have presented contradicts the strong gender distinctions in the imagery from Çatalhöyük. In the imagery the realms of influence seem distinct. In many societies, the politics of representation lead to masking of gender relations. At Çatalhöyük many of the paintings appear to concentrate on men. There are a few possible women (see Plate 16 from the lower part of Plate 15), but many of the figures are sexless. In one of the teasing or hunting scenes, all the figures wearing leopard skins are bearded. Some of the painting is masculine in that bulls and stags have erect penises. Most of the cattle heads fixed to the walls of the houses have proven to be those of wild bulls, although in the recent excavations it is possible that some exceptions exist. I have already noted the link between feasting deposits and wild bulls.

While most figurines are sexless, there are some that are bearded and others that clearly show breasts.[15] Most of the latter, and others that are probable women (Figure 94 and Plate 21), occur in the upper levels of the site and some are found in house contexts around hearths. This contrasts with the majority of the figurines which occur in midden and other discard locations. There is a possible and weak association with plants. The very small figurine shown in Figure 90 has a wild seed lodged in its back, in a way that suggests intentional inclusion. And the famous female figure on a seat of felines (Plate 24) was found in a grain bin by Mellaart. There is also a painting that could be interpreted as women gathering plants. But there may also be a symbolic association between women and death. In 2004 we discovered the clay figurine shown in Plate 22 in the fill of a burnt house. The front of the figurine looks very much like others found in the upper levels of the site, with full breasts on which the hands rest, and the stomach is extended in the central part. There is a hole in the top for the head which is missing. As one turns the figurine around one notices that the arms are very

94 This clay figurine is unusual in that it is naturistically and delicately modelled, particularly in the detail of the hands and breasts; it is also painted with a meander pattern.

thin, and then on the back of the figurine one sees a depiction of either a skeleton or the bones of a very thin and depleted human. The ribs and vertebrae are clear, as are the scapulae and the main pelvic bones. The figurine can be interpreted in a number of ways – as a woman turning into an ancestor, as a woman associated with death, or as death and life conjoined. Whatever the specific interpretation, this is a unique piece that extends our knowledge about the associations of female imagery.

As noted earlier, much of our evidence for similar lifestyles and diets and ways of treatment in burial for men and women comes from the lower and middle levels of the site (up to Level V). At the time of writing we have not excavated burials from the upper levels. But most of the art which shows clear gender differentiation occurs in Level V and above. I will argue in Chapter 11 that there were social changes that took place during the later occupation of the East Mound and that these changes included gender relations. In Chapter 8 I described an emphasis on prowess, animal spirits, hunting and feasting that can be identified at earlier sites like Göbekli and at Çatalhöyük. This social focus downplayed the role of agriculture and domestic, hearth-centred production. But in the upper levels of Çatalhöyük the increasing importance of the house and domestic and agricultural production led to gradual change. As part of these changes pottery becomes more central to domestic life and there is other evidence of specialization of domestic production (very large ovens for example). One component of these changes may have been that male and female roles diverged more than they had done. Perhaps we will find, when we look at the bones from skeletons now being excavated in the upper levels of the site, that male and female diets and ways of life had started to differentiate more clearly. But whatever the evidence proves to suggest, it seems at present that the changes occurred very slowly. The gender changes were brought about by infinitesimal changes in the way people cooked, made stone tools, made pottery, used houses and so on.

AGE

If gender differentiation is slight at Çatalhöyük, especially in the earlier levels, there is more evidence of age-related distinctions. In a society with minimal status differentiation, the role of elders must have been important in regulating social norms. In a society in which hunting wild animals was a central focus of social life, the role of fit and strong younger people must have been significant. In a society based on ancestry and the passing down of rites and rights within houses, age must have been an important consideration.

I have throughout this book emphasized the role of daily life within the house in transmitting social rules to the young. It was through the movement of the body around these highly differentiated spaces that one learnt the rules and roles of social categories of people and things. For the Tikopia, Firth describes the taboos

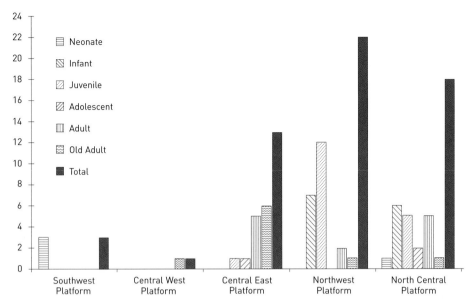

95 Distribution of ages of those buried beneath the different platforms in Building 1. There is a higher concentration of young people buried beneath the northwest platform than beneath the north central and central east platforms.

regarding how people should behave in front of relatives of various types. Children are taught they must not take things from above the head of an in-law. They are taught that certain behaviour will break decorum and cause real shame. 'Thus a command constantly given to young children in any company is "Nofo fakalaui," "Sit properly," that is for boys with legs neatly crossed, for girls with legs tucked away at the side or stretched straight out in front. Squatting, hunched-up or kneeling postures are not encouraged. A strong reason for this is that such positions are not proper' in the presence of certain types of relative.[16]

The best way for us to see whether different parts of the main rooms of the houses were associated with different ages of people is to examine the burial patterning. How old were the people buried under each platform? Our best evidence comes from Building 1 where the large sample size (62 burials) allows patterning to be explored. Theya Molleson and her colleagues have identified a clear pattern of age-related burial in Building 1 in relation to primary and secondary burial[17]. As discussed in Chapter 5, primary burial involves burial of the fleshed body in a grave. Secondary burial occurs when a body that has been buried or exposed elsewhere is dug up or obtained and reburied in a second grave. While primary burial occurs at all ages in Building 1, secondary burial is restricted to the north-central platform, and it is restricted to adolescents and adults. Young children or infants are not treated in this way. Amongst the primary burials, more younger people are buried under the northwest platform than are buried under the east-central platform (Figure 95).

As already noted, we have found what seem to be carbon residues on the insides of ribs that probably derive from the inhalation of smoke in smoke-filled houses. And certainly the plaster walls of the main rooms are usually soot-covered. The carbon residues on ribs occur only on older people and many older people have such residues.[18] This suggests an association between older people and indoor life in the houses. It is also of interest that the burials in the latest phases of use of Building 1 are mainly adults. It is perhaps their association with the house that needs to be dealt with at death by cleaning and rebuilding.

It may be the case at Çatalhöyük that status was largely attained with age, although we have seen above some evidence for cross-cutting differences based on inherited status and gender. But in fact, one of the most distinctive groups in society as far as burial is concerned seems to be children. And it may be the case that much of their special treatment is not related to status but to the development of ways of dealing with child mortality at a site in which domestic labour and lineal descent were increasingly important.

A high mortality rate for children is claimed by Theya Molleson and her colleagues in the human remains team.[19] While high child mortality seems likely in a packed 'town' of humans, animals and refuse, there is a need for caution as the large number of children found buried in houses may result from a cultural choice to bury children more commonly than adults in houses, as is the case in many cultures. We have seen that in Anatolia and the Middle East more widely, burial in houses is less common than at Çatalhöyük. There is little evidence elsewhere that all adults were buried in houses and we need to be careful about making such assumptions at Çatalhöyük, especially given the depictions in the art of the removal by vultures of the flesh of headless corpses – a practice for which there is no evidence on site. It is quite possible that large numbers of adults were buried off site, and calculations by Craig Cessford have shown that there are not enough adult burials at Çatalhöyük to account for the population of the site.[20] So the large numbers of children buried in buildings is more likely to be a cultural choice than an indication of high child mortality.

Any society like Çatalhöyük, in which domestic labour and lineal descent seem so important, is likely to place special importance on children. It is thus not surprising that so much attention is given to child burial. It is in such burials that large numbers of beads are often found. Burial baskets containing neonates are often made from a distinctive wild grass that is not used for other baskets. These baskets probably emphasize the floral aspects of the plant.[21] In several examples, burial of children is associated with shells and colouring. As we saw in Chapter 8, all this use of flowers, decoration and colouring could be read as indicating apotropaism. The ornaments and decoration may have 'protected' the child, or 'protected' the living from the associations of the child's death. It is also of interest that there is a link between the focus on younger burials beneath the northwest platform in Building 1 and the painting on walls around that platform. Again, the painting could be seen as 'protective'.[22]

Further study is needed on whether a distinct period of 'childhood' existed at Çatalhöyük, and at what age 'childhood' ended, although we have to be careful about our assumptions here as the concept of childhood as we know it today is a fairly recent phenomenon. Naomi Hamilton and Theya Molleson note that a number of different types of evidence converge to suggest late weaning for children.[23] Certainly, the stable isotope evidence suggests that weaning started as late as 18 months of age.[24]

The evidence discussed above would suggest that young children were treated differently, and certainly neonates and very young children stand out in the evidence. Neonates were buried in the foundations by an entry way into the main room in Building 1. In the South Area, neonates and very young children were occasionally buried near hearths and ovens in the 'dirty areas' of the main rooms, contravening the normative rules for burial. James Mellaart had found a young child burial in a brick in a house wall, and this could be interpreted as apotropaic. But it could also be interpreted in rather different terms. In 2004 a skeleton of a child was found in the infill in Space 227 in the 4040 Area in the North part of the mound. The bones suggested an age of rather less than 2. What was intriguing was the way the body had been stuffed into an overhang beneath a collapsing wall, in amongst building collapse and debris. This did not suggest a careful burial. Perhaps the burial was supposed to 'strengthen' the wall in some way so that future walls built on top would be secure. Perhaps it was not as casual as appeared. But whatever the precise interpretation it seems that a young child was again being treated in a distinctive way.

If very young people were clearly treated differently, it is also possible that some of the art can be interpreted in terms of the initiation of older children into adult life, although many stages of initiation may have been involved. The emphasis on baiting and teasing wild animals, and the evidence that heads, skulls, claws, skins and teeth of these animals were brought into the house and installed on walls, may relate to coming-of-age ceremonies and their memorialization in the fabric of the house. It may be the case that the status of older individuals was partly based on these objects and their histories, and that the handing down of these objects was part of the right of elders.

CONCLUSION

In earlier chapters (especially Chapters 2 and 7) I have described a society based not only on domestic production and feasting and exchange, but also on the control of knowledge. In these various realms or spheres, we might expect people of different ages to have taken different roles. In particular, the hunting and killing of wild bulls for feasts may have been both a gendered and an age-related activity. The focus on ancestry may have been age-related. But the overall focus on the control of knowledge (about where people and heads and obsidian are buried, about the significance of the art and myth, about the treatment of skulls) is likely to have favoured the role of elders, especially given the relative lack of other forms of status differentiation.[25] It is thus not remarkable that the major patterning we see at Çatalhöyük in terms of burial and other evidence is in terms of age-related distinctions. In particular, there are clear differences between younger and older people. Very young children are also treated very differently. A special concern about the death of very young children could be said to be the result of unhealthy conditions in a crowded 'town', but in fact we have little evidence of high degrees of poor health.[26] More likely the focus on young burial in the house is a cultural choice related to the social importance of domestic production (the need for labour in small house groups), lineage (the need for the transmission of rites and resources) and exchange ('marriage' of sons and daughters). The placing in the houses rather than outside, and the special relationship of young burials to the hearth/oven areas, indicate the association between the very young and the hearth and separate this sphere from the northerly area of the house associated with ancestry and art. Perhaps children were not treated as full persons until they had reached a certain age when they could be expected to survive and become part of the ancestral lines.

All this focus on young children and their loss might be thought to suggest a particular role for mothering.[27] But in fact there are few, if any, clear depictions of women caring for, holding, or nursing children. Such images do occur later in Anatolia, for example at Hacılar.[28] But despite the widespread use of the term 'Mother Goddess' in relation to the clay statuette shown in Plate 24, there is very little evidence that mothering was central to symbolic life, and there is really nothing in the lump of clay between the legs of this seated woman to suggest that it is the head of a baby being born, as Mellaart had claimed.[29] There are no clear images of birthing in the representational repertoire. In fact, as we have seen in this chapter, we have little evidence of distinct roles for men and women throughout the early and middle occupation of the site. There is little evidence that gender was of central importance in assigning social roles. Of course men and women must have carried out some different roles, and probably dressed differently. But there is little evidence that such differences meant that one gender was privileged above the other in terms of the transmission of rites and resources or in terms of social status and lifestyle.

In the uppermost levels of the site, however, gender relations may have become more demarcated as part of wider changes in society at that time. Men and women may increasingly have become associated with specialist tasks and spheres. I will explore these changes more fully in Chapter II.

CHAPTER TEN

Selfhood and Individuality

No two leopards are alike, either in the markings or the ground colour.[1] The rosettes on the body take an infinite variety of forms. The markings on the bodies of the Çatalhöyük reliefs mirror this diversity with spots, rosettes, crosses and various other markings. On the other hand at Çatalhöyük the leopard is often used to represent balance or pairing, and large numbers of leopard skins occur in the animal teasing and hunting scenes. A tension surrounding balance and control is best seen in the tail of the leopard. The tail is a balancing instrument, especially when the leopard is leaping, swerving or changing direction. The tail is also indicative of the mood of an individual leopard – it is highly expressive.[2] For example, a gentle beating of the tail is a sign of tension, irritation or excitement. What was the relationship between the individual and the group at Çatalhöyük? Was there a strongly developed sense of self? We cannot assume a priori that people at Çatalhöyük saw themselves as we do – as atomized individuals with agency. How did they see themselves and their personhood?

The notion that the origins of agriculture see the origins of private property goes back to Engels and Rousseau, and to a long tradition of Western thought.[3] I have argued throughout this book that by the time of Çatalhöyük individual houses were the focus of social life and have pointed to the fact that each house had its own walls and its own storage, and much production and exchange occurred at the domestic scale. But does all this evidence of house-based property and activity have any relationship to the sense of individual self? Is it the case that we can identify a greater sense of the individual self emerging at Çatalhöyük in contrast to the emphasis on collectivities that is presumed to exist earlier?[4] A number of archaeologists, such as Chris Fowler in his work on the Neolithic of Britain, now argue that personhood in the Neolithic was less whole, more divided and more continuous with the surrounding object world than in modern Western thought.[5] How were the individual and the self construed at Çatalhöyük?

INDIVIDUAL LIVES

We have had some success in charting the lives of individuals that lived at Çatalhöyük 9,000 years ago. As already noted (Chapter 6), Building 1 was found directly over Building 5 in the North part of the site. Dating of this sequence is based on high-precision (AMS) radiocarbon determinations on a large number of samples, and on the numbers of replasterings of the walls in the main rooms. There is general evidence for the length of use of buildings from the correlations that have been identified from AMS dating, dendrochronology and replastering sequences.[6] In the site as a whole, buildings were occupied for an average of 45 to 90 years. The main North Area excavation sequence (Buildings 5 and 1) spans a period of decades and probably represents a period of just over a century. The

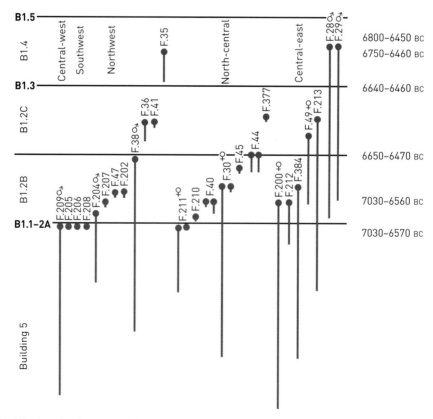

96 Life duration for some of those buried in Building 1 in relation to the phases of Buildings 1 and 5.

excavated and unexcavated phases of Building 5 show that it was occupied for probably over half a century and perhaps around 70 years. Both buildings underwent numerous phases of occupation during this period (excavation of the earlier phases of occupation of Building 5 has not been completed as the building has been put on long-term display).

But what of the people who lived in or knew these buildings during their occupation? About 62 people were buried overall in the several phases of Building 1. By using their approximate ages at death, and by noting their phase of burial, it has been possible for Craig Cessford to work out how many of them would have been alive at different times in the use of the building (Figure 96 and see Figure 44).[7] In the description that follows I make extensive use of the report by Craig Cessford on the excavations of Buildings 5 and 1.[8]

From Figure 96 we can see that individual 'A' (2529) in grave F.209, buried during the earlier phases of Building 1, was probably alive for most, if not all, the lifespan of Building 5. In addition, individual 'B' (1378) in burial F.28 may well have been alive for

the entire lifespan of Building 1, and he and individual 'C' (1466) in burial F.29 were certainly alive for most of it. I want therefore to look at these three individuals more closely.

The burial of 'A' (Figure 97) occurred in the central-western part of Space 71. It proved difficult to be certain about the precise point when 'A' was deposited, but it was almost certainly in Subphase B1.1B. The latter represents a series of infilling events plus wall construction after Building 5 and before Building 1 – a sort of liminal in-between time. The body was a crouched, articulated old adult male, bound with much textile strapping/tape (to judge from the phytoliths found). The femur heads had been pulled out of their sockets by the flexion, suggesting that the binding was very tight. The inside surfaces of the upper ribs had dark soot-type black staining. The sexing of this individual was quite difficult since the post-cranial bones are gracile and very light owing to osteoporosis. The left

97 Burial 'A' (F.209) from Space 71 in Building 1. 'A' was an elderly male who was alive for most, if not all, the lifespan of Building 5.

humerus had a bowed appearance caused by the strong development of the triceps muscle insertion, which suggests the arm lifted heavy weights. The hand bones had marked ridges along the length of both proximal and medial phalanges, character- istic of a task that required a strong gripping action. The femora showed strong gluteal attachment areas, which may indicate some form of squatting was usual. The teeth had an unusual amount of calculus (tartar) for this population, implying a change in diet or mouth acidity in the months before death, although we cannot say what these changes were. A fragment of textile was found next to and parallel to the lower legs.

Several decades later, towards the end of the occupation of Building I, in Phase BI.4, two burials (F.28 and F.29) were placed in a small room (Space 110) which had earlier been the main eastern platform. These burials, which are the last in the building, contained individuals 'B' and 'C' respectively.

The burial of 'B' (Figure 98) occurred in the northeastern corner of the space. The tightly flexed primary complete articulated skeleton of an old man (1378) was placed in the grave in a crouched position lying on its left side with its head to the west. The burial was tightly packed into the burial cut, with the right foot and scapula forced into unnatural positions. A white fibrous material which was laid down in lines both vertically and horizontally was found and, in combination with the tight packing of the bones, this suggests the body was wrapped. The upper ribs and vertebrae had a black amorphous carbon substance coating their internal surfaces indicating carbon-related anthracosis, due to inhalation from open fires in poorly ventilated areas. The skeleton showed remarkably few signs

98 Burial 'B' (F.28) in Building 1. Like 'A', 'B' was an old man; he would have witnessed many of the burials and changes in Building 1 that occurred over its lifetime.

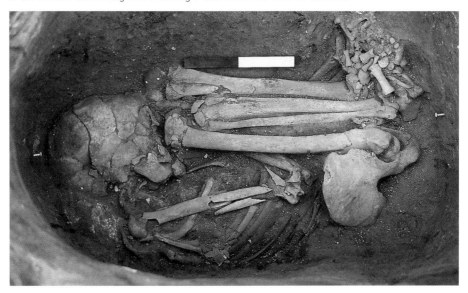

of degenerative change except to the hands. Extensive and extreme osteoarthritic changes to the wrist and finger bones are long standing and probably due to repeated minor trauma associated with some habitual activity. The first sacral vertebra also shows degenerative changes, which may have an infective element. There is a healed parry fracture of the left ulna that is more than two years old, perhaps sustained when the arm was raised to ward off a blow to the face. Morphological features of the leg bones indicate the habitual adoption from childhood of a squatting position with the heels off the ground and the thighs as widely splayed as possible.

The burial of 'C' (Figure 99) occurred in a more central part of the small room. The articulated primary skeleton (1466) of a mature adult man lacking a skull was lying on its side. Some disarticulated skeletal elements were also found. The body

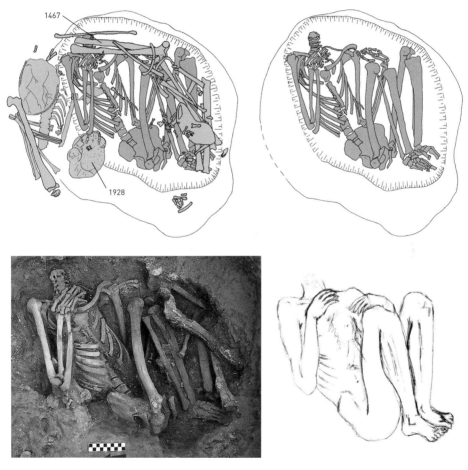

99 Burial 'C' (F.29) in Building 1. Disarticulated skeletal elements (above left) covered this mature male's headless but otherwise articulated skeleton. It seems likely that the head was removed at some point after the initial burial.

was probably placed in the grave and then the head removed prior to infilling. There must have been some time between death and interment to allow initial decay to take place. Part of the axis vertebra, which is relatively robust, is not present. There are no traces of cut marks on the vertebrae from the head removal, but there is a single chop mark on a fragment of possibly human bone found when cleaning the skeleton in the laboratory. The cut associated with this is likely to have been made by a heavy-duty chopping implement used during head removal, either a large piece of obsidian similar to those discovered in hoards or a ground-stone axe. The upper body of 'C' was twisted on to its back, and the skull must have been pressed forwards onto the chest because of the skeleton's position close to the edge of the burial cut. In this position the chop mark must have been made while the skull was in place to gain access to the ventral side of the vertebral column. Asymmetry of the vertebrae suggests the carrying of heavy weights from an early age. Unlike other mature adults there were no traces of black sooting on the ribs of this individual.

The burial of 'C' disturbed various earlier burials; the disarticulated and possibly burnt bones of a male adolescent (1467) were lying around the edges of the grave. It is likely the initial burial of this individual occurred during phase B1.2 in this building. There was also the skull of an old individual (1928) in the northwest part of the grave under the right elbow of 'C'; both these elements appear deliberately placed. As the old individual (1928) is solely represented by a skull this raises the possibility that this is not a disturbed earlier burial, but a skull that was used in some way. The lack of use-related polish argues against this, but might indicate that the skull was not handled often. The deliberate placement of a skull (1928) in a burial where 'C' had his head removed at some stage is an interesting phenomenon. Was there some form of changeover between skulls?

The radiocarbon determinations are not capable of separating the two individuals 'B' and 'C', but suggest that 'B' is marginally more likely to be the later of the two (53.8 per cent probability versus 45.2 per cent). 'B' is also older, possibly as old as the structure itself, and is in a location that may have been in some sense reserved for him as there were no earlier burials here, which may indicate that he was the more significant individual. Stable isotope analysis indicated that cattle may have been a more important part of the diet for 'B' and 'C' than for most other individuals in Building 1. It is reasonable to suggest that these two had a special status, at least within this small house group. We know that consumption of cattle had a special link to feasting. We also know from the art that removal of heads had a special significance. And the two burials occur in the area of the main room that was initially the highest and most clearly demarcated platform, and then became its own room (Space 110).

Taking these three individuals ('A', 'B' and 'C'), we can say that their lives spanned the period of use of Buildings 5 and 1. We can say quite a bit about their lives from the skeletal evidence. However, we cannot assume that these people would have 'lived' in any simple sense in these buildings even if they were buried in them. More people were buried in Building 1 than could have lived in it directly; and those buried in the buildings could have married into this social group from outside. So we cannot say with certainty that they would have seen or known about or been involved in making all the architectural changes that the buildings went through. But there is a good probability that they did.

So we can say that individual 'A' would probably have known about the way that Building 5 was arranged (Figures 42 and 43). He had probably passed down the stairs above the oven on the south wall. It was probably this oven that produced the soot that filled his lungs. It was probably on these floors that he used to squat. Individuals 'B' and 'C' would likely have seen many of the changes that took place in Building 1 (Figure 44). They would probably have seen the first oven in the main room, located in much the same place as the one known by 'A' in Building 5. As children they could have known several people, including the old woman buried in grave F.200, who in turn would have known individual 'A' (see Figure 96). They would have seen the main occupation phase (what we call Subphase B1.2B) with many burials placed under the northwest platform. In their lives they would have seen the oven moved into the small side room, would have witnessed the wall paintings and reliefs (Figures 59 and 83). They would have known about the demolition and burning of the southern part of the building, and the remodelling and reoccupation of the northern part. Individual 'C' had spent less time indoors, and he probably knew that he would have his head removed and kept after death (see Chapter 6). He himself may have been buried with a skull that he retained from an earlier ancestor and may have had a special role in relation to ancestry. Perhaps he arranged the burial rituals in the house, organized the bringing in of skeletons that had been initially buried elsewhere and reburied them under the north-central platform, and even did the paintings around the northwest platform. Both he and 'B' may have been especially involved in feasting (seen in their isotope values) and in making feasting deposits. They may have first encountered feasts when the southwestern platform in the main room of Building 1 was used for a feasting deposit in their youth, in Subphase B1.2B.

REMEMBERING INDIVIDUAL LIVES

So we can use archaeological evidence to say something about the lifestyles of particular prehistoric individuals. But how were such individuals perceived and identified? A key point here is memory. To what extent were the acts of individuals woven together in accounts that constructed memories of individual lives? In archaeology we can at least explore this question in relation to death. To what extent were individual people remembered and memorialized after their death?

Were ancestors remembered in general, or were specific ancestors remembered? How much of the individual was there in the concept of ancestry? There is of course, throughout the Middle East and Anatolia in the 9th and 8th millennia BC (roughly equivalent to the PPNB in the Levant) much evidence of skull cults and ancestor rituals. Some of these, such as at Çayönü, are clearly collective cults, with large groups of skulls involved. The purpose of disarticulating and mixing bones at such sites seems to be to assert the collective over the individual memory (as has been argued for the Neolithic in Britain[9]).

But I argued in Chapter 6 that there is good evidence to suggest that at Çatalhöyük individual lives were remembered. It is difficult to say how individualized the 'portrait' of the plastered skull in Figure 7 is. The face is finely executed, showing the details of nostrils for example. And the nose is very distinctive in shape, although there has been some movement due to the pressure of the earth in the grave and disturbance by an animal burrow. I argued in Chapter 6 that the individual deposition of skulls indicates that individual skulls and people were remembered.

The nature of the skull removal at Çatalhöyük suggests that memories were retained of the exact locations of particular skulls beneath the floors. Whole bodies were not disturbed – only the skull was located and cut off. Skull removal is shown in the wall art (headless bodies with vultures, such as Figure 22) and there is some evidence that those from whom heads were removed were buried originally with special rites. All this suggests that not just any skull was retrieved – but that the skulls of particular remembered individuals were retrieved. After retrieval, the skulls were used as part of foundation and abandonment rituals, and may have been in circulation for some time.

None of this is of course conclusive, but it does intimate that specific memories of individuals were constructed, at least after death. In general terms, people were buried whole in individual graves at Çatalhöyük, rather than having secondary, disarticulated and collective burial as in the tombs of northwest Europe. The emphasis on individual memory construction at Çatalhöyük is contextual. Figurines and their depicted clothes and hairstyles (small as the samples of the latter are) show little evidence of individualized features. In Chapter 8 I argued that the function of many of the figurines at Çatalhöyük is less to do with death than with protection and apotropaism. In the latter contexts there is little need for a focus on representing individuals, but this does not mean that in other contexts, such as death and social memory, individuals were not identified.

The process of memorializing individual houses was discussed in Chapter 5. On the whole, each house has different brick composition, suggesting individualized house construction activities. There is evidence for a largely domestic mode of production for lithics and food preparation and storage. There is much evidence, summarized in Chapters 5 and 6, that houses were built on top of each other in such an exact way, replicating earlier arrangements of space so closely, that memories can be seen as constructed of individual house histories.[10] The 'art' found in a house sometimes replicates that found in an earlier house beneath it. There is evidence of people digging down from later phases to retrieve sculpture from walls of earlier buildings beneath – with such precision that memories of specific individual houses must have been retained. Such evidence refers to house 'inhabitants' (of say 3 to 10 people) rather than to individuals themselves. But it nevertheless suggests a context in which individualized memories could have been constructed.

The Self and Body Boundaries

The emphasis on socialization within the house, as discussed in Chapter 5, could indicate that individuals did not have a strong sense of separate atomized selves.[11] People were probably closely allied to family, lineage and to the materiality of the house.[12] Their life cycles and those of houses were closely tied. Identity was closely tied to ancestors and to social memory. While people may have increasingly had a sense of an individualized self, perhaps as part of the emergence of 'private' storage and property, at the same time they were increasingly being highly socialized into group norms. I argue that this socialization both produced a very regulated social person that was embedded within the house, was almost part of its fabric, and it also produced a partitioning and a greater sense of bodily boundaries.

In Chapter 5 I showed how the internal arrangements of the house are very structured. There are often two or more rooms, but it is the central room which is most clearly divided up into small segments by the use of platforms, ridges, benches and pedestals. In fact, moving around these rooms as we dig them forces one to be especially careful where one moves and steps. There are bulls' horns sticking out from benches and walls, and the ridges between platforms are often fragile. Of course, with familiarity one moves around more easily – but that is the point, that one's bodily movement is channelled by the physical space so that it becomes habituated.

These structured practices as people went about their daily lives were repeated over decades, centuries and even millennia. While there are examples of shifts through time, the repeated plasterings of the walls and floors are remarkably consistent. The same platforms and types of use of space tend to be repeated over enormous expanses of time in some houses. This again suggests a strong emphasis on using movement around space in socialization. As the body moved around space it repeated earlier practices, and became social in the process.

It is important to note that there is evidence that the spatial segmentation of practices had social meaning. Where sufficient numbers of burials have been found in houses, it has been possible to identify tendencies for different social categories to be buried beneath different platforms (see Chapter 9). It seems likely that these distinctions made at burial related in some way to distinctions in life – regarding who could eat, sleep or carry out activities on different platforms.

So as a child grew up in these houses it would learn that certain things could be done here but not there, that some people could sit there but not here, and that movement around space mirrored and created social distinctions. Indeed, it might be argued that social roles may have been thoroughly embedded in the uses of the house, in the fabric of its platforms and ridges. I have also pointed out that the 'art' in the buildings is related to the structural and practical distinctions. It occurs in specific places and in specific relationships to platforms and activities and burials. So symbolic and mythical representations are also linked into the fabric of the house and into the social distinctions found there.

It would thus be possible to argue that there was little sense of individual self at Çatalhöyük because the self was so thoroughly embedded in plasters and platforms and spatially located activities and symbolic references. The self formed in the practices and relationships of the house, entirely embedded within the social and indistinguishable from it. And yet on the other hand the processes I have been describing also produce a partitioning and a greater sense of difference as the practices are carried out. The individualized self does emerge as identified in its difference from others, and from the very emphasis on boundaries themselves – the ridges, edges, pedestals, and the distinctions in symbolism, burial and activity. This is a social process that creates individual difference.

One further way in which we can explore this idea is in relation to bodily functions – of which archaeologists have special ability to monitor defecations preserved as coprolites. There is a possibility that the northeast corner room in Building 1 was used as a latrine,[13] perhaps laid with straw and periodically cleaned out. But until recently we did not know where defecation was cleaned out to. Recent chemical analysis of the bile acids in coprolites in the midden areas around and between houses has shown that they include human markers.[14] The careful cleaning of the spotless floors inside the houses, and the cleaning out of faecal material contrasts with the dense concentrations of hearth and floor sweepings, butchery debris, and human excretions immediately outside. Presumably the faecal material in the house was swept up, taken up the stairs onto the roof, and discarded on a nearby midden. Such practices draw attention to the physical boundaries of self. The daily toing and froing of bodily excretions perhaps draws attention to body boundaries and to the boundaries of an individual self.

There is other evidence to support this idea that there was a distinct or emerging sense of self as individualized at Çatalhöyük. In her account of the bone tools from the site, Nerissa Russell describes the occurrence of whole pendants in burials.[15] She shows that they were at least sometimes worn around the neck. Together with their variability of form, this suggests that the pendants were a part of personal identities. Russell also notes the striking frequency of repair of these items in contrast to other bone artifacts. There is evidence of use after repair, and in some cases pendants that had lost their perforation and could no longer be worn were kept, perhaps as amulets. All this suggests that the pendants were linked to individual and shorter-term memories, and that they would have been associated with and formed a sense of individual self.

Possible evidence of a stronger sense of self is provided by the obsidian mirrors (Figures 101 and 102). Experimental work by Jim Vedder has shown that these do not function well as signalling devices, and would not be useful to start fires, but that they do reflect images well.[16] They may have been used to 'see' and 'divine' the spirit world, but it is tempting to suggest that, whatever their specific function, they could have been used to look at one's own body. There is a new technology of the body seen in a set of equipment related to bodily decoration (grinding stones used to grind ochre, and shells containing ochre associated with a small spatula in graves, although we cannot be sure these were used for body painting, and they often occur in graves with children so they may have had more of an apotropaic function – see below). Some of the skulls have red paint that may parallel painting of the face in life, and the plastered skull in Figure 7 was replastered and painted red at least three times. We know from the figurines that people had elaborate hair styles and hat styles (although as noted above the figurines themselves do not seem highly individualized). All this attention to facial and bodily presentation fits well with a focus on individual self image.

I have for some time been intrigued by what was put in graves and what was not. Right at the start of this book I pointed to patterning in the way that pots and clay figurines were not put in graves. At least part of the explanation for these distinctions might be the separation of spheres discussed in Chapter 2, in particular the separation of domestic production from ancestry. But another way of looking at the patterning is in terms of closeness to the body. The main things that we find in burials are items of bodily adornment or bodily preparation. It is in burials that we find boar tusk necklaces, belt hooks (Figure 100), huge numbers of beads from

100 A finely crafted bone belt hook and fastener.

101, 102 A number of obsidian mirrors have been found at Çatalhöyük, including this fine example (left) which has a plaster backing. The final stages of the polishing process are reconstructed above. Experimental work along with some unfinished examples found at the site give some clues to the manufacturing process.

necklaces, pendants, finger rings (in some cases still on the fingers) and bracelets (often still on the arm). We find obsidian mirrors and bits of cloth from clothing and binding. It is true that we also sometimes find baskets in which bodies are placed, and we sometimes find obsidian points and tools – but at least in some cases the obsidian is closely associated with the skeleton as if it was tied to the leg or placed on the back or shoulder. So people were mainly buried with material which is closely associated with the bodies and skin – things which were close to them. What seems rare or absent from burials is material that was less close but might have been thought to be part of what one owned – things like pots and figurines. The sense of self does not extend out very far – it seems to be close in.

I argue, therefore, that people at Çatalhöyük were very strongly and immediately socialized into rules and roles, and that their sense of self was primarily associated with the house and its members and social categories. But as part of this process, some sense of individual self, and the construction of individual bodily boundaries became more marked. This sense of self did not extend out very far into the world – that was still largely dominated by a strong corporate ethic. But yet the seeds of individual selves were being sown.

In fact, there is some evidence that this process of individuation increases through time in the upper levels of the site. My impression, although not yet backed up with empirical evidence, is that there is more adornment of burials in the upper levels. The stamp seals from the site are not well understood as to function, but the most likely explanation is that they were used in some way to identify individuals – either by stamping cloth and clothes or by stamping bodies.[17] Stamp seals become common in the upper levels of the site (especially from Level V onwards), and again they are found in burials, supporting the notion that burial goods concentrate on things close to the body.

CONCLUSION

I argue that there is enough evidence from Çatalhöyük to suggest that an important locus of socialization (there were undoubtedly others) was the house, and that the sense of self that resulted must have been formed to some degree by the regulating of the body in the practices of the house. But within, and as part of this social self, there were practices that distinguished individual selves within the house group.

The individual identity of the house was formed in many ways – through the use of memory, burial, use of different types of brick and so on. But within this strong overarching formation of bodies and selves, individual histories were woven. Particular individuals might have been seen as representing the whole, but nevertheless, individual selves came to be discerned, at least in some domains.

This evidence of an emphasis on individual houses and individual persons (constituted in distinct practices and memories) can be seen as located at a particular historical moment. Although there is much work that needs to be done, the emphasis on individuals can be seen as part of a larger process in which storage and ownership were increasing. Other factors too play a role. The Neolithic involves holding groups together over longer periods, in order to protect a joint investment in land and crops and animals. There is a potential for dispute over rights to shared resources. So the self in relation to the whole becomes of concern. Longer-term systems also imply longer memories. As we have seen, memory construction seems central to the constitution of individual house units and individual selves. Individual bodies may have become more central to alliance building through ancestry and the exchange of sons and daughters. Individuals were thus increasingly produced as part of the changing social whole. Through time, in the upper levels of the site, there is more specialization of production, and so again individuation is encouraged. Houses become more self-sufficient and internally differentiated. All this produces atomization.

Overall, we see at Çatalhöyük a tension between the individual and the group, seen most clearly in the standardization of house layout, while at the same time each house is slightly different in its internal arrangement. Burial too follows certain rules, but on the other hand each burial is different in the way that the body is laid out and accoutrements added. As part of this general tension, there is an increasing sense of contradiction between self and society. People were buried with personal accoutrements well back into the Palaeolithic, but the self was probably closely tied to giving, sharing and reciprocity. As accumulation and history increased in importance, so too the tensions of self in relation to society increased. This productive set of interactions moved forward incrementally, by infinitesimal steps. It is this movement that will be the subject of the final chapter.

CHAPTER ELEVEN

Changing Material Entanglements, and the 'Origins of Agriculture'

This chapter is about change – both at Çatalhöyük itself and over the longer term in Anatolia and the Middle East. Figure 103 shows a clay stamp seal, probably used for stamping designs on cloth or skin, that we discovered in the 4040 Area of the North hill of the East Mound in 2003. Stamp seals at Çatalhöyük almost always show geometric designs, although some are in the shape of hands.[1] But this particular example almost certainly depicts a leopard. The tail rests on the back, and the head and front legs have been broken off. This example could take us back to the question of individual selves that was explored in the last chapter: the stamp can be used to make a print, and it is sometimes in the shape of a hand print, and the markings on a leopard also have an individual imprint.

103 The front face of a stamp seal in the form of a leopard from the 4040 Area.

However, it is a related but rather different point that I wish to make with regard to the leopard stamp seal. The pairings of leopard reliefs that we have previously explored occur in Levels VIII, VII and VIB. But the stamp seals as a whole are found mainly in Levels V and above. In his research on the stamp seals as part of the Çatalhöyük team, Ali Türkcan has convincingly argued that the designs used on the stamp seals in the upper levels of the site derive from those used throughout the sequence on the wall paintings.[2] There is a shift here from wall art to include mobiliary art (that is, art on movable objects). Throughout this book I have been describing the Neolithic East Mound. But on the other side of the river by which the East Mound sat, there grew up another mound during the following Chalcolithic period (in the late 7th and 6th millennia BC). This later West Mound had no figurative wall paintings or reliefs as far as we can discern,[3] but it did have elaborately painted pottery (unlike the unpainted pottery on the earlier Neolithic East Mound). Jonathan Last, who has studied the pottery from both mounds, argues that the focus of decoration shifted from house walls to pottery, often with the same motifs in use. What has changed here? Why this shift from wall to mobiliary art (the stamp seals and pottery decoration)? And why the shift to a greater emphasis on marking individual difference?

SMALL THINGS AND THE SLOW MOVEMENT OF THE MASS

In this book, I have been describing a world in which little things are important. I do not just refer here to the miniaturization that one sees in the figurines, although that is an aspect of what I mean. And I do not just refer to the careful attention to cleaning up every speck of dirt on house floors, although that too is part of it. Rather I mean that little acts are part of and can have an impact on a totality. There was a great attention to detail as society reproduced itself through the practices of daily life.

I have described the way in which people lived their lives at Çatalhöyük, and I have tried to discuss some of their basic orientations and perspectives. I have tried to build up from small daily acts to see how their world was organized and embodied. I have said something of change through time in many of the chapters, but in this chapter I want to take a broader view and look backwards and forwards in time from Çatalhöyük in order to identify longer-term trends. I want to look back into the Palaeolithic to show how slowly and gradually things changed – the slow emergence of sedentary life, the slow appearance of greater intervention in the environment and of non-reciprocal relationships between people and things. I will look back to the earlier Neolithic and the amazing new sites that have emerged in Anatolia and the Middle East such as Göbekli Tepe, Nevali Çori, Çayönü and Aşıklı Höyük, to show how storage, burial, the centrality of the house and the changed relationship with the past gradually emerged by slow small changes in everyday activities. The 'origins of agriculture' and settled life are seen as nowhere but also everywhere, distributed in countless small changes that make agriculture and settled life possible – new senses of time, place, self and identity.

THE RISE OF THE PROWESS-ANIMAL
SPIRIT-HUNTING-FEASTING NETWORK

The shifts that included cultivation, herding and settled life started emerging thousands of years before Çatalhöyük, and the processes continued on after it, but the detailed evidence from the site does allow a perspective on these larger and longer-term changes. In the preceding chapters I have described a tension that seems to dominate the evidence from Çatalhöyük. On the one hand much of the evidence seems to be related to a network of symbolism and social practices linked to hunting and baiting wild animals, as well as to feasting, ancestry, death and exchange. On the other hand there is the sphere of domestic production. Both are brought together in the house, and they seem interdependent. And yet there is a tension between them. It is this tension that produces the avoidances and distinctions that made up the puzzle with which this book began. It is this tension that places wild animals and the sharp dangerous parts of wild animals and birds in the art, but not domesticated sheep. It is presumably this tension that keeps leopard bones from being brought on site – especially since the leopard was probably not perceived as a useful feasting animal (since difficult to obtain and with a relatively small amount of meat when compared to a wild bull[4]). It is the same tension that focuses decoration in the north parts of houses where burial occurs, and which keeps southern oven areas of houses undecorated. And so on.

I have already pointed out (Chapter 8) that the network of practices involved in the prowess-animal spirit-hunting-feasting social network emerges very early in archaeological sequences in Europe and the Middle East. From the earliest sites in the PPNA, there is evidence of cattle head and horn placements,[5] feasting at a wide range of sites, wild cat and other animal symbolism,[6] and symbolism of raptors and vultures.[7] Much of this symbolism emerges in the context of large elaborate ritual centres such as Göbekli,[8] and the ritual buildings at other PPNA and early Aceramic sites (see Chapter 5). It is even possible that one route to settled village life was the participation in ritual events and feasting. There is investment in public works, as at Jericho. Nigel Goring-Morris and Anna Belfer-Cohen show that in the Levant early Natufian architecture includes large structures, including those with plastered benches and slabs at Eynan.[9] A large incised monolith was found in the early Natufian site of Wadi Hammeh 27 in the Jordan Valley. A monolith was also found at the late Natufian site of Rosh Zin in the central Negev, and a large solitary structure was constructed of massive slabs at the late Natufian site of Rosh Horesha.[10] The size of these structures and monoliths, certainly by the time of the late 10th millennium BC at Göbekli, suggests some public participation beyond the individual household. We can argue that the first agglomerations of people were closely linked to the sociality of public ceremony, feasting, prestige, status. Similar arguments were earlier made by Barbara Bender and Brian Hayden,[11] and it is now clear that a central component of the process is that people came together for ceremonies and rituals, and to control the alliances that were set up through them (as was argued in Chapter 4).

This emerging picture of the growth of settled village life is very different from what we have been used to. There has long been an assumption that we should be able to see an evolutionary sequence that progresses from primitive hunter-gatherer windbreaks, to shelters and houses, to the more settled rectangular architecture of early farming villages, and then on to the palaces and temples of urban civilizations in the Middle East.[12] What we now see instead is the early emergence of collective ritual, large-scale investment in ritual centres, feasting and prowess/display.

I should emphasize that I do not argue that feasting and public ceremony began with settled life. They began earlier and I would suggest that they gradually increased in scale towards the Neolithic. Indeed, I suggest that it was this slow process that was one factor underpinning the drive to sedentism. By the time of the first settled villages in the Middle East, the process had reached a scale that became clearly visible archaeologically.

So a prime motivation for forming early settled agglomerations may have been public ritual, feasting and exchange and the control of social and economic relations that such public ceremonials allowed. The focus is on the collective and the communal. Houses, on the other hand, are initially often relatively unelaborated with few internal divisions. And yet the engagement in longer-term agglomerations must have involved much more than just the ascendance of the prowess-animal spirit-hunting-feasting network. It also involved shifts in daily practice and in the ways people lived their daily lives. I will argue below that the shifts in the ways people lived their lives, including their construction of houses, were part of a long-term process of slow gradual change that made the adoption of public ceremony possible.

In exploring this notion of a long-term process of change in small daily practices I will return to many of the themes I have visited in this book. An underlying process is that of material and social entanglement. But in more specific terms I will talk of processes of bodily constraint and restriction in the use of space in houses, and I will return to the idea that this was associated with an increased sense of self. I will also return to the idea that by objectifying the social world so clearly in house walls, platform edges, baskets and muds, the sense of human agency, paradoxically, increased. By crafting community it became more possible to change it. I will talk about shifts towards a sense of history linked to relationships with the dead placed beneath floors. I will return also to the ways in which material objects were increasingly engaged as delegates in the spirit world. But all these transformations in practice and orientation emerged very slowly and not all at once. They emerged through infinitesimal moves in daily life and daily practices.

The Example of the Enlightenment

To get a sense of what I mean by the slow movement of the mass and the importance of small daily shifts leading to major fault-line change, we can look at some approaches to the major shifts we call the Enlightenment and the Industrial

Revolution. Central to these were events such as the French Revolution. There were also major reformulations of economic and social relations, transformations of elites, the emergence of a strong middle class, the emergence of greater roles for civil society and so on. But many people now argue that there were underlying changes in the ways people behaved in daily lives. We have already seen some of this when talking of Norbert Elias and Michel Foucault in Chapter I.

It is perhaps archaeologists who are best placed to explore how major change is embedded within small shifts in daily practice. Historical archaeologists have for some time been making the point – that major social and political change is embedded within, and may be presaged by, the many small acts of the mass. James Deetz, in his book *In Small Things Forgotten*,[13] provided one of the most telling examples for the 18th century in North America. He showed how changes in the way people threw away rubbish, buried their dead, built their houses, ate from plates all led to the greater individualism which we might see as the defining characteristic of the Enlightenment. For example, people started throwing their rubbish not in collective spreads but in individual pits, and rather than eating from communal plates they had sets of plates so that each person could eat from her or his own plate.

An even longer set of shifts in daily practices leading up to the major upheavals of the 18th and 19th centuries is provided by Matthew Johnson in his book on the *Archaeology of Capitalism*.[14] In this he shows that many of the changes we associate with the Enlightenment and the Industrial Revolution, in particular the shift to a greater sense of private property and individual rights, can be seen to emerge over the very long term. He shows how for centuries, rural houses had being going through a process of division of communal space (the 'hall' in the house) into separate rooms and private places. Similarly, one can explore the way that over the same period land was increasingly divided and enclosed – even spaces within churches went through comparable shifts. In these ways, people's daily lives changed towards greater privacy, seclusion, and individual property. In these small shifts over many centuries, society was being prepared for, or was moving towards, the great political changes that so mark our history books.

Material Entanglements

As noted above, I have been describing in this book a world of small things, a world in which great attention was paid to the details of daily life and to the minutiae of material matters. I now want to argue that we can apply what we have learned at Çatalhöyük to a wider discussion of a changing relationship with material things that occurs very widely in the Middle East after the end of the Ice Age. This changing relationship with things is the slow process that lies behind the shifts we call the emergence of village life, agriculture and social inequality.

In many small-scale hunter-gatherer societies, humans have a view of themselves as involved in immediate short-term relationships with the environment, with other people, and with the gods and spirits.[15] For example, after killing an animal a sacrifice may be made to thank the spirits of the woods, the food may be shared, but long-term commitments are not involved. The emphasis is on giving, sharing and immediate reciprocity. People are minimally entangled with each other and with things. This system has long-term evolutionary advantages because it is flexible and small scale. It is presumably some version of this system that dominated the early millennia of human existence.

At the other end of the scale, I have throughout this book pointed to the numerous long-term entanglements that people were involved in at Çatalhöyük. Every act seems to have entailed social and material commitments and dependencies.[16] There is a greater involvement of people and society with durable materials, and these involvements with durable materials lead to further social entanglements. I have shown how an emerging sense of history is linked to the retrieval and curation of material 'documents' such as human skulls and animal installation art (Chapter 6). The central notion of revelation involved in such practices extends to the retrieval of other cached material objects such as obsidian (Chapter 7). Material objects are also central to the ability of people to affect the spirit world and the ancestors as seen in the use of paintings and figurines (Chapter 8). A sense of self is constructed from objects, using a material technology of the body (Chapter 10). In Chapters 3 and 4 we saw how social relations are embedded in the landscape, in exchange patterns, and in the layout of the 'town'. Above all, in Chapter 5, we saw how the social world is embedded within the house, in its platforms, edges and ridges, in its mats, and in the types of containers placed on the floors. Every small act in the house had some relevance for socialization and social structure and social change.

We saw how living for a long time in a dense mud-brick agglomeration led to slumping house walls and so to the need to rebuild. In more general terms, the material entanglement led to greater labour investment and further social collaboration – as we also have seen with issues of drainage, sewage and discard. Switching to cooking with pottery involves needs for new types of temper and new, possibly more specialized productive technologies – and thus new social investments. What evidence we have for social centralization and specialization involves investments in materials such as pottery and obsidian and figurines.

So what we have seen at Çatalhöyük is a social world heavily engaging with durable materials as part of the social process. But as it does so, it becomes yet more dependent on long-term social commitments. This is what I mean by entanglement: that increased investment in materials also increases social commitments. Perhaps the clearest example I have used involves the plastering of house walls and floors. Just the simple act of plastering a wall involves access to quarry sites, to technical and ritual knowledge, to tools, to animals and so on (Chapter 2). All these entailments have social components, such as the exchange links to obtain tools (Figure 104), the learning networks within houses and within other social units, the power to organize labour and the authority to gain access to rituals.

This greater entanglement with a material-social world, this greater link between the social process and durable material objects, can be described as an increased 'objectification' of the social process. I also argue that by materializing and objectifying social relations, it became more possible to change them. Thus one of the most profound shifts that one sees after the end of the Ice Age is a greater sense of human agency, and a parallel increase in the use of the idea of material agency (Chapter 8). The explosion of materiality that can be associated with the early settled villages of the Middle East is thus associated with a gradual increase in the rate of change that we see about the same time.

104 Obsidian tools found in a hoard or cache beneath the floor of a building in the South Area of the site. Extensive social links and networks were in place to bring obsidian onto the site.

In the most general of terms and going back into the Palaeolithic, material entanglement would seem to have evolutionary disadvantages. It limited flexibility of response – for example, restricting the option of fissioning. It required greater investments of labour. So why did people ever get involved in material entanglement? I think the answer lies in the link between materiality and sociality. If we accept that anatomically modern humans are quintessentially social, then materiality has selective advantages. By engaging in material things more fully, humans were able to extend social ties in the giving of gifts. By providing 'enchanting objects' for each other, humans became tied more completely – to things and to each other. They also had more scope to manipulate social relations.[17] Indeed, Clive Gamble notes how during the Upper Palaeolithic networks of exchange gradually increased.[18] The whole Upper Palaeolithic can be seen as a gradual increase of materiality as people invested in material things as a way of creating social status, social ties and ritual events. So the social world produces the material explosion, but we have also seen that materiality involves sociality. We have seen that material entanglement involves social relations. For example, in the case of providing material gifts, people had to depend on the social links that allowed exploitation of sources of rock or shell. The more that people became socially entangled in materials, the more they became materially entangled in social relations. So there was a dual process of social and material entrapment pushing entanglement forward in a positive feedback loop.

Yet it happened incredibly slowly. After the appearance of anatomically modern humans (*Homo sapiens sapiens*) about 150,000 years ago, the degree of social and material entanglement that we see in the Blombos Cave in southern Africa and in the later caves of Iberia and southwest France[19] did not emerge until 70,000–40,000 years ago. And then the changes we associate with the yet fuller entanglement of early settled farmers did not happen until around 12,000 years ago. The slowness was perhaps partly because humans, despite our flexibility and adaptability, have a tendency to be bound by habituated practices and dispositions.[20] At a deeper level than day-to-day adaptation we get very embedded in ways of doing things and in repetitive practices. Early humans had a deep commitment to giving and to immediate reciprocity which meant they could not horde, keep, dominate, own. But perhaps more important, as I have already suggested, material entanglement may have had deep disadvantages in evolutionary terms. It implied less flexibility and adaptability. However, the socially selective value of material entanglement ultimately led to change in the period from 70,000–40,000 years ago onwards. Art became more common. Bone and stone tools showed technological change. Burial became more frequent. Exchange networks expanded. People increasingly lived in complex houses. By the time of Ohalo II, 20,000 years ago by the Sea of Galilee, there is possible evidence of year-round use, a midden area, burial and hearths.[21] There is also repeated reconstruction of a hut, although repeated long-term use of space is more clearly seen in cave sites. It is not a long way from these Palaeolithic sites to the more settled villages of the Natufian in the Levant (12th to 10th millennia BC) and to the greater entanglements of fully sedentary village life and agriculture. It is all these small shifts in the way people behaved that provided the basis for the large changes we see in the construction of ceremonial buildings in the Holocene. The construction of ceremonial buildings and the holding of large collective feasts and rituals depended on long-term social-material dependencies as much as they recreated them.

I would argue then that increased material entanglement occurs during the millennia that lead up to the appearance of settled villages in the Middle East, and that by the time of Çatalhöyük we see a heavy human-material dependency.[22] In a series of papers, Colin Renfrew has described the shifts in materialization at the start of the Neolithic.[23] Renfrew defines a phase of symbolic material culture which has two subphases. The first subphase is associated with sedentism and early farming. Here the storage of symbolic information in monuments and other material culture creates collective memory and socially cohesive groups and ranks. The second subphase is associated with the early use of metals. Gold, copper and bronze help to create notions of value and commodity on which wealth, prestige and further social ranking become based. It is especially the first subphase which is relevant to Çatalhöyük, although it could be argued that the exchange of beads and obsidian created value and prestige at the site.

In both subphases, the point emphasized by Renfrew is that the material objects do not just express social facts. Rather they constitute social concepts and relations. Thus they have an active role.[24] Renfrew tries to develop an approach which focuses on material 'engagement' in which materials and the human mind are codependent.[25] While arguing that these are general processes associated with humans, he is also arguing that the processes go into a higher gear at the transition to farming and in the Bronze Age. For a long period after the appearance of anatomically modern humans, there was little change. But then, in his two subphases, material engagement became more marked and social complexity increased.

Certainly I endorse the view put forward by Renfrew that the material world is inseparable from cognitive and social worlds. This view is for me related to the claim by Maurice Merleau-Ponty that consciousness is always 'consciousness of' something.[26] But the links made by Renfrew between things, value, commodity and exchange seem to be very general. The notion that an object becomes a gift through exchange, and thus comes to have value in further interactions seems at the basis of most exchange and must have been in play in the Upper Palaeolithic at the very least. According to Renfrew it was only with the Neolithic that materials took on a symbolic power so that the process of engagement led to social and economic change.[27] But in the Upper Palaeolithic and earlier, objects certainly had symbolic power. So the problem becomes: what changes in material engagement occurred at the transition to farming and sedentism? Can we take Renfrew's insight that something significant happened at this juncture in human development and understand something of the changes that occurred? How did materiality shift?

One thing that happened was that there just became a lot more of it – a lot more things made by people. This is a point well made by Renfrew, that 'human culture became more substantive, more material'.[28] He recognizes that this is related to sedentism. Those following a mobile existence are limited in terms of the accumulation of materials. But once people have settled, the potential for surrounding oneself with material things increases. This is not just a set of symbolic relations with things – it is also a material entanglement.[29] Humans get increasingly caught up in society through their involvement with objects.

Çatalhöyük occurs many millennia after the emergence of sedentism in the Middle East and Anatolia.[30] But as a fully sedentary society, it provides a good example of the degree of entanglement that had occurred in large settlements by the 7th millennium BC. I have provided examples in this book of the material-social entanglement created by simply plastering a wall or changing from clay balls to pots in cooking (Chapter 2). Also in Chapter 2, I gave the examples of burial beneath house floors, and moving an oven. One could imagine the same analysis extended over a wide range of things that emerge in the Neolithic – making pots, polishing stone axes (and mirrors at Çatalhöyük), making bricks, storing grains, looking after the herds. In each case, greater dependence on material things involves greater dependence on people. And vice versa. The degree of entanglement implied by the time of fully settled village life is massive, but I want to argue that it really continues on from what had been happening since anatomically modern humans emerged.

Rather than seeing sedentism as the cause of greater materiality, I would argue that the ongoing process of material entanglement led to sedentism. As already noted, there are trends towards longer-term occupation of sites, increasingly elaborate buildings, and more evidence of ritual collective acts throughout the Upper Palaeolithic in Europe and the Middle East. By the time of Ohalo II there is possible year-round occupation, even if this still involves intermittent use. The increasing use of a wide range of materials, the greater involvement in long-distance exchange, the increase of burial in or near houses – all this requires and allows longer-term social engagement. Objects tie people together in the practicalities of their use. The objects are pursued because they allow greater sociality. But they also mean greater dependencies (material and social), and thus further shifts in practices, concepts, beliefs and orientations.

The daily spiralling of material-social engagements ultimately produced the major changes that can be associated with the Aceramic or Pre-Pottery Neolithic and with early Çatalhöyük. These include changes in approaches to agency, an increased sense of history, a changed self image. Many of these changes themselves are linked to the increasing social centrality of the house. As people settled down in the last millennia of the Pleistocene and in the early Holocene, the house became more and more a focus of social life. Its walls and fittings created boundaries and continuities. Those buried in or near it created links with the past. Its construction involved social ties. More and more was brought into the house. Nigel Goring-Morris and Anna Belfer-Cohen have described the long slow development of houses and associated ritual structures in the Levant.[31] In central Anatolia at Aşıklı Höyük in the late 9th and early 8th millennia BC, there are ceremonial buildings but houses are much less elaborate than at Çatalhöyük in the ensuing millennia. At Çatalhöyük a wide range of functions from burial, ritual and art to storage, manufacture and production are more clearly drawn into the house.

As I have argued, many of the early large-scale agglomerations in Anatolia and the Middle East may be linked to social and ceremonial events.[32] But such social events and public constructions imply long-term and complex social relations. The latter had been built up over millennia by the gradual process of material entanglement. It was that slow 'march of the mass' that created the conditions for ceremonial constructions and large-scale agglomeration. It was this slow move of the mass that allowed the elaboration of the prowess-animal spirit-hunting-feasting network.

AGRICULTURE AS THE UNINTENDED PRODUCT OF MATERIAL ENTANGLEMENT

The notion of material and social entanglement between people and things is also a useful framework for making sense of the 'origins of agriculture'. It is now widely accepted that climatic and vegetational change at the end of the Pleistocene provided a context in which sedentism could occur. As warming happened, large stands of wild cereals grew in parts of Anatolia, the Middle East and the Levant.[33] The availability of these grasses was undoubtedly a factor in allowing greater sedentism. There is much evidence of collecting and processing (grinding for example) of wild plants in the Natufian sites of the Levant in the period starting from the 12th millennium BC.

But the actual shift to domesticated cereals occurs slightly later – in the PPNA of the 10th millennium BC. The late Natufian was in a climatic phase recognized worldwide as a return to glacial conditions and termed the Younger Dryas.[34] Incipient agriculture occurred in the Levant towards the end of this Younger Dryas phase. Thus people have argued that environmental changes triggered by climatic changes produced the origins of agriculture.[35] Settlements had increased in size during the warming at the end of the Pleistocene, but the setback of the Younger Dryas forced intensification in order to maintain settled life in agglomerated villages. The result of that intensification was that people domesticated plants and animals – perhaps unintentionally. Simply the process of harvesting, storing and replanting the now less available seeds would have led to the selective processes that we call domestication. In particular, the keeping and replanting of seeds would have selected for those plants with a tough rachis. The rachis attaches the grain head to the plant stem and this is brittle in the wild cereal so that the seed can fall off and re-sow itself. But, as we will see further below, during harvesting of wild cereals, there will be a tendency for the harvester to select out, by accident, plants with a tough rachis that does not break easily. It is the presence of a tough rachis that defines domesticated wheat and barley since such plants are no longer able to propagate themselves successfully in the wild.

This overall account is probably largely correct in general outline. Recent biomolecular studies have, however, suggested that the first domestication of einkorn wheat occurred somewhere near Karacadağ in southeastern Turkey, rather than in the Levant.[36] As Steve Mithen has suggested,[37] the first domestication of wheat may have been connected with nearby sites such as Göbekli Tepe which have produced such clear evidence for public ritual and the prowess-animal spirit-hunting-feasting network that I have described. Indeed, it seems quite possible that people who had come together largely because of the benefits (prestige, exchange, status, control over resources) that this network allowed, ended up 'accidentally' domesticating plants and animals. The large agglomerations of people would have depended on a wide range of local resources which would increasingly have had to be more intensively collected (just because of the large numbers of people exploiting the same landscape). Part of that intensity would have involved keeping grains and replanting them. At Göbekli Tepe itself it is argued that there are still no domesticated plants or animals.[38] But the intensification would likely have produced the selective environment in which domestication could have occurred at some site in the region.

Domestication provides an extremely good example of entanglement. Indeed, one can argue that domestication is entanglement. Once cereal varieties have been produced with a tough rachis they become entirely dependent on humans. Unlike the wild cereals which have a brittle rachis which scatters the grains so that they regrow, the domesticated cereals cannot reproduce on their own as the rachis is tough and the heads do not break off or shatter – the seeds stay trapped in the plant. The domesticated plants depend on humans to thresh out their seeds and replant them. The humans in their turn need to engage in greater material and social investment (for example, threshing) if they want to reap the social and economic advantages (such as providing food for increasingly sedentary families) of growing domesticated plants.

But the role of entanglement is rather greater than this – as has been shown in a series of experimental studies conducted by Gordon Hillman and colleagues. Hillman has shown that in some ways the most efficient way to harvest wild cereals is by beating the heads of the plant into a basket.[39] This is the most efficient method in terms of amount harvested per unit of time. But the beating method does not produce the conditions for the genetic change to a tough rachis, since the harvesting process selects for a brittle rachis. What does produce the conditions for genetic change more effectively is harvesting lower down the stalk with a sickle. We know that sickles were used in the Natufian because blades with a polish or gloss have been found and the gloss probably results from cutting grasses. By harvesting lower down the stalk of the plant and then threshing, people were selecting for plants with a tough rachis. So, if we want to understand what caused the domestication of plants, we have to explore why people might start harvesting the stalks with sickles rather than just beating the heads. Ofer Bar-Yosef and Anna Belfer-Cohen[40] argue that harvesting wild stands with a sickle is more efficient in terms of the amount harvested per unit area.[41] Thus the shift to sickle harvesting, and the domestication of plants, may have resulted from the decreased availability of land for wild cereal growth produced by the Younger Dryas.

This is possible, but in my view there is no good evidence that there was a major pressure on land availability at this time. It seems to me more likely that the pressure to shift to sickle harvesting was a product of the wider shift to entanglement. One of the ways that people became entangled in grasses was for a variety of non-food purposes, from making baskets and mats to roofing houses to tempering bricks to providing fuel. In all these ways people would have increasingly wanted to make use of the stalks of grasses. So shifting to the use of sickles rather than beating would have been necessary in order to get access to the stems and stalks. It was this shift, apparently minor and carried out for quite different reasons, that could have produced what we call the domestication of plants.

Probably the specifics of the process varied from place to place. It increasingly seems that the cultural sequences leading to agriculture in the southern Levant, southeastern Turkey, the Zagros Mountains and central Turkey were rather different. And even within each of these regions the specific processes that led to domestication must have been varied. The example of the shift to sickle blades is just that – an example from probably a great variety of instances. But I would argue that the underlying process was much the same: that people became entangled with objects, and in the process, often inadvertently, they caused processes of sedentism and domestication that had irretrievable effects.

By the time of Çatalhöyük in central Anatolia, that is, after 7400 BC, the process had not only led to the domestication of cereals, sheep, goat and dog, but it had also produced a very specific set of practices and orientations. People and society had become thoroughly entangled in the materiality of the house – in its construction, use, abandonment, rebuilding and so on. Children grew up in a world in which small things mattered – where one cooked, how one swept up, where one hid little figurines, and so on. There were new relationships with a more historical past, and new senses of individual and material agency. Social life centred around the house, and around a set of values associated with hunting, sexual and other prowess, feasting and ancestry. All these went alongside settled 'town' life and the domestication of plants and animals. And they were in turn to lead to the domestication of cattle, as we shall see.

INCREASING MATERIAL ENTANGLEMENT IN THE ÇATALHÖYÜK SEQUENCE

The smallest of actions, such as the decision to plaster the house floors with fine muds, or the decision to keep obsidian pre-forms below the floors, had as much impact as the first planting of a seed or the first tethering of a cow. This is because the small decisions involved changes in material-human relations that also changed the ways people interacted with each other and with the spirit world. In other words, they contributed to changes in discourse and practice that were part of and necessary for the longer-term delayed-return systems that underpinned settled village life and farming.

Previously, the pace of cultural, economic and social change in the Upper Palaeolithic had been extremely slow. In the early Neolithic mound sites in Anatolia and the Middle East, there is remarkable continuity, with house built on house over centuries, even the hearths staying in the same place in the deep sounding at Aşıklı Höyük.[42] In PPNA Jericho, there are 32 occupation horizons associated with the monumental tower.[43] Even in the 8th and 7th millennia at Çatalhöyük, there is remarkable continuity. One component of this slow pace of change may have been that social structures were embedded within the material world. As people were socialized at Çatalhöyük, they learnt social rules in the practices of daily life, moving around houses and stepping between pots, baskets and wooden containers.[44]

This emphasis on continuity is seen in house rebuilding, and in the repetition of what is done where in the houses. The codification of internal space into 'clean' and 'dirty' areas inside Çatalhöyük houses was discussed in Chapter 5. Although a

105 Two flint daggers with carved bone handles found at Çatalhöyük. The upper example with the handle in the form of a boar's head is from a small room by Building 3 in the BACH Area. The lower example with the handle in the form of a snake was found by James Mellaart in Level VIA.

rather different perspective is presented by Adnan Baysal and Karen Wright[45], the overall evidence for the codification of construction, use and discard activities in different parts of the houses is strong. Codification is also seen in relation to lithic projectile points.[46] These were predominantly made of obsidian and rarely of flint; on the other hand, the two daggers that have been found with carved bone handles were both made of flint (Figure 105). Another example of codification is provided by the bone tools – these were mainly made from distal ends of metapodials of sheep/goat, rather than on hunted wild animals.[47] All these codified and practical rules may have inhibited change.

An overall lack of change in the lower levels of the site[48] so far excavated and studied by the current project is seen in subsistence. There is great stability in plant use during the early occupied phases as shown by the archaeobotanical data and few major shifts in the faunal data. According to Nerissa Russell there are no dramatic changes in the bone tool assemblage through time in these levels. Adnan Baysal and Karen Wright do not see any clear variations in materials or types of ground stone artifacts from the early levels to later ones.[49]

But there is also change, and I have suggested that increased material entanglement and objectification of the social structure may have allowed that structure to be re-crafted. By moving an oven one can confront social status or gender relations. By scuffing some dirt into a 'clean' area one could challenge accepted roles. An increasing focus on history rather than myth may have encouraged change also. I have also described an increasing sense of material and human agency.

Detailed anatomies of the buildings at Çatalhöyük show an endless cycle of movement and reorganization. In particular, the ovens and hearths and bins keep moving around the building, shifting from one side to the other along the south wall, or being blocked up and shifted into side rooms, and then back into the main rooms.[50] There is an endless restlessness through the sequence as pottery comes in, obsidian becomes more specialized, stamp seals are introduced, figurines change in style, social differentiation becomes more marked, and houses become more independent.

There are many examples of material change which in various ways must have confronted highly codified practices. For example, between Levels XII and VIII pottery changed hardly at all; between VI and II most stylistic elements changed, though without further technological 'ruptures' like the Level VII transition[51]: Jonathan Last relates the major Level VII shift to the increased use of pottery in cooking, alongside a contemporary decline in clay balls which had been used for cooking in the earlier levels of the site.[52] While the bone tool industry is quite stable through the occupation of the site, there seem to be some minor changes around Level IX.[53] These include the use of a somewhat wider range of taxa and elements and a slight decline in splitting in the points; a change from cut to drilled perforations in the needles; and the appearance of worked boar's tusk and some minor tool types, many of them associated with woodworking. There is also change in obsidian. During the Pre-XII levels, there is a decline in the use of a technology[54] based on very small or micro-blades. Inscribed obsidian points only occur in Pre-XII levels. The Göllü Dağ-East source of obsidian had a long use from at least Level IX, whereas Nenezi Dağ comes in in a major way in Levels VII to VI.[55] The latter is associated with a specific technology – unipolar pressure-flaked blade technology which becomes the mainstay industry at Çatalhöyük. In Levels VIA–B there is a shift from flake- to larger blade-based assemblages,[56] and from percussion to pressure-flaking technologies. Also production became more restricted or specialized. As another example of change in obsidian, burials with mirrors occur in Levels VIB, V and IV.

Many of these changes involved increasing material-social entanglements. The greater specialization of production in pottery and obsidian from about Level VI onwards must have involved a series of material and social investments and entanglements. More specialized labour and knowledge were involved and so people's commitments to and dependencies on each other increased. The population of the 'town' too was changing. The most dense phases so far excavated seem to be in Levels VII and VI. The largest numbers of burials occur in houses in Levels VII and VI, on both the South and North hills. The investment in 'town' living must have been considerable during these dense phases.

I discussed the case of the shift from clay balls to pottery in Chapter 2. The shift to the use of pottery in cooking at Çatalhöyük had many implications for the cooking process itself. Cooking could become more varied, complex, controlled. It became dependent on the technology of pot production. The shift also involved a more elaborate and longer, or more intensive pottery productive process – ageing the clay etc. Also, the clay now used from Level VII onwards had to be obtained from farther away. So, through time, people became more and more involved in a complex network, both material and social, surrounding cooking and clay production and exchange. In the scheduling of tasks inside the house, the use of pottery instead of clay balls allowed greater flexibility – since the pot took over some of the tasks of cooking itself. It acted as a material delegate of human agency. Again people and things had become codependent.

In these examples, people at Çatalhöyük became increasingly involved in a seamless web of material-social interactions. They became entangled in the social relations necessary to obtain material goods, and material goods were necessary to provide the materials and media for increasingly complex social interactions. The examples given so far show how material entanglements led into social entanglements. But equally, social structures are needed for the material engagements to be possible. A good example is provided by the introduction of pottery itself. The reasons may have been largely social but whatever the reasons it is clear there was a delay. People clearly had the technology to make fired clay figurines and to fire lime plaster well before they fired pots. Why the delay? I suggest that the primary reason was that people were not yet socially 'ready'. By this I mean that they were not sufficiently 'entangled' in long-term social relations. They were not yet sufficiently networked into a web of specialized entanglements to sustain the production and use of pottery. They were not sufficiently involved in long-term durations, to maintain the long-term involvements and entanglements involved in rights to dig clay, knowledge to find temper, time and tools to form clay, and time and social relations to obtain fuel to fire pottery. It was only when larger social changes occurred – in the direction of multi-tasked, larger households – that it made sense to invest in pottery production.

The House and the Upper Levels at Çatalhöyük

I talked earlier about the hunting-feasting-prowess-ancestry network and how that emerged over the long term and dominated much of the symbolism at Çatalhöyük. I showed that this network was a driving force behind the 'origins of agriculture'. But I also argued that an equally important long-term process was that people, materials and society became increasingly entangled in daily life in the house. I want to look at an aspect of this now – the increasing importance of the house and domestic production at Çatalhöyük.

The house at Çatalhöyük is already distinctive in relation to other and earlier sites. It brings everything, including the symbolism, inside. I explained this in Chapter 5 as part of a shift from the collective to house-based social strategies. The latter include the focus on burial and ancestry in the house. They also include the way in which the house plays a role in exchange (in the burial of obsidian), and in socialization. Although Çatalhöyük is distinctive in its degree of emphasis on the house, it is also part of a wider process throughout Anatolia and the Middle East. Brian Byrd has noted that as one moves into the PPNB in the Levant, domestic building size increases, and there are more internal features and divisions of space.[57] Byrd sees an increased use of the insides of buildings for activities, and a shift to more house-based and less communal forms of ownership. Although this sequence has been challenged by Nigel Goring-Morris and Anna Belfer-Cohen, similar sequences are visible in southeastern Anatolia, for example at Çayönü.[58]

This general shift in the nature of the house can be seen in terms of material entanglement. I have given the example of burial. Simply by burying the dead near or in the house, there are opportunities to create ancestry and links to the past through the fabric and memories of the house. The handing down of rights is part of the repeated use of the same building in densely packed agglomerations. None of these links are assured. We know from mound sites in southeast Europe that houses do not have to be built directly on each other,[59] and we know from later sites in the Middle East that burial can occur outside houses or settlements. The entanglement that leads to the increased importance of the house relates to social production and reproduction. Through the later Pleistocene and into the early Holocene we have seen increased sedentism, and increased investment in ceremony. The hunting-feasting-prowess-ancestry network allowed or encouraged sedentism and agglomeration. The house which was already important at Ohalo II and in the Natufian gained importance in the Pre-Pottery Neolithic (10th to 8th millennia BC), partly because many aspects of life were organized at the domestic scale. Obtaining food, making objects, arranging burial, producing and reproducing were largely domestic tasks, although early Neolithic houses remained relatively small and unelaborated and there was a

106 The build-up of houses above and around VII.44 (with the leopard reliefs) as excavated by James Mellaart. The house was very much the focal point of social life at Çatalhöyük.

strong focus on communal ritual. As societies became more materially entangled in the Holocene, they increasingly did so through what Marshall Sahlins termed 'the domestic mode of production'.[60]

In this book I have suggested that by the time we get to Çatalhöyük, rights and resources were handed down within houses, groups of houses, sections of the community, and the community as a whole, but that the main focus was the transmission of rights within houses. Rights, resources, status, prestige were obtained in a number of ways: through (1) domestic production, (2) domestic reproduction and socialization, (3) feasting, (4) prowess in hunting, baiting and with the animal spirits, (5) exchange, (6) control of knowledge about and the objects of the spirit world, (7) control of access to knowledge about and remains of the ancestors, and (8) revelation of controlled knowledge and objects. All these processes were channelled through the house in some way. By the time of Çatalhöyük, the house had become a main focus of social life (Figure 106). Everything had to be brought into the house. And yet we have also seen a tension between the sphere of hunting-feasting-prowess-ancestry associated with the north part of the house, and the sphere of domestic production in the oven areas to the south. I have pointed to the ways in which the production and storage areas of houses are often less or undecorated. There are undecorated screen walls in front of storage and food preparation areas. There are unelaborated grain storage bins.

And the pots, often associated with the oven areas, are undecorated. Domesticated animals and plants occur rarely in the art. As much as the hunting-feasting-prowess-ancestry network must have been linked to domestic production, that link was initially unelaborated in the house.

I want to show now how the sphere or area of domestic production came to be elaborated and made central in the upper levels at Çatalhöyük, as a result of a myriad small steps, and closely connected to wider changes in society.

A clear example of this shift was found while excavating in the 4040 Area of the North hill in 2004: the first building we had seen on the East Mound with the hearth in the middle of the floor. At the time of writing we are not sure of the phasing of this building, but it is probably Level IV. In fact we had already seen such an arrangement on the Chalcolithic West Mound. Here, the team headed by Jonathan Last and Catriona Gibson had found a large building with multiple rooms – completely different from the buildings on the Neolithic East Mound – and in the central, plastered room was a central hearth. (In fact Mellaart's plans do show examples of central features in the uppermost levels of the East Mound, and there are some hearths in the upper levels that seem to wander close to the centre of the main rooms.)

In the main sequence of levels on the East Mound, from Level XII to IV (we have so far not excavated houses from the Pre-XII levels), hearths and ovens are always by or close to walls. They normally occur near south walls, but they can occur elsewhere – but always near walls. This strong code is weakened or changed in the upper levels and into the ensuing West Mound. Just the movement of a hearth a few feet seems to change the world. Rather than being marginal to the main room, domestic food preparation becomes central. Rather than the focus of the main room being records of feasting and baiting (in the paintings and installations), or being links to the ancestors (in the burials beneath floors), the focus shifts to domestic production.

There are related shifts. On the West Mound there is no evidence of burial beneath floors. It seems likely that burial now occurs off site, less immediately tied to house-based ancestry. Also there is no evidence that the walls were painted with geometric or figurative designs. Rather, the focus of 'art' shifts to domestic pottery (Figure 107). This change begins in the upper levels of the East Mound. In Levels IV and above, a greater variety of pottery forms is found,[61] with some coloured slips. We also begin to find very large pots in the upper levels that were probably used for storage.

107 On the West Mound, Chalcolithic pottery was often painted in elaborate designs, whereas there is no evidence of complex wall-painting.

So the small, and apparently insignificant shift in the location of a hearth leads and is part of a major social change. Another example of long slow change in small daily acts that moves in a similar direction is provided by the plastering of walls and floors. Fired lime plaster floors occur on the East Mound up to Levels XII and XI. The early hard lime plasters produce floors of a single, or very few, layers. The practices of making and using them were very different from the later levels. Although the firing of lime does not seem to have been on a very large scale,[62] it still involved a longer process of preparation and wider collection of resources such as dung for fuel than the later use of mud plasters. During use there was not the frequent need to replaster as was found in the later levels. Thus, in the early use of lime plaster floors, major construction events were followed by plastering and painting of the floors and then less repetitive remakings.

From Levels XII and XI through the main sequence on the East Mound, mud or marl plasters were used. These were soft and had to be resurfaced on a yearly, seasonal, and even monthly basis. This process of endless replastering could have been more house-based as it involved less labour. It would have been less easy to control (for example through ritual external to the house) because so frequent and so dispersed and so small scale.

But in the uppermost levels of the East Mound, there is a further shift. In Level V and above, there are often fewer and thicker layers of plaster, with thicker preparation layers. This suggests less emphasis on continuous maintenance of the plaster surfaces, and still less investment in the house wall surfaces. On the Chalcolithic West Mound, the plaster on the walls does not have the multiple layerings found in the main Neolithic East Mound sequence.[63]

These gradual shifts in the ways in which the walls were plastered take the emphasis away from the ritual and symbolic importance of the house walls and floors. The early lime plasters are similar to those used in the PPNB in the Levant. They are part of the tradition of elaborate houses that we see leading up to Çatalhöyük. The multiple replasterings in the main part of the sequence are closely linked to the frequent burial (since floors were replastered after graves had been closed), the intermittent paintings, the remaking of installations and so on. The wall plasters become less important in the upper levels as the emphasis shifted to domestic production.

A similar move is found in relation to bricks. At the base of the mound the bricks are very long (up to 1.5 m (4.9 ft)) and very thin (often just a few centimetres). To make them and carry them to the house and place them on the wall would have needed more than one person. The bricks get gradually smaller through time until in the upper part of the sequence there are small rectangular bricks that can be held in one hand. Placing them on the wall with mortar could be done more quickly and with just one person. This is just one small example of how houses became more example of the degree of entanglement that had occurred in large settlements by the 7th millennium BC. I have provided examples in this book of the material-social entanglement created by simply plastering a wall or changing from clay balls to pots in cooking (Chapter 2). Also in Chapter 2, I gave the examples of burial beneath house floors, and moving an oven. One could imagine the same analysis extended over a wide range of things that emerge in the Neolithic – making pots, polishing stone axes (and mirrors at Çatalhöyük), making bricks, storing grains, looking after the herds. In each case, greater dependence on material things involves greater

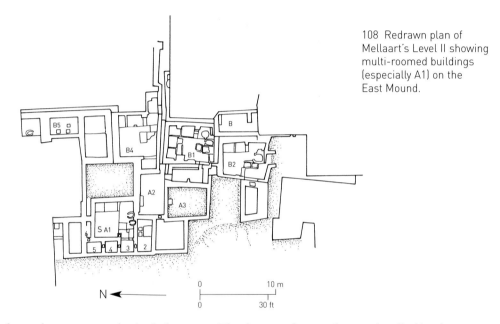

108 Redrawn plan of Mellaart's Level II showing multi-roomed buildings (especially A1) on the East Mound.

N

0   10 m

0   30 ft

dependence on people. And vice versa. The degree of entanglement implied by the time of fully settled village life is massive, but I want to argue that it really continues on from what had been happening since anatomically modern humans emerged.

Rather than seeing sedentism as the cause of greater materiality, I would argue that the ongoing process of material entanglement led to sedentism. As already noted, there are trends towards longer-term occupation of sites, increasingly elaborate buildings, and more evidence of ritual collective acts throughout the Upper Palaeolithic in Europe and the Middle East. By the time of Ohalo II there is possible year-round occupation, even if this still involves intermittent use. The increasing use of a wide range of materials, the greater involvement in long-distance exchange, the increase of burial in or near houses – all this requires and allows longer-term social engagement. Objects tie people together in the practicalities of their use. The objects are pursued because they allow greater sociality. But they also mean greater dependencies (material and social), and thus further shifts in practices, concepts, beliefs and orientations.

from Level VI onwards. It seems likely, given the radiocarbon dating, that the West Mound begins to be occupied during the last phases of occupation on the East Mound – again giving a sense of dispersal of housing, and indicating a clear move away from the close huddling of buildings that seems so characteristic of Çatalhöyük. Perhaps this suggests less of an emphasis on links to ancestors in houses (because people are less concerned to huddle round the ancestral house), and less emphasis on communal identities. There may be less continuity between houses,[66] and certainly by the time of the West Mound there is less or no burial in houses. The rate of change between phases or levels as measured by Craig Cessford shows a speeding up in the upper levels.[67] The overall length of occupation of the East Mound in all likelihood was 950–1,150 years. There are probably 18 levels overall although the definition of levels is somewhat arbitrary, and some levels are better defined than others. The average length of level is 50–80 years, but they are longer earlier and shorter later.

There may also be shifts in gender relations. Age and gender organization at the site were discussed in Chapter 9. Here I wish to point only to possible evidence of a change in gender through time. Naomi Hamilton notes a *slight* increase in numbers of female burials in houses in upper levels[68] – and there is also a greater emphasis on female figurines in the upper levels, and there are clusters of the famous seated female figurines around hearths and in buildings (Figure 109). Mary Voigt notes a shift in Level VI from male stone figurines in the lower levels to female clay figures in the upper levels.[69] This increased representation of women may be partly linked to the craft specialization and 'industrialization' of food preparation (with external large ovens) that we see in the upper levels. It is often the case that as craft specialization increases, women become more clearly identified with domestic production and men focus on other spheres of production and exchange.[70] This may be relevant at Çatalhöyük, but there are other ways of interpreting the shift.

I have shown that a network of social practices and symbolism centred around hunting and baiting, prowess including spiritual prowess, feasting, ancestry and exchange. I argued that this human-material network was visible from early on in the settled villages of Anatolia, particularly at Göbekli Tepe where sexuality, especially male sexuality, seems to have had a central role. I have also shown that this same network, brought into the house, underlies most of the symbolism at Çatalhöyük. And here too there is strong phallic imagery seen in the paintings of animals with erect penises and in phallic figurines. Many aspects of status at Çatalhöyük, throughout the sequence, depended on the provision of wild bulls for feasting.

But we have seen in the upper levels of the site, and on into the West Mound, the increasing importance of production in the house. The female figurine on or by felines (Plate 24) was found in a grain bin in Level II. We have also seen the small naked female figurine with a wild seed in her back (Figure 90) from a midden in the uppermost levels, and there are paintings perhaps showing women collecting

109 Clay figurines found by James Mellaart in buildings in the upper levels of the site, often around the hearth. These female representations are often seated and the head rarely survives.

plants in the upper levels. The possibly greater presence of female and plant symbolism suggests a new emphasis in the upper levels. This can be linked to all the other evidence for the increased importance of domestic production. Rather than women and fertility being tied to the origins of agriculture,[71] female representations become more marked much later alongside the hunting/baiting symbolism, as domestic production becomes more socially central.

It is of great interest that domesticated cattle have emerged by the time of the upper levels of the West Mound.[72] We have not yet been able to study sufficient numbers of cattle bones from the upper levels of the Neolithic East Mound. We do know that cattle were wild up to Level VI,[73] but we do not know whether there was any domestication by the end of the occupation of the East Mound. But at least we can say that by the 6th millennium on the West Mound, feasting must have come to depend on domestic animals, including domestic cattle. In fact the need to provide cattle for feasting may have been the motivation for domestication/control of cattle.[74] But as this shift to domesticated cattle occurred, so did part of the basis for the hunting-feasting-prowess-ancestry network diminish. Wild bulls became less available. The control of feasting depended now more on the provision of domesticated animals – and thus on the house as a productive unit.

Thus, in general terms at the Çatalhöyük East Mound, we see a shift from an earlier (pre-Çatalhöyük) importance of communal relations to a focus at Çatalhöyük on ancestry, feasting, the control of the spirit world and exchange in the house. But in the later levels at Çatalhöyük there is more of a focus on production in houses which become larger and more functionally differentiated and linked to other houses by exchange and through the specialization of production.

CONCLUSIONS

So, at the broadest of scales Colin Renfrew was right to point to important changes in human engagement with materiality in the Neolithic. But this was not so much a shift in symbolic power, as a shift in the degree to which people became so entangled with material objects that these objects came to have greater impact or agency in their lives. And it was a long slow process. Making slow infinitesimal changes in their engagements with things, for social reasons, people became more dependent on things and on each other. This greater engagement increasingly trapped people and society in longer-term dependencies. One product was sedentism, since this allowed a major expansion in material and social investment and accumulation. Another product was domestication. But both sedentism and domestication were also causes of further entanglement, as the spiral moved onwards.

With this perspective, we can see how a small decision, such as to use clay to make a brick, can have just as much long-term significance as the decision to plant seeds. All such decisions are linked by the shift towards greater entanglement between people, society and things. If we bring things into the picture, explore their materiality and the social implications they involve, we get away from the idea that people produced sedentism and agriculture. They did so only because of their entanglement with things.

There were other, and perhaps more important, shifts that lay within these minor shifts leading to entanglement and major structural change. In this book I have pointed in particular to changing notions of self and material and human agency. I have pointed out that the long-term process of material entanglement involved people becoming increasingly associated with things, and things with people. This 'objectification' was related to a centrality of the human in daily and spiritual life. Through this shift it became more possible to move away from giving and reciprocity (with people, spirits, things, animals, plants) and engage in change and accumulation and domination (of people, spirits, things, animals, plants). I have shown, as part of this process, how people increasingly became involved in making interventions in the world – by using things like figurines to act as delegates.

I have tried to show too how senses of time and relations with the past changed – how a sense of 'history' emerged, and how people started using more 'documents' of what had happened in the past in order to conduct their social negotiations in the present. People started digging up things and reusing them, and they did this as part of a new sense of historical time.

These changes in self, material and human agency, temporality, seem to have happened with icy slowness in the Middle East, emerging over the millennia at and after the end of the Pleistocene. They occur alongside and as part of increased material entanglement, and they change most dramatically along with the marked increase in material entanglement that goes along with sedentism. It is these shifts in the orientation of people that are needed for sedentism and agriculture, but the shifts are also enhanced by 'town' life and domestication.[75]

Greater material entanglement means that to do the smallest of things involves more dependencies on other people and on other things. As a result, people and things become mutually entangled and codependent. Relationships get 'stretched out' over time and people and things get embedded in long-term relationships. It is this long-termness that lies at the basis of both sedentism and agriculture. So the major social shift that we see in the early Holocene is towards the handing down of rights within social units such as the house. But overall, the 'thingness' of things – that is their duration and specificity – seems to be involved in the social processes of Çatalhöyük in two contradictory ways. There is a continual tension at the site between continuity and change. On the one hand, the increased materiality of life leads to a greater potential for constructing continuities, especially based in the house as it is reused and rebuilt over centuries. There is repeated replastering, there is burial beneath floors, there are installations of animal heads and sculpture on walls that last through the occupation of houses and may be taken for reuse in later buildings (Figure 110). On the other hand, the increased material- ity of life allows that life to be endlessly re-crafted by shift- ing an oven here, by changing foodways, pot and obsidian types there.

110 Splayed figure on the west wall of Mellaart's building EVI.8. As usual the head and extremities of the limbs have been removed.

I have argued that more material entanglement and objectification lead to faster change. As material entanglement increased in the upper levels at Çatalhöyük, so the rate of change increased, even though the overall rate remained slow and incremental – the slow movement of the mass. No individual would have been aware of the large picture that I have sketched out. Individuals may have been aware of the movement of a hearth into the centre of a house. But not all houses do the same thing at exactly the same time. Individuals come to find that certain things feel appropriate as circumstances gradually change. And their own parts in the overall process may have been difficult and contested. There would have been individual struggles as change in hearth location, for example, was brought about. But these individual acts only gained larger significance because the whole mass gradually and incrementally moved in the same direction. Any individual life would have been unlikely to appreciate how the whole was moving. The movement of the mass, like the movement of a very large crowd, has a character of its own, that is not visible to the individual participants caught up in their own struggles. This larger movement is made up of those struggles, but it responds in waves and flows. Circumstances change (local resources become used up, vegetational shifts occur, population densities increase, there is no room to bury any more people under a certain platform, and so on) and certain behaviours seem appropriate given existing orientations and bodily customs, while others come to seem uncomfortable. Much of this shifting occurs without real recognition of how it fits into the larger picture. The mass seems to move with a life of its own. But the movement is built up from the little micro-details of life – where and when and how one sits by a hearth, how one plasters a wall, how one cooks, what one does with the leopard bones.

'We Have Found a Leopard Bone'

This book was largely written in 2003 and 2004. I finished the first draft during the excavation season in 2004 and sent out copies to some of the people on the Çatalhöyük project. During the autumn of 2004 I began to receive comments back. In particular I heard back from Nerissa Russell who has been an important player throughout this book as one of the leaders of the faunal analysis team. She said that she had identified the first leopard bone at the site.

She had not told me about it during the excavation season because, while it was clearly the perforated claw (third phalanx) of a large felid, the team could not definitely identify it as a leopard in the laboratory at the site since they did not have examples of leopard bones with which to compare the archaeological find. Nerissa brought back measurements and a thorough set of digital scans to her laboratory at Cornell University in the United States. There she found that the specimen compared pretty well to a snow leopard skeleton in the comparative collection at Cornell.

But she was still not sure, and when she read the draft of the book and realized what a central part the leopard had in it, she asked Louise Martin, her co-director of the faunal team at Çatalhöyük, if she could help. Louise works at the Institute of Archaeology in University College London. She was able to walk over to spend a day in the carnivore section of the British Museum, looking at leopard, lion, tiger, cheetah and lynx skeletons. The Çatalhöyük example was definitely not from a cheetah which is unusual among felids as it does not retract its claws. Louise found that the best fit was with the leopard.

While I was grateful to Nerissa and Louise for going to all this trouble to identify one bone, my initial thought was that the argument surrounding the importance of the leopard in the book would be undermined. The supposed taboo about bringing leopard bones on site had here clearly been broken. But Nerissa convinced me that the circumstances of the find might even strengthen my argument. In the first case, the bone was not the direct product of consumption for food. It had been made into a pendant. In her field description of the claw, Nerissa wrote that it had been 'drilled, in fact not precisely in the centre but practically on the edge of the base of the claw part. This and the surface condition suggest that the claw sheath was on when the hole was drilled, or they would have put the perforation a little further in. It leaves a very thin wall of bone. The perforation was made with a cylinder drill, and shows little or no wear. The claw sheath would have extended the length 2-3 times, making it rather impressive.' The drilling suggested that the claw as a whole had been used as a pendant. The evidence did not indicate that a leopard had been brought on site to eat.

Second, the leopard claw pendant had been found in a very remarkable context. In Chapter 6 I described the discovery in 2004 of a burial in which a woman was holding a plastered human skull to her chest and face. This burial in Building 42 (Level IV) is shown in Figure 7 and Plates 13 and 14. As noted in Chapter 6, this was a very unusual find. There is only one other site with a plastered skull in Turkey. The best parallels are in the Levant in PPNB contexts. I have argued in this book that the removal of human heads and the circulation of skulls were associated with people with special social significance. In the field the claw was given the number (11306.x2) and it was found near the lower right arm of the female skeleton – the arm that goes under the plastered skull. The claw was thus found very close to both the right arm of the whole skeleton and to the plastered skull. So two of our most exceptional finds (the leopard claw pendant and the plastered skull) were found in intimate association with each other. This was too much to be coincidence. It was not possible to say whether the pendant was most closely

111 The perforated leopard claw from a burial in Building 42.

associated with the skull or the female skeleton. Since it seems unlikely that the pendant could have been 'worn' by the plastered skull, perhaps an association with the whole skeleton is more likely. Either way, the special significance of the claw (and the plastered skull) is reinforced.

In a way, finding this one leopard bone after the faunal team had recorded over 650,000 pieces of animal bone and had identified well over 24,000 to taxon was a relief. I had begun to worry that perhaps the complete lack of leopard bones on the site meant there were just no leopards in the environment at all at the time – perhaps all the depictions of leopards in the symbolism were distant memories of a species that had been hunted out. My argument about taboos against bringing leopards on site to eat would have been rather undermined. So the discovery of at least one bone confirmed our assumptions (based on historic evidence of leopards in Turkey) that there were leopards in Turkey at the time of Çatalhöyük. In a way this one bone made the taboo or high social value even more striking. If they could bring leopard bones on site in the form of a pendant (and we have seen they may have brought on leopard skins), why did they not bring leopard bones and skeleton parts more often, and in what contexts could a bone be brought in? Why is there no evidence of use of leopards in feasting or in other meat consumption?

I have argued in this book that leopard bones were not brought on site because of a set of taboos that separated off the domestic realm. But I have also argued that the symbolism in the house dealt with prowess, animal spirits, hunting and feasting. I showed how this set of imagery often involved the sharp, pointed, dangerous parts of wild animals. And I argued in Chapter 8 that this set of associated symbolism was also linked to ancestry. Bulls were centrally involved in feasting, and the heads of bulls were kept in houses and may have been passed down from house to house, creating historical connections within house and ancestral groups. In a similar way human heads were passed down.

Many of these same themes come together in this one new find of a bone pendant. In this one bone and the context of its discovery, many of the themes that have dominated this book are highlighted and reinforced. Once again in the burial or northern part of a house we have the focus on the sharp pointed part of a wild animal. And the bone is associated with a woman holding a plastered skull that seems to have been replastered several times, handed down through time. The prowess or spiritual power of the claw are associated with ancestry. The pendant was worn and may have been associated with specific memories and histories.

The find also contributes to the issue of the role of women at Çatalhöyük, as discussed in Chapter 9. The claw and its context evoke in an uncanny way the most iconic image from Çatalhöyük – the woman seated on a seat of felines shown in Plate 24. In the burial the woman is associated with a leopard claw. Perhaps she wore it, while in the sculpture her hands rest on the heads of the large cats. Whether she wore the pendant or held the skull wearing the pendant, the central role of powerful images of women in the upper part of the site is reinforced.

But like any good archaeological find, the leopard claw pendant raises new questions as much as it may illustrate existing arguments. As I looked back at the image of the woman seated on large cats in the light of the new discovery of a woman buried with a skull and leopard claw pendant, it occurred to me that perhaps the rounded shape between the legs of the woman in Plate 24 was a detached human head or skull. James Mellaart had interpreted the shape in the sculpture as a child being born, fitting in with his focus on the female as nurturing mother. But we have seen that from eastern Turkey to Çatalhöyük in central Turkey there is little evidence in the early Neolithic of a nurturing, mothering female role. I have suggested that the splayed figure at Çatalhöyük seen in Plate 18 (and also Figures 87 and 110) may have represented a dangerous human-animal hybrid or bear rather than a woman giving birth as interpreted by Mellaart. Looking at the rounded shape between the legs of the woman in the sculpture I have never been able to see any evidence that it represented a child, but its simple rounded shape might indicate the top of a skull. Perhaps in both the sculpture and the burial a woman is associated with a leopard and with a human head. The central but balanced role of women in the later occupation at Çatalhöyük would in this way be confirmed.

Notes

PROLOGUE

1 Dates in this volume are given as BC, meaning years before the Christian or Common era, but corrected or calibrated against tree ring data
2 Estes (1991)
3 See Shankland (1996; 2000; 2005)
4 Lloyd (1956, 53)
5 *ibid.*
6 Roger Matthews (2003)
7 Mellaart (1959)
8 Mellaart (1967, 27)
9 Mellaart (1959, 33; 1967, 27)
10 Mellaart excavated at Çatalhöyük in 1961, 1962, 1963 and 1965 publishing interim accounts in *Anatolian Studies* (Mellaart (1962; 1963; 1964; 1966)) and a popular book on the 1961 to 1963 seasons (Mellaart (1967); see also reports in the *Illustrated London News* from 1962 to 1966). He published the West Mound excavations in 1965. For Hacılar see Mellaart (1970)
11 Wheeler in his Foreword to the Mellaart book (Mellaart (1967, 10))
12 Çatalhöyük occurs at the very end of the Aceramic Neolithic and in the Ceramic Neolithic, that is ECA (Early Central Anatolian) II and III in the terms of Özbaşaran and Buitenhuis (2002). Aşıklı Höyük in central Anatolia is a complex densely packed site that covers the millennium before Çatalhöyük (Esin & Harmankaya (1999)). Sites in eastern Anatolia such as Göbekli Tepe and Çayönü begin in the late 10th and 9th millennia BC, and they have rich and elaborate artistic traditions of their own (Özdoğan & Özdoğan (1990, 1998); Schmidt (2001)). In the Near East, by the time of the PPNB (partially contemporary with early Çatalhöyük) there are sites as large as Abu Hureyra (11.5 hectares (28.5 acres), but possibly as large as 16 hectares (39.5 acres); Moore *et al.* (2000, 269–70)) and

'Ain Ghazal (12 to 13 hectares (30 to 32 acres); Rollefson *et al.* (1992, 444))

CHAPTER ONE

1 Lowenthal (1985)
2 Giddens (1992)
3 Elias (1994 [1936]). See Foucault (1977) for changing systems of punishment in France
4 For Egypt see Meskell (2002; 2004); and for Mesopotamia see Bahrani (2003)
5 Giddens (1992); Lowenthal (1985)
6 Fabian (1983)
7 Lane (1994)
8 For a summary of this ethnoarchaeological work see Hodder (1982)
9 Firth (1936; 1967)
10 As noted in the Prologue, Çatalhöyük was inhabited by 3,000 to 8,000 people at any one time
11 Lewis-Williams (2004; 2005)
12 Schmidt (2000; 2001)
13 Bataille (1955; 1962)
14 Bloch (1992)
15 Malhi *et al.* (2005). For a more general account of ancient DNA analysis see Jones (2001)
16 Yalman (2005)
17 Özdoğan (2002)
18 The case for regional variation is put by Özdoğan (2002). For Göbekli and Köşk Höyük see Schmidt (2001) and Özkan (2002)
19 Renfrew (1987)
20 Matero (2000)
21 Bartu (2000) and Bartu Candan (2006)
22 Fabian (1983)
23 Gimbutas (1982)
24 Swogger (2000)
25 *ibid.*, 149
26 Leibhammer (2000)
27 Hodder (2000)
28 Harris (1989)
29 Hodder (1996; 2000; 2005a, b, c; 2006)
30 Gibson and Last (2003)

CHAPTER TWO

1 Richards *et al.* (2003) and Richards

and Pearson (2005)
2 See Boyd (2005) for a different view in the Levantine Neolithic
3 Russell and Meece (2005)
4 Russell and McGowan (2005)
5 Russell and McGowan (2003)
6 The use of pots for cooking the fat of small ruminants has been indicated by residue analysis published by Copley *et al.* (2005)
7 Last (1998 and 2005)
8 In a recent article, Nerissa Russell and Bleda Düring (2005) have pointed to a burial in Space 112 (Mellaart's E.VII.9) in the South Area containing an adult male and a complete lamb, probably domestic and female. They point to other examples in the Neolithic of the Middle East of burials of young domestic animals. There is only one such example at Çatalhöyük, but the lamb burial does indicate that there could be associations of death and burial beyond the symbolic link in the art with vultures. After all, burials do normally occur in the domestic context of the house, even if normally in the part of the main room away from the hearths and ovens
9 The work on the clay balls at the site has been carried out by Sonya Atalay (2005)
10 Hamilton (1996, 248)
11 The stamp seals from the site have been studied by Ali Türkcan (2005)
12 Mellaart (1967, Plate 115) referring to a grave in VIB.20
13 Hamilton (1996, 249)
14 This statement is based on the statistical work of Sarah Cross May (2005)
15 Last (2005)
16 See Last (1996) and Conolly (1996)
17 For Göbekli, Çayönü, Aşıklı Höyük and Musular see Schmidt (2001), Özdoğan and Özdoğan (1990), Esin and Harmankaya (1999) and Özbaşaran (1999)
18 Gibson and Last (2003)

19 Judging by Can Hasan I, the upper storeys at that site were probably painted in the Early Chalcolithic and so the appearance of painted pottery may be an expansion rather than a shift in symbolic elaboration. It should also be recognized that the changes at Çatalhöyük are part of a wider change throughout the Middle East towards more elaborately decorated pottery

20 For other discussions and definitions of entanglement see, for example, Nicholas Thomas (1991), Timothy Mitchell (2002) and Bruno Latour (1996; 1999)

21 Jenkins (2005)

22 Russell (2005)

23 The exchange of obsidian from the site has been studied by Carter et al. (2005b)

CHAPTER THREE

1 Bailey (1993), Turnbull-Kemp (1967)

2 Nerissa Russell, pers. comm.

3 Firth (1967, 191 and 264)

4 Baird (2002) and pers. comm.

5 Mellaart (1967)

6 Baird (2005)

7 Some archaeological writings on the topic of the lived environment include Tilley (1994), Thomas (1996) and Edmonds (1999). The primary influence has been from phenomenology (a branch of philosophy dealing with how humans experience the world) and Heidegger's concepts of 'being-in-the-world' and 'dwelling' (Heidegger (1927)). Another important influence has been Tim Ingold's (1995) notions about practical engagements with environments and 'taskscapes'

8 The environmental and climatic context of Çatalhöyük is summarized in a number of recent publications (Kuzucuoğlu (2002); Kuzucuoğlu & Roberts (1997); Roberts et al. (1999)) and by Rosen and Roberts (2005). The account presented here is closely based on their work

9 Roberts (1995), Roberts et al. (1996; 1999; 2001)

10 Kuzucuoğlu (2002, 41)

11 Roberts et al. (2006)

12 Russell and McGowan (2005)

13 Asouti (2005)

14 Roberts et al. (1999)

15 Fairbairn et al. (2005a). The wetland species in the flora recovered in the carbonized remains include club-rush and *Alopecurus* sp.

16 Russell and McGowan (2005)

17 Asouti (2005)

18 Jenkins (2005)

19 Sherratt (1972; 1980); Van Andel & Runnels (1995)

20 This claim about the nature of the flooding of the Çarşamba river is based on long-term studies of the behaviour of the river in recent centuries (Rosen and Roberts (2005))

21 Rosen (2005) studied 250 wheat-husk phytoliths, primarily from Building 1

22 Fairbairn et al. (2005a)

23 Asouti (2005)

24 Sherratt (1972; 1980); Van Andel & Runnels (1995)

25 Roberts et al. (2006)

26 Tung (2005)

27 Russell and McGowan (2005)

28 Matthews (2005)

29 Fairbairn et al. (2005b)

30 For an explanation of this term see the discussion earlier in this chapter

31 For the phytolith data see Rosen (2005), for shells see Reese (2005) and for obsidian trade see Carter et al. (2005)

32 Esin & Harmankaya (1999)

33 Asouti & Fairbairn (2002) and Fairbairn et al. (2005a)

34 Esin & Harmankaya (1999)

35 Helbaek (1964)

36 Stable isotope analysis has been used throughout the research discussed in this volume, mainly to analyse human bones and animal bones. The main work has been carried out by Mike Richards and Jessica Pearson (Richards et al. (2003), Richards and Pearson (2005) and Pearson, pers. comm.). The method of stable isotope analysis for palaeodietary reconstruction is based on the idea that 'you are what you eat'. Carbon and nitrogen is taken from various foods and used to build body tissues over an individual's lifetime. We can determine the sources of the carbon and nitrogen (and therefore the foods consumed) by measuring the ratios of the two stable carbon isotopes, 13C and 12C (the ratio is called the δ_{13}C value) as well as the ratios of the two stable nitrogen isotopes, 15N and 14N (the δ_{15}N value). We know the range of stable isotope values in a variety of foods and know, at least generally, how these values are preserved in body tissues. Therefore, if we measure the body tissue δ_{13}C and δ_{15}N values we can then infer what foods provided the carbon and nitrogen used to make up the body tissues. The technique can be used to reconstruct the diet of both humans and animals by examining their bones. Mike Richards and Jessica Pearson have studied over 50 human individuals and a still larger sample of animal bones from the site. By comparing the results from human and animal bones it is possible to evaluate which animals were most important in the diet. It is also possible to determine the relative importance of plant food in the human diet and Richards and Pearson have also studied the stable isotopes of carbonized seeds from the site

37 The porous nature of unglazed pottery vessels ensures that during the processing of food (e.g. cooking) lipids are absorbed into the vessel wall. In this state animal fats, plant oils and plant waxes are known to survive burial for several thousand years (Evershed et al. (1999)). Following excavation, these lipids can be analysed using a suite of modern analytical techniques, including high temperature-gas chromatography (HTGC) and HTGC/mass spectrometry (Evershed et al. (1990)). Copley et al. (2005) analysed 28 sherds but only 5 (from several different levels on the site) yielded significant abundances of lipid. All are typical of degraded animal fats, rather than plant oils, and most are probably from ruminants.

Many plants, such as cereals, are difficult to identify using this technique, and more research will be needed before we can say whether the pots were used to contain and cook plants
38 Atalay (2005)
39 On the basis of the animal bones collected from the site by Mellaart, Perkins (1969) had argued that the cattle at Çatalhöyük were the main source of meat and that they were domesticated. But this claim was based on poor recovery of smaller bones, resulting in the impression that cattle were a much larger part of the diet than has been shown to be the case using modern recovery techniques
40 Russell and Martin (2005)
41 See note 36
42 Buitenhuis (1997), Martin *et al.* (2002)
43 Peters *et al.* (1999)
44 Russell and Martin (2005)
45 Richards *et al.* (2003)
46 Yeomans (2005)
47 Russell and McGowan (2005)
48 Asouti (2005)
49 See note 39
50 Mellaart (1967, 64)
51 Richards and Pearson (2005) and see note 36
52 Russell and Martin (2005)
53 Andrew Sherratt, pers. comm. (at time of writing)
54 Evershed *et al.* (2005) and see note 37
55 Molleson *et al.* (2005) and Boz (2005)
56 Atalay (2005)
57 Cessford (2006)
58 Childe (1952)

CHAPTER FOUR
1 Mellaart (1967)
2 Estes (1992)
3 Russell and Martin (2005)
4 Mellaart (1966a, 184–91 and Plates LI–LXIII)
5 Estes (1992)
6 Tung (2005); Matthews (2005a)
7 Cessford (2005b)
8 Matthews (1996); Shell (1996)
9 Dobbs and Johnson (2005); see also Shell (1996)
10 Özdoğan (2002)
11 Mellaart (1967, Plate 6)

12 Baird (2005)
13 Based on Wobst (1974)
14 Mellaart (1967)
15 Düring 2001; Cutting (2005)
16 This claim is based on the evidence for the dating of the East and West Mounds (Cessford 2005a)
17 Jenkins (2005)
18 Cessford (2006) discusses evidence for infestation in Building 5 in the North Area
19 Matthews (2005a)
20 Cessford (2006)
21 Yalman (2005)
22 Molleson *et al.* (2005) have identified secondary burial beneath the north-central platform in Building 1 in the North Area
23 Cross May (2005)
24 Mellaart (1967, 68)
25 Cessford and Mitrovic (2005), and see Chapter 1
26 Yeomans (2005)
27 Yeomans (2005)
28 Bull *et al.* (2005)
29 Rosen (2005)
30 Sidell and Scudder (2005)
31 Asouti (2005)
32 Farid (2006)
33 Esin & Harmankaya (1999)
34 As in the case of Building 3 (Stevanovic and Tringham (1998))
35 Carter *et al.* (2005a)
36 Fairbairn *et al.* (2005a)
37 Carter *et al.* (2005a)
38 I refer here to the middens in Space 181
39 In Space 181
40 Matthews (2005a) worked on micromorphological soil sequences taken from the site
41 Farid (2006)
42 Matthews *et al.* (1996, 321–4); Matthews and Farid (1996)
43 Russell and Martin (2005)
44 Space 181 in the South Area
45 The KOPAL Area has deposits which cover the early development of the site, and the only contemporary deposits we have excavated on the mound are the middens in Space 181. We have not excavated buildings in these Pre-XII Levels. If we had found buildings in these early levels they might give a different picture from the middens. It is thus possible that the apparent differences between

KOPAL, Space 181 middens and other on-site locations might be temporal in nature
46 Although the Space 181 sequence may be nearer the heart of the settlement in the early levels than the KOPAL Area
47 Perlès (2001)
48 Baysal and Wright (2005)
49 Cessford (2005b; 2006)
50 For example, Bar-Yosef (1986)
51 Baird (2005)
52 Schmidt (2001). There appear to be classic PPNA domestic structures at Göbekli contemporary with the ritual buildings, rather as at Jerf el Ahmar

CHAPTER FIVE
1 Firth (1936, 76)
2 *ibid.*, 78
3 *ibid.*
4 *ibid.*, 79
5 Matthews (2005b)
6 Düring (2001)
7 Mellaart (1967)
8 *ibid.*
9 The building is Building 4 in Level VIII and the wall is F.262
10 Cessford (2006)
11 Space 71 in Building 1 in Subphase B1.1B
12 Space 199, F.525
13 Examples are Space 106 and between Building 8 and Space 168 in Level VII; and in relation to Building 6 in Level VIII, and Building 2 in Level IX
14 Subphase B1.2C
15 F.203 is the hole in the south wall of Space 71 in Building 1, and the plastering over occurs in Subphase B1.2A
16 The oven is F.360 in Space 187 in Building 1 in Subphase B1.2C
17 The plaster feature is F.26 on the wall of Building 1 in Subphase B1.2A
18 Building 17, Space 170 in Phase B
19 In Building 17 (Phase D, Subphase (iv)) there is hearth F.545
20 Hearth F.538 in Phase B in Building 17
21 Space 156 (northwest room) in Building 5
22 This is Phase A at Beidha
23 Byrd (2000, 87)
24 Byrd (2000, 79)
25 Esin & Harmankaya (1999)

26 Building 42

27 Atalay (2005)

28 Firth (1936, 97)

29 This claim is based on the statistical integration of artifact data (Cross May (2005)) and the analysis of heavy residue distributions (Cessford and Mitrovic (2005))

30 Carter *et al.* (2005a)

31 Russell and Martin (2005)

32 Fairbairn *et al.* (2005a)

33 Middleton *et al.* (2005)

34 Cessford and Mitrovic (2005)

35 Matthews (2005a)

36 Farid (2006); Carter *et al.* (2005a)

37 Russell (2005)

38 This is Space 109

39 There is an infant (nine months old) burial in the southwest platform in Building 6, Level VIII, as well as an infant burial F.537 on the edge of the 'dirty' area in this same building. In Space 109, Level VII, burial F.264 is of a neonate near a hearth or oven. There is another example of a neonate burial close to the oven/hearth in the 'dirty' occupation area in Space 112, Level VII. In Building 18 there is a neonate burial F.493 near ovens in the southern part of the building

40 Cauvin (1994), and see box on page 20 for chronology of the Natufian

41 Özdoğan (1999). The Round Building phase at Çayönü has burial in open areas or in buildings without grave goods. The Skull Building occurs in the phase with Grill Buildings. Basement floors were used as graves in the phase with Cell Buildings

42 Hauptmann (1999; 2002)

43 Esin & Harmankaya (1999)

44 Large Roomed PPNC phase

45 Özdoğan (2002)

46 Mellaart (1970)

47 Perlès (2001)

48 Andrews *et al.* (2005); Molleson *et al.* (2005). Since 2001 the palaeo-anthropology team has been led by Clark Larsen and Simon Hillson

49 As already noted, the north-central floor area in the main room (Space 71) in Building 1 does have a concentration of secondary burial (although not with any

evidence of the exposure to vulture activity suggested by the paintings). This same area in Building 1 has no grave goods (Hamilton 2005). It is tempting to suggest that these bodies were first buried in another house or area and then relocated and that burial goods were lost or recirculated when this happened

50 Esin & Harmankaya (1999)

51 Rosen (2005)

52 *Agropyron* sp.

53 Space 181 in the South Area

54 For example, at the Natufian site of 'Ain Mallaha in the Levant new structures were built directly over earlier ones (Valla 1994). Naveh (2003) in his discussion of PPNA Jericho, notes that there are 32 PPNA occupation phases during the use of the tower (plus two which predate the tower). Kenyon's (1981) sections through the PPN deposits at Jericho show evidence of repeated building of walls in the same location. Özdoğan (1999) notes that in the Grill Building phase at Çayönü grill buildings may have five or six consecutive rebuildings at slightly different orientations. Persistent maintenance and rebuilding are also seen very early (PPNA) at Qermez Dere (*ibid.*). At Nevali Çori, Hauptmann (1999, 70) notes that one fact 'also seen in the houses at Çayönü, is a direct sequence of the individual structures throughout Levels I to IV. When a new house was erected, the foundation platforms of the previous house were used again after demolition and leveling'

55 Cessford (2005a)

56 Esin & Harmankaya (1999, fig. 9)

57 For example, Duru (1999)

58 Perlès (2001)

59 Tringham (2000)

60 Düring (2001)

61 A careful and detailed restudy of depositional processes in the Natufian levels of the Levantine site of El-Wad showed the complexities of trying to understand spatial and temporal patterning (Weinstein-Evron (1998)). Byrd (2000, 88) describes a 'dearth of detailed studies of floor

artifacts' although he discusses Epipalaeolithic sites in the Levant with multiple floors. Multiple resurfaced floors are found in semi-subterranean buildings with claimed public functions at Hallan Çemi (Rosenberg (1999)), and they are also found in PPN Jericho (Kenyon (1981))

62 Farid (2006)

63 Although digging through hard lime floors to bury the dead is found at, for example, PPNB 'Ain Ghazal (Rollefson (2000))

64 Basin/bin F.280

65 Mellaart (1964, 116–17; 1967, 50)

66 Cessford (2006)

67 Matthews (2005a)

68 Düring (2001)

69 Hodder (1990); Hodder & Cessford (2004)

70 Bourdieu (1977)

71 Byrd (1994), but for a critique of Byrd and the idea that there is a gradual progression from smaller to larger domestic houses in the Levant see Goring-Morris and Belfer-Cohen (2003)

72 The latest burials in Building 1 include people who seem to have been distinctive in some way (e.g. with the head removed), but there is some uncertainty about which of the burials is latest and there is some replastering of floors over the latest burials

73 Cessford and Near (2005)

74 Cessford (2006)

75 As well as the Building 1 examples, a cattle scapula was placed over hearth F.592 in the southeast corner of Building 17 in Phase B (Level IX). In Building 23, Subphase 3, two cattle scapulae were found associated with hearth F.809. A large number of scapulae have been found near a hearth in the abandonment phase of Building 3 (Stevanovic and Tringham (1998)). However, scapulae were also abandoned elsewhere – for example, in Building 5, near basins, in a bin and in a post-retrieval hole (Cessford (2006))

76 The doorway is between Spaces 154 and 155 in Building 5

77 The lentil bin is F.215

78 Phase B1.3

79 Phase B5.B

80 The main room is Space 154

81 Part of Space 155

82 At the southern end of wall F.225

83 Space 157

84 In addition, Space 173 in Building 6, Level VIII had been heavily truncated prior to infilling, as had the floors in Building 4, Level VIII

85 Mellaart (1967, 82)

86 Mellaart (1967, fig. 16)

87 Space 117

88 The buildings referred to here are 'Grill Buildings' as defined by Özdoğan (1999)

89 Özdoğan (1999)

90 These practices are seen at the Çayönü Skull Building and at Qermez Dere, Beidha and Abu Hureyra (Özdoğan (1999))

91 Cross May (2005)

92 The refitting evidence comes from Phase D, sub-phase (ii) in Building 17

93 The adjoining room is Space 182

94 The oven is F.87 in Phase 3 in Building 4

95 Byrd (1994; 2000), but see note 71 for a different view. There are dangers in suggesting general trends in Anatolia and the Middle East as many PPNB buildings earlier than Çatalhöyük are much more complex than those found at the site

96 Schmidt (2001)

97 Özdoğan (1999); Stordeur et al. (2000)

98 Kenyon (1981); Naveh (2003)

99 Durkheim (1893)

100 Blanton et al. (1996); Feinman (1995)

101 Andrews et al. (2005)

102 Mellaart (1967)

103 Russell and Meece (2005)

104 Elias (1994)

105 Elias (1994, 52)

CHAPTER SIX

1 Schmidt (2001)

2 Mellaart (1966b); Todd (1976, 57)

3 Mellaart (1966a)

4 Schmidt (2001)

5 But see the useful summary and discussion by Helmer et al. (2004) who argue that the splayed figure is a leopard

6 Goring-Morris and Belfer-Cohen (2002)

7 Wiessner and Tumu (1998)

8 ibid., 27

9 ibid., 25

10 There has been much recent discussion in archaeology about how objects, sites and landscapes can be used to construct memories (e.g. Alcock et al. (2003), Mills (2004)). My concern in this chapter is with a particular type of memory construction that I argue is historical, involving specific genealogical links and material evidence

11 Farid (2006) referring to Space 105. The eastern wall that was added was F.56 and the southern wall F.78

12 The underlying walls and middens were Level VII and VIII middens and a Level VIII wall F.63

13 This earlier wall was the Level IX wall of Building 2

14 Connerton (1989)

15 The filled-in phase is termed Subphase B1.5B in Building 1

16 The phases that saw disturbance or destruction of the sculpture on the west wall of Building 1 are Phases B1.3 and B1.4

17 Back in Subphase B1.2C

18 The period covers Phases B1.3 to B1.5B

19 The pit is F.223 in Space 154 in Building 5

20 In Building 4 pit F.91 was dug into Space 150 in Level VIII

21 Mellaart (1967)

22 Cessford (2006)

23 Cessford (2005a) found that the bones had a 51 per cent probability of being earlier than the lentils by up to 150 (95 per cent probability) or 80 (68 per cent probability) years

24 Mellaart (1967, 84)

25 Rollefson (2000)

26 Silistreli (1991) and Bonogofsky (2005)

27 Solecki (1977)

28 Stordeur et al. (2000)

29 Cauvin (1994)

30 Although see Cessford (2006) for a rather different interpretation of the Building 1 example

31 Bonogofsky (2005) has suggested that the plastered skulls from the Levant and from Köşk Höyük in Anatolia do not support the hypothesis of ancestor cult

veneration because the plastered skulls include men, women and children. While she is right to point to the fact that a wide range of people were treated in this way, I think it quite possible that the skulls of children in important lineages could be used to 'stand for' ancestral ties. I also find the specific context of the plastered skull from Çatalhöyük difficult to interpret except in terms of the construction of links to the past

32 Özdoğan and Başgelen (1999)

33 Weiner (1992)

34 Baysal and Wright (2005)

35 Wright (2000)

36 The stamp seals at the site have been studied by Ali Türkcan (Türkcan (2005)), and the figurines by Naomi Hamilton (Hamilton (2005)). The figurines are now being studied by Lynn Meskell, Caroline Nakamura and Ali Türkcan

37 Russell (2005)

38 Joyce (2000)

39 See Hodder and Cessford (2004) and Hodder (2005d)

40 Ritchey (1996) and Düring (2001)

41 This evidence for a concentration of bifacially flaked points in more elaborate buildings is based on the re-analysis of 1960s data which has many difficulties (Conolly (1996)). The current project has not excavated a large enough sample of buildings to be able to confirm the pattern. A similar point can be made about the apparent concentration of certain types of figurines in more elaborate buildings (Hamilton (1996))

42 The number of people buried in Building 1 who were probably alive at the same point in time has been estimated by Craig Cessford (2006) on the basis of the age at death of the interred individuals in relation to the radiocarbon-dated phases of the burials

43 Hamilton (1996)

44 Ritchey (1996)

45 The quotes in this paragraph are from Firth (1936, 299 and 309)

46 Özbaşaran (1999)

47 Özdoğan (2002); Gérard and Thissen (2002)

48 Cauvin (1994)

49 Stordeur *et al.* (1977)
50 Cauvin (1994)
51 Schmidt (2001)
52 Özdoğan and Başgelen (1999)
53 Cauvin (1994) has claimed a PPNB expansion of this sort
54 Cessford (2005a) has calculated that the deep sounding at Aşıklı Höyük was occupied for 250–530 years (68 per cent probability) or 180–600 years (95 per cent probability), excluding level 3 which is undated
55 Esin and Harmankaya (1999, fig. 9)
56 Esin and Harmankaya (1999)
57 Levi-Strauss (1982, 174)
58 Carsten & Hugh-Jones (1995), Joyce & Gillespie (2000)
59 Joyce (2000)
60 Kirch (2000)
61 By politics of history I mean the ways in which history and memory were given political purpose. At Çatalhöyük I have argued that history was largely controlled in the interests of house-based groups
62 Woodburn (1980)
63 Painted walls occur probably in upper storeys of buildings in the Chalcolithic at Can Hasan

CHAPTER SEVEN

1 Mellaart (1967, 119)
2 Todd (1976, 57)
3 Stevanovic and Tringham (1998)
4 Julia Hendon (2000) provides a wide range of examples from the Trobriand Islands, Neolithic Europe and Mesoamerica showing how household storage (including of obsidian) can be used to create memory and social prestige
5 For a discussion of shamans at Çatalhöyük see Lewis-Williams (2004)
6 Firth (1967, 213). The following quote is from Firth (1967, 215)
7 Stevanovic and Tringham (1998)
8 Mellaart (1967, 102)
9 Cauvin (1994)
10 Naveh (2003)
11 Stordeur *et al.* (2000); Cauvin (1994)
12 Such as Weiner (1992)
13 Bender (1978); Hayden (1990); Dietler and Hayden (2001)
14 Russell and Martin (2005)
15 Spasojevic is part of the team

working on the obsidian at Çatal-höyük – see Carter *et al.* (2005a). She is referring here to Space 105
16 Conolly (1996) and Carter *et al.* (2005a)
17 See Hendon (2000) and note 4 above
18 Cessford (2006)
19 Benjamin (1969)
20 Turner (1969)
21 Reese (2005); Rosen (2005)
22 Jackson (2005)
23 Carter *et al.* (2005a)
24 As well as the links to the neonates below the floors, an aspect of the suite of meanings connected to obsidian hoarding may be a link to hunting. Tristan Carter and other members of the team studying the struck stone suggest that obsidian was made into hunting and killing points, whereas flint was not. In many small-scale societies, there are strong taboos surrounding hunting points and spears. Perhaps the obsidian had to be buried because it was seen as 'dangerous' – because it was a material used to kill animals. Perhaps the location of the hoarding near fire and entry/exit areas can also be made sense of in this way. However, obsidian was also used for many other, non-hunting activities, and the hoards are not just of projectile points
25 Mellaart (1967); Türkcan (2005)
26 Carter *et al.* (2005a)
27 Hodder (1990)
28 A long programme of work by French and Turkish scientists has concentrated on chemical characterization of the Neolithic obsidian found on archaeological sites, and has matched the chemical signatures of the archaeological obsidian with the different sources such as the mountains Göllü Dağ-East and Nenezi Dağ in Cappadocia. A summary of this work and its application to Çatalhöyük is provided by Carter *et al.* (2005b)
29 Balkan-Atlı *et al.* (1999)
30 Wright (1978) argued for social stratification in Natufian burials at El-Wad, but this was questioned by Belfer-Cohen (1995) and Byrd and Monahan (1995) (see also

Weinstein-Evron 1998)
31 See Kuijt (2000) for a full review of this debate
32 Naveh (2003)
33 Rosenberg (1999)
34 Cauvin (1994); Hauptmann (1999); Schmidt (2001); Stordeur *et al.* (2000)
35 Esin & Harmankaya (1999)
36 Özdoğan (1999)
37 Ranking has also been claimed by Wasson (1994)
38 Yalman (2005)
39 Conolly (1996; 1999a, b)
40 Hamilton (1996, 217–18)
41 Özdoğan (2002)
42 Hamilton (2005a)
43 Özdoğan (2002)
44 Perlès (2001, 270)
45 The lime burning evidence is from Level Pre-XII.B in Space 181 in the South Area (Farid (2006))
46 Baysal and Wright (2005)
47 Obsidian industry 1 is house based (Carter *et al.* (2005a))
48 Russell and Martin (2005)
49 Fairbairn *et al.* (2005a)
50 Space 157
51 Wendrich (2005) argues, however, that the 'coaster' mats that we find on the floors are unlikely to be the surviving bases of baskets
52 Rosen (2005)
53 As in Space 156
54 Atalay (2005)
55 Hamilton (2005) discusses the beads from the site and the evidence for manufacture near hearths or ovens in Buildings 17 and 18
56 Baysal and Wright (2005)
57 Mellaart (1962, 55)
58 Hamilton (2005c)
59 Russell (2005)
60 Vedder (2005)
61 Mellaart (1967)

CHAPTER EIGHT

1 Turnbull-Kemp (1967)
2 Last (2005)
3 Wendrich (2005)
4 Copley *et al.* (2005)
5 Gebel *et al.* (2002); Verhoeven (2000; 2002)
6 Latour (1996); Gell (1998)
7 Gebel (2002)
8 Morsch (2002)
9 For a similar argument at Çatalhöyük see Voigt (2000)

10 Mellaart (1967, 149–50)
11 Matthews (2005a)
12 Although Cessford (2006) argues for a rather more cautious interpretation of this evidence
13 Stevanovic and Tringham (1998)
14 Jenkins (2005)
15 Douglas (1966; 1972)
16 Hamilton (2005c)
17 Nakamura and Meskell (2004)
18 Cessford and Mitrovic (2005)
19 Krotschek (2004) referring to Space 100 in the 4040 Area
20 Voigt (2000)
21 Hamilton (2005c) is here referring to deposit (4321) at the interface of Spaces 159 and 173
22 Carter et al. (2005a) are here referring to (1387) and (1388), part of F.364 in Building 1
23 For example, a large sharp obsidian flake was placed behind oven F.473 in Building 18. In addition a flint perforator was placed in bin F.515 with red ochre as part of the abandonment of Building 18
24 Carter et al. (2005a) note such cases in Buildings 1, 2, 5, 17 and 23
25 Lewis-Williams (2004)
26 Lewis-Williams (2004); Thomas and Humphrey (1996)
27 Cessford (2006)
28 Russell and Martin (2005)
29 Bender (1978); Hayden (1990); Dietler and Hayden (2001)
30 PPNA roasting pits occur at Mureybet and Jerf el Ahmar (Cauvin (1994)), and public feasting is claimed at Hallan Çemi in Anatolia (Rosenberg (1999))
31 The sites are Nevali Çori, Cafer Höyük and Çayönü (Cauvin et al. (1999); Hauptmann (1999))
32 At Musular (Özbaşaran (1999))
33 I refer here to the walls around Buildings 8 and 20 in Level VII (Farid (2006))
34 Level VIB
35 Schmidt (2001)
36 Hauptmann (1999; 2002)
37 Cessford (2006)
38 Mellaart (1967)
39 Hauptmann (1999); Schmidt (2001)
40 Goring-Morris and Belfer-Cohen (2002)
41 Rollefson (1986)
42 Schmidt (1999)
43 At Middle PPNB Wadi Ghwair

and in Late PPNB burials at 'Ain Ghazal (Simmons and Najjar (2000); Rollefson (2000))
44 Goring-Morris and Belfer-Cohen (2002) refer to Hallan Çemi and Nemrik
45 Goring-Morris and Belfer-Cohen (2002, 70)
46 Bataille (1962)
47 Bloch (1992) and see Chapter 1
48 Schmidt (1999)
49 The term 'taphonomic' refers to the processes of decay and transformation that affect artifacts and carbonized seeds after deposition in the ground
50 Mellaart (1964, 45)
51 Hodder (2004)
52 Fairbairn et al. (2005a)
53 See also Winnicott (1958)
54 Although female representations occur already in the earlier Khiamian culture in the same area (Cauvin (1994))
55 Perlès (2001) is here referring to phases EN1, EN2 and EN3 in Thessaly
56 Hauptmann (2002)
57 Helms (2003)
58 Meskell (2004)

CHAPTER NINE
1 Estes (1991, 411)
2 Mellaart (1967)
3 Rudebeck (2000)
4 Firth (1936, 93 and 95)
5 The female cranium in Building 17 is referred to as (5022)
6 Stevanovic and Tringham (1998)
7 Kuijt (2000)
8 Cessford (2006)
9 Molleson et al. (2005)
10 Boz (2005)
11 Richards and Pearson (2005)
12 Molleson et al. (2005)
13 Hamilton (1996; 2005a)
14 Mellaart (1967)
15 Hamilton (2005c)
16 Firth (1936, 267)
17 Molleson et al. (2005)
18 Molleson et al. (2005)
19 Molleson et al. (2005)
20 Cessford (2005b)
21 Rosen (2005)
22 Gell (1998)
23 Hamilton (2005a) and Molleson et al. (2005)
24 Richards and Pearson (2005)
25 Although, as I described in

Chapter 6, some houses (and perhaps mainly the elders in some houses) became dominant in terms of the control of knowledge, ancestry and feasting
26 However, many forms of ill health will not be visible in skeletal data. We only see chronic conditions in the skeletons
27 There are various reactions to high infant mortality, and not all stress good mothering (see Nancy Scheper-Hughes (1987), and Alma Gottlieb (2004))
28 Mellaart (1970)
29 See Epilogue for an alternative interpretation of this protuberance

CHAPTER TEN
1 Estes (1992)
2 Turnbull-Kemp (1967, 31 and 32)
3 Rudebeck (2000)
4 There is a danger in assuming some overarching evolutionary trend from collective sharing and a lack of emphasis on individual selves towards greater individuation. In fact, people are buried with beads and body decoration from much earlier times, indeed way back into the Palaeolithic. The shifts through time are complex, nuanced and contextual. My aim is to understand the particular situation at Çatalhöyük in relation to earlier sites in Anatolia and the Middle East
5 Fowler (2004)
5 Kuniholm and Newton (1996) and Cessford (2005a)
6 Cessford (2006)
7 Cessford (2006). Cessford's account is itself based on and quotes from the reports of those that excavated in these buildings from 1995 to 1998, especially Gavin Lucas, Roger Matthews, Naomi Hamilton and Tona Majo
8 Shanks and Tilley (1982). For the Levant see Kuijt (2001)
9 See also Hodder and Cessford (2004)
10 For an ethnographic and anthro-pological discussion of varying notions of body boundaries, indivi-duals and relational individuals or 'dividuals' see Strathern (1988)

11 In many societies humans and selves are seen relationally in terms of their contextual links to other humans and non-humans (for example, see Bird-David (1999))

12 Matthews (2005a)

13 Bull *et al.* (2005)

14 Russell (2005)

15 Vedder (2005)

16 Türkcan (2005)

CHAPTER ELEVEN

1 Türkcan (2005)

2 *ibid.*

3 Last (1998)

4 Leopard flesh may also have been thought to be less palatable. Carnivores have strong tasting meat, but in some societies the meat is still thought to be tasty and is valued. We cannot assume that people at Çatalhöyük simply disliked leopard meat. Taste is always socially embedded

5 For example, at Hallan Çemi (Rosenberg (1999))

6 For example, Göbekli Tepe (Schmidt (1999; 2001))

7 As at Jerf el Ahmar (Stordeur *et al.* (1996)) and at Zawi Chemi Shanidar in northern Iraq in the 9th millennium BC (Solecki (1977))

8 Schmidt (2001)

9 Goring-Morris and Belfer-Cohen (2003; see also 2002)

10 *ibid.*

11 Bender (1978); Hayden (1990)

12 Goring-Morris and Belfer-Cohen (2003, 76)

13 Deetz (1977)

14 Johnson (1996)

15 Woodburn (1980); Ingold (1995); Bird-David (1990, 1999)

16 Chapman (2000)

17 Gell (1998)

18 Gamble (1999)

19 For Blombos see Henshilwood (2002) and for France and Iberia see Mithen (1996)

20 I am referring here to Bourdieu's (1977) idea of habitus

21 Nadel and Werker (1999)

22 The notion of 'materiality' has become of widespread interest in archaeology in recent years (e.g. Tilley (1999, 2004), Chapman (2000), Meskell (2004), Myers (2001)). These new interests in material culture have a complex heritage. They partly derive from structural Marxism and the importance of objective conditions (Friedman and Rowlands (1977)), and from anthropological studies of material culture (Miller (1987; 1998)), but they also come from practice theories (Bourdieu (1977)), and from attempts to break down mind/body, subject/object oppositions in the phenomenological tradition (Thomas (1996)). A similar emphasis on breaking down mind/object distinctions is found in the cognitive development and evolutionary psychology perspectives that have been championed by cognitive-processual archaeology (Mithen (1996), Donald (1991), Demarrais *et al.* (1996)). Another important contribution is from the French emphasis on technologies (e.g. Lemonnier (1993), Dobres (2000))

23 Renfrew (1998; 2001; Renfrew and Scarre (1998)) has based his phases, which he sees as cognitive, on the work of Donald (1991)

24 Renfrew wishes to escape from mind/matter dichotomies, and to argue, in a tradition that extends back and across to Cartesian critics (Merleau-Ponty (1962), Heidegger (1927), Latour (1996)), that mind and object are mutually constitutive

25 Renfrew (2001, 128)

26 Merleau-Ponty (1962)

27 Renfrew (2001, 127)

28 Renfrew (2001, 128)

29 I have taken and generalized this concept of material entanglement from Thomas (1991)

30 Belfer-Cohen and Bar Yosef (2000); Özdoğan (2002)

31 Goring-Morris and Belfer-Cohen (2003)

32 See also Mithen (2003)

33 Hillman (1996)

34 Grosman and Belfer-Cohen (2002, 50)

35 Grosman and Belfer-Cohen (2002)

36 Heun *et al.* (1997); Jones (2001)

37 Mithen (2003, 67)

38 Schmidt (2001)

39 Hillman and Davies (1990)

40 Bar-Yosef and Anna Belfer-Cohen (2002)

41 Hillman and Davies (1990)

42 Esin and Harmankaya (1999)

43 Kenyon (1981)

44 Hodder and Cessford (2004)

45 Baysal and Wright (2005)

46 Carter *et al.* (2005a)

47 Russell (2005)

48 Levels Pre-XII to VI

49 Fairbairn *et al.* (2005a); Russell and Martin (2005); Russell (2005); Baysal and Wright (2005)

50 Farid (2006); Cessford (2006)

51 Last (1996; 2005)

52 Atalay (2005)

53 Russell (2005)

54 Carter *et al.* (2005a)

55 Carter *et al.* (2005b)

56 These larger blades differ from the micro-blades in the lower part of the sequence

57 Byrd (2000, 79)

58 Goring-Morris and Belfer-Cohen (2003); Özdoğan and Özdoğan (1990)

59 Tringham (2000)

60 Sahlins (1972)

61 Last (1996)

62 Farid (2006)

63 Painted plaster does occur on other Chalcolithic sites such as Can Hasan I. It is possible that painted wall plasters at this time occurred in upper storeys, indicating an overall extension of decoration, including pottery decoration

64 Mellaart (1967)

65 Hodder (1996)

66 Düring (2001), though see Cutting (2005) for a rather different view

67 Cessford (2005a)

68 Hamilton (2005a)

69 Voigt (2000)

70 Silverblatt (1988)

71 Cauvin (1994)

72 Frame (2002)

73 Russell and Martin (2005)

74 Russell and Martin (2005)

75 I refer here only to the Middle East. In Mesoamerica, for example, agriculture developed before sedentism. The relevance of theories based on materiality to theories about the adoption of agriculture and sedentism outside the Middle East needs further research

Bibliography

Alcock, S., Van Dyke, R. and Keeble, N. H. (eds.) 2003. *Archaeologies of memory*. Blackwell, Oxford.

Andel, van. T. and Runnels, C. 1995. The earliest farmers in Europe. *Antiquity* 69, 481–500.

Anderson, B. 1991. *Imagined communities: reflections on the origin and spread of nationalism*. Verso, London

Andrews, P., Molleson, T. and Boz, B. 2005. The human burials at Çatalhöyük. In Hodder, I. (ed.) *Inhabiting Çatalhöyük: reports from the 1995–1999 seasons*. McDonald Institute for Archaeological Research/British Institute of Archaeology at Ankara Monograph, Cambridge. (In press).

Asouti, E. 2005. Woodland vegetation and the exploitation of fuel and timber at Neolithic Çatalhöyük: report on the wood charcoal macro-remains. In Hodder, I. (ed.) *Inhabiting Çatalhöyük: reports from the 1995–1999 seasons*. McDonald Institute for Archaeological Research/ British Institute of Archaeology at Ankara Monograph, Cambridge. (In press).

Asouti E. and Fairbairn, A. 2002. Subsistence economy in Central Anatolia during the Neolithic. The archaeo-botanical evidence. In Gérard, F. and Thissen, L. (eds.) *The Neolithic of Central Anatolia. Internal developments and external relations during the 9th–6th millennia cal BC, Proceedings of the International CANeW Round Table, Istanbul 23–24 November 2001*, pp. 181–92. Ege Yayınları, Istanbul.

Atalay, S. 2005. Domesticating clay: the role of clay balls, mini balls and geometric objects in daily life at Çatalhöyük. In Hodder, I. (ed.) *Changing materialities at Çatalhöyük: reports from the 1995–1999 seasons*. McDonald Institute for Archaeological Research/British Institute of Archaeology at Ankara Monograph, Cambridge. (In press).

Bahrani, Z. 2003. *The graven image: representation in Babylonia and Assyria*. University of Pennsylvania Press, Philadelphia.

Bailey, T. 1993. *The African leopard*. Columbia University Press, New York.

Baird, D. 2002. Early Holocene settlement in Central Anatolia: problems and prospects as seen from the Konya Plain. In Gérard, F. and Thissen, L. (eds.) *The Neolithic of Central Anatolia. Internal developments and external relations during the 9th–6th millennia cal BC, Proceedings of the International CANeW Round Table, Istanbul 23–24 November 2001*, pp. 139–52. Ege Yayınları, Istanbul.

Baird, D. 2005. The history of settlement and social landscapes in the Early Holocene in the Çatalhöyük area. In Hodder, I. (ed.) *Çatalhöyük perspectives: themes from the 1995–1999 seasons*. McDonald Institute for Archaeological Research/British Institute of

Archaeology at Ankara Monograph, Cambridge. (In press).

Balkan-Atlı, N., Binder, D. and Cauvin M.-C. 1999. Obsidian: sources, workshops and trade in Central Anatolia. In Özdoğan, M. and Başgelen, N. (eds.) *Neolithic in Turkey: The cradle of civilization. New discoveries*, pp. 133–45. Arkeoloji ve Sanat Yayınları, Istanbul.

Balter, M. 2005. *The goddess and the bull*. Simon and Schuster, New York.

Banning, E. B. and Byrd, B. F. 1987. Houses and the changing residential unit: domestic architecture at PPNB 'Ain Ghazal, Jordan. *Proceedings of the Prehistoric Society* 53, 309–25.

Bartu, A. 2000. Where is Çatalhöyük? Multiple sites in the construction of an archaeological site. In Hodder, I. (ed.) *Towards reflexive method in archaeology: the example at Çatalhöyük*, pp. 101–110. McDonald Institute for Archaeological Research/British Institute of Archaeology at Ankara, Cambridge.

Bartu Candan, A. 2006. Entanglements/encounters/ engagements with prehistory: Çatalhöyük and its publics. In Hodder, I. (ed.) *Çatalhöyük perspectives: themes from the 1995–1999 seasons*. McDonald Institute for Archaeological Research/British Institute of Archaeology at Ankara Monograph, Cambridge. (In press).

Bar-Yosef, O. 1986. The walls of Jericho. An alternative interpretation. *Current Anthropology* 27, 157–62.

Bar-Yosef, O. and Belfer-Cohen, A. 2002. Facing environmental crisis. Societal and cultural changes at the transition from the Younger Dryas to the Holocene in the Levant. In Cappers, R. T. J. and Bottema, S. (eds.) *The dawn of farming in the Near East*. Studies in Early Near Eastern Production, Subsistence, and Environment 6, 55–66. Ex Oriente, Berlin.

Bataille, G. 1955 *Lascaux; or, The birth of art: prehistoric painting*. Skira, Lausanne.

Bataille, G. 1962. *Erotism : death and sensuality*. Walker, New York.

Baysal, A. and Wright, K. I. 2005. Cooking, crafts and curation: ground stone artefacts from Çatalhöyük (1995–99 excavations). In Hodder, I. (ed.) *Changing materialities at Çatalhöyük: reports from the 1995–1999 seasons*. McDonald Institute for Archaeological Research/British Institute of Archaeology at Ankara Monograph, Cambridge. (In press).

Belfer-Cohen, A. 1995. Rethinking social stratification in the Natufian culture: the evidence from burials. In Campbell, S. and Green, A. (eds.) *The archaeology of death in the ancient Near East*, pp. 9–16. Oxbow Monograph 51, Oxford.

Bender, B. 1978. Gatherer-hunter to farmer: a social

perspective. *World Archaeology* 10, 204–22.

Benjamin, W. 1969. *Illuminations.* Schocjen, New York.

Bird-David, N. 1990. The giving environment: another perspective on the economic system of gatherer-hunters. *Current Anthropology* 31, 189–196.

Bird-David, N. 1999. "Animism" revisited. Personhood, environment, and relational epistemology. *Current Anthropology* 40 Supplement, 67–90.

Blanton, R. E., Feinman, G. M., Kowalewski, S. A. and Peregrine, P.N. 1996. A dual-processual theory for the evolution of Mesoamerican civilization. *Current Anthropology* 37, 1–14.

Bloch, M. 1992 *Prey into hunter. The politics of religious experience.* Cambridge University Press, Cambridge.

Bonogofsky, M. 2005. A bioarchaeological study of plastered skulls from Anatolia: new discoveries and interpretations. *International Journal of Osteoarchaeology* 15, 124–35.

Bourdieu, P. 1977. *Outline of a theory of practice.* Cambridge University Press, Cambridge.

Boyd, B. 2005. *People and animals in Levantine prehistory: 20,000–8,000 BC.* Cambridge University Press, Cambridge

Boz, B. 2005. The oral health of Çatalhöyük Neolithic people. In Hodder, I. (ed.) *Inhabiting Çatalhöyük: reports from the 1995–1999 seasons.* McDonald Institute for Archaeological Research/British Institute of Archaeology at Ankara Monograph, Cambridge. (In press).

Bradley, R. 2002. *The past in prehistoric societies.* Routledge, London.

Buck, C.E., Christen, J. A. and James, G. N. 1999. BCal: an on-line Bayesian radiocarbon calibration tool. *Internet Archaeology* 7 (http://intarch.ac.uk/journal/issue7/buck_toc.html).

Buitenhuis, H. 1997. Aşıklı Höyük: a 'protodomestication' site. *Anthropozoologica* 25/26, 655–62.

Bull, I.D., Elhmmali, M. M., Perret, P., Matthews, W., Roberts, D.J. and Evershed, R.P. 2005. Biomarker evidence of faecal deposition in archaeological sediments at Çatalhöyük. In Hodder, I. (ed.) *Inhabiting Çatalhöyük: reports from the 1995–1999 seasons.* McDonald Institute for Archaeological Research/British Institute of Archaeology at Ankara Monograph, Cambridge. (In press).

Byrd, B. F. 1994. Public and private, domestic and corporate: the emergence of the Southwest Asian village. *American Antiquity* 59, 639–66.

Byrd, B. F., 2000. Households in transition: Neolithic social organization within Southwest Asia. In Kuijt, I. (ed.) *Life in Neolithic farming communities: Social organization, identity, and differentiation,* pp. 63–102. Kluwer Academic/Plenum, New York.

Byrd, B. F. and Monahan, C. M. 1995. Death, mortuary rituals and Natufian social structure. *Journal of Anthropological Archaeology* 14, 251–287.

Carsten, J. and Hugh-Jones, S. (eds.) 1995. *About the house: Levi-Strauss and beyond.* Cambridge University Press, Cambridge.

Carter, T., Conolly, J. and Spasojević, A. 2005a. The chipped stone. In Hodder, I. (ed.) *Changing materialities at Çatalhöyük: reports from the 1995–1999 seasons.* McDonald Institute for Archaeological Research/British Institute of Archaeology at Ankara Monograph, Cambridge. (In press).

Carter, T., Poupeau, G., Bressy, C. and Pearce, N. J. G. 2005b. From chemistry to consumption: towards a history of obsidian use at Çatalhöyük through a programme of inter-laboratory trace-elemental characterization. In Hodder, I. (ed.) *Changing materialities at Çatalhöyük: reports from the 1995–1999 seasons.* McDonald Institute for Archaeological Research/British Institute of Archaeology at Ankara Monograph, Cambridge. (In press).

Cauvin, J. 1994. *Naissance des divinités, Naissance de l'agriculture.* CNRS, Paris.

Cauvin, J., Aurenche, O., Cauvin M.-C. and Balkan-Atlı, N. 1999. The Pre-Pottery site of Cafer Höyük. In Özdoğan, M. and Başgelen, N. (eds.) *Neolithic in Turkey: The cradle of civilization. New discoveries,* pp. 87–103. Arkeoloji ve Sanat Yayınları, Istanbul.

Cessford, C. 2005a. Absolute dating at Çatalhöyük. In Hodder, I. (ed.) *Changing materialities at Çatalhöyük: reports from the 1995–1999 seasons.* McDonald Institute for Archaeological Research/British Institute of Archaeology at Ankara Monograph, Cambridge. (In press).

Cessford, C. 2005b. Estimating the Neolithic population of Çatalhöyük. In Hodder, I. (ed.) *Inhabiting Çatalhöyük: reports from the 1995–1999 seasons.* McDonald Institute for Archaeological Research/British Institute of Archaeology at Ankara Monograph, Cambridge. (In press).

Cessford, C. 2006. Neolithic excavations in the North Area, East Mound, Çatalhöyük 1995–98. In Hodder, I. (ed.) *Excavating Çatalhöyük: reports from the 1995–1999 seasons.* McDonald Institute for Archaeological Research/British Institute of Archaeology at Ankara Monograph, Cambridge. (In press).

Cessford, C. and Mitrovic, S. 2005. Heavy residue analysis. In Hodder, I. (ed.) *Changing materialities at Çatalhöyük: reports from the 1995–1999 seasons.* McDonald Institute for Archaeological Research/British Institute of Archaeology at Ankara Monograph, Cambridge. (In press).

Cessford, C. and Near, J. 2005. Fire, burning and pyrotechnology at Çatalhöyük. In Hodder, I. (ed.) *Çatalhöyük perspectives: themes from the 1995–1999 seasons.* McDonald Institute for Archaeological Research/British Institute of Archaeology at Ankara Monograph, Cambridge. (In press).

Chapman, J. 2000. *Fragmentation in archaeology: people, places and broken objects in the prehistory of southeast Europe.* Routledge, London.

Childe, V. G. 1952. *New light on the most ancient East.* Routledge and Paul, London.

Connerton, P. 1989. *How societies remember.* Cambridge University Press, Cambridge.

Conolly, J. 1996. The knapped stone. In Hodder, I. (ed.) *On the surface: Çatalhöyük 1993–95*, pp. 173–198. McDonald Institute for Archaeological Research/British Institute of Archaeology at Ankara Monograph, Cambridge.

Conolly, J. 1999a. *The Çatalhöyük flint and obsidian industry. Technology and typology in context.* British Archaeological Reports, International Series 787, Oxford.

Conolly, J. 1999b. Technical strategies and technical change at Neolithic Çatalhöyük, Turkey. *Antiquity* 73, 791–800.

Copley, M., Clark, K. and Evershed, R. 2005. Organic residue analysis of pottery vessels and clay balls. In Hodder, I. (ed.) *Changing materialities at Çatalhöyük: reports from the 1995–1999 seasons.* McDonald Institute for Archaeological Research/British Institute of Archaeology at Ankara Monograph, Cambridge. (In press).

Cross May, S. 2005. Statistical integration of contextual data. In Hodder, I. (ed.) *Changing materialities at Çatalhöyük: reports from the 1995–1999 seasons.* McDonald Institute for Archaeological Research/British Institute of Archaeology at Ankara Monograph, Cambridge. (In press).

Cutting, M. 2005. The architecture of Çatalhöyük: continuity, households and the lost upper levels. In Hodder, I. (ed.) *Çatalhöyük perspectives: themes from the 1995–1999 seasons.* McDonald Institute for Archaeological Research/British Institute of Archaeology at Ankara Monograph, Cambridge. (In press).

Deetz, J. 1977. *In small things forgotten.* Anchor Books, New York.

DeMarrais, E., Castillo, J. L. and Earle, T. 1996. Ideology, materialization and power strategies. *Current Anthropology* 37, 15–31.

Dietler, M. and Hayden, B. (eds.) 2001. *Feasts. Archaeological and ethnographic perspectives on food, politics, and power.* Smithsonian Institution Press, Washington (DC).

Dobbs, C. A. and Johnson, D. W. 2005. Magnetic, radar and resistivity studies at Çatalhöyük. In Hodder, I. (ed.) *Inhabiting Çatalhöyük: reports from the 1995–1999 seasons.* McDonald Institute for Archaeological Research/British Institute of Archaeology at Ankara Monograph, Cambridge. (In press).

Dobres, M-A. 2000. *Technology as social agency.* Blackwell, Oxford.

Donald, M. 1991. *Origins of the modern mind.* Harvard University Press, Cambridge.

Doody, M. A. 1980. Introduction. In Richardson, S. (originally published 1740) *Pamela; or, virtue rewarded,* pp. 7–20. Penguin, London.

Douglas, M. 1966. *Purity and danger.* Routledge & Kegan Paul, London.

Douglas, M. 1972. Deciphering a meal. *Daedalus* 1972, 61–81.

Durkheim, É. 1893. *De la division du travail social: étude sur l'organisation des sociétés supérieures.* Alcan, Paris.

Duru, R. 1999. The Neolithic of the Lake District. In Özdoğan, M. and Başgelen, N. (eds.) *Neolithic in Turkey: The cradle of civilization. New discoveries,* pp. 165–91. Arkeoloji ve Sanat Yayınları, Istanbul.

Düring, B. 2001. Social dimensions in the architecture of Neolithic Çatalhöyük. *Anatolian Studies* 51, 1–18.

Ebron, P. 1998. Enchanted memories of regional difference in African American culture. *American Anthropologist* 100, 94–105.

Edmonds, M. 1999. *Ancestral geographies of the Neolithic: landscapes, monuments and memories.* Routledge, London.

Elias, N. 1994 [1936]. *The civilizing process: the history of manners.* Blackwell, Oxford.

Esin, U. and Harmanakaya, S. 1999. Aşıklı in the frame of Central Anatolian Neolithic. In Özdoğan, M. and Başgelen, N. (eds.) *Neolithic in Turkey: The cradle of civilization. New discoveries,* pp 115–32. Arkeoloji ve Sanat Yayınları, Istanbul.

Estes, R. D. 1992. *The behaviour guide to African mammals.* University of California Press, Berkeley.

Evershed, R. P., Heron, C. and Goad, L. J. 1990. Analysis of organic residues of archaeological origin by high-temperature gas-chromatography and gas-chromatography mass-spectrometry. *Analyst* 115, 1339–42.

Evershed, R. P., Dudd, S. N., Charters, S., Mottram, H., Stott, A. W., Raven, A., van Bergen, P. F. and Bland, H. A. 1999. Lipids as carriers of anthropogenic signals from prehistory. *Philosophical Transactions of the Royal Society of London Series B-Biological Sciences* 354, 19–31.

Fabian, J. 1983. *Time and the other: how anthropology makes its object.* Columbia University Press, New York.

Fairbairn, A., Near, J. and Martinoli, Daniéle 2005a. Macrobotanical investigation of the North, South and KOPAL Area excavations at Çatalhöyük East. In Hodder, I. (ed.) *Inhabiting Çatalhöyük: reports from the 1995–1999 seasons.* McDonald Institute for Archaeological Research/British Institute of Archaeology at Ankara Monograph, Cambridge. (In press).

Fairbairn, A., Asouti, E., Russell, N. and Swogger, J. 2005b. Seasonality. In Hodder, I. (ed.) *Çatalhöyük perspectives: themes from the 1995–1999 seasons.* McDonald Institute for Archaeological Research/British Institute of Archaeology at Ankara Monograph, Cambridge. (In press).

Farid, S. 2006. Neolithic Excavations in the South Area, East Mound, Çatalhöyük 1995–99. In Hodder, I. (ed.) *Excavating Çatalhöyük: reports from the 1995–1999 seasons.* McDonald Institute for Archaeological Research/British Institute of Archaeology at Ankara Monograph, Cambridge. (In press).

Feinman, G.M. 1995. The emergence of inequality: a focus on processes and strategies. In Price, T. D. and Feinman, G. M. (eds.) *Foundations of social inequality,* pp. 255–80. Plenum Press, New York.

Firth, R. 1936 *We, the Tikopia.* George Allen and Unwin, London (1968 edition, Beacon Press, Boston)

Firth, R. 1967. *Tikopia ritual and belief.* George Allen and Unwin, London.

Forty, A. and Kuchler, S. (eds.) 1999. *The art of forgetting.* Berg, London.

Foucault, M. 1977. *Discipline and punish*. Vintage Books, New York.

Fowler, C. 2004. *The archaeology of personhood*. Routledge, London.

Frame, S. 2002. The animal bone (West Mound). *Catal News* 9, 15–16.

Friedman, J, and Rowlands, M. (eds.) 1978. *The evolution of social systems*. Duckworth, London.

Gamble, C. 1999. *The Palaeolithic societies of Europe*. Cambridge University Press, Cambridge.

Garfinkel, Y. 1994. Ritual burial of cultic objects: the earliest evidence. *Cambridge Archaeological Journal* 4, 159–88.

Gebel, H. G. K. 2002. Walls. Loci of forces. In Gebel, H. G. K., Hermansen, B. D. and Jensen C. H. (eds.) *Magic practices and ritual in the Near eastern Neolithic*, pp. 119–132. Ex Oriente, Berlin.

Gebel, H. G. K., Hermansen, B. D. and Jensen C. H. (eds.) 2002. *Magic practices and ritual in the Near eastern Neolithic*. Ex Oriente, Berlin.

Gell, A. 1998. *Art and agency*. Clarendon, Oxford.

Gérard, F. and Thissen, L. 2002. *The Neolithic of Central Anatolia. Internal Developments and External Relations during the 9th-6th Millennia CAL BC*. Ege Yayınları, Istanbul.

Gibson, C. and Last, J. 2003. Excavations of the West Mound. *Çatal News* 10, 8–9. (http://catalhoyuk.com).

Giddens, A. 1992. *Transformations of intimacy*. Stanford University Press, Stanford.

Gimbutas, M., 1982. *The goddesses and gods of Old Europe*. Thames & Hudson, London.

Goring-Morris, N. 2000. The quick and the dead: the social context of aceramic Neolithic mortuary practices as seen from Kfar HaHoresh. In Kuijt, I. (ed.) *Life in Neolithic farming communities: social organization, identity, and differentiation*, pp. 13–36. Kluwer Academic/Plenum Publishers, New York.

Goring-Morris, N. and Belfer-Cohen, A. 2002. Symbolic behaviour from the Epipalaeolithic and Early Neolithic of the Near East: preliminary observations on continuity and change. In Gebel, H. G. K., Hermansen, B. D. and Jensen, C. H. (eds.) *Magic practices and ritual in the Near Eastern Neolithic*. Studies in early Near Eastern production, subsistence and environment 8, 67–79.

Goring-Morris, N. and Belfer-Cohen, A. 2003. Structures and dwellings in the Upper and Epi-Palaeolithic (ca 42–10k BP) Levant: profane and symbolic uses. In Vasil'ev, S. A., Soffer, O. and Kozlowski, J. (eds.) *Perceived landscapes and built environments*. British Archaeological Report International Series 1122, 65–81.

Gottlieb, A. 2004. *The afterlife is where we come from : the culture of infancy in West Africa*. University of Chicago Press.

Grosman, L. and Belfer-Cohen, A. 2002. Zooming onto the 'Younger Dryas'. In Cappers, R. T. J. and Bottema, S. (eds.) *The dawn of farming in the Near East*. Studies in Early Near Eastern Production, Subsistence, and Environment 6, 49–54. Ex Oriente, Berlin.

Hamann, B. 2002. The social life of pre-sunrise things: indigenous Mesoamerican archaeology. *Current Anthropology* 43, 351–382.

Hamilton, N. 1996. Figurines, clay balls, small finds and burials. In Hodder, I. (ed.) *On the surface: Çatalhöyük 1993–95*, pp. 215–264. McDonald Institute for Archaeological Research/British Institute of Archaeology at Ankara Monograph, Cambridge.

Hamilton, N. 2005a. Social aspects of burial. In Hodder, I. (ed.) *Inhabiting Çatalhöyük: reports from the 1995–1999 seasons*. McDonald Institute for Archaeological Research/British Institute of Archaeology at Ankara Monograph, Cambridge. (In press).

Hamilton, N. 2005b. The beads. In Hodder, I. (ed.) *Changing materialities at Çatalhöyük: reports from the 1995–1999 seasons*. McDonald Institute for Archaeological Research/British Institute of Archaeology at Ankara Monograph, Cambridge. (In press).

Hamilton, N. 2005c. The figurines. In Hodder, I. (ed.) *Changing materialities at Çatalhöyük: reports from the 1995–1999 seasons*. McDonald Institute for Archaeological Research/British Institute of Archaeology at Ankara Monograph, Cambridge. (In press).

Harris, E. C. 1989. *Principles of archaeological stratigraphy*. Academic Press, London.

Hauptmann, H. 1999. The Urfa region. In Özdoğan, M. and Başgelen, N. (eds.) *Neolithic in Turkey: The cradle of civilization. New discoveries*, pp. 65–87. Arkeoloji ve Sanat Yayınları, Istanbul.

Hauptmann, H., 2002. Upper Mesopotamia in its regional context during the Early Neolithic. In Gérard, F. and Thissen, L. (eds.) *The Neolithic of Central Anatolia. Internal developments and external relations during the 9th–6th millennia cal BC*, *Proceedings of the International CANeW Round Table, Istanbul 23–24 November 2001*, pp. 263–74. Ege Yayınları, Istanbul.

Hayden, B. 1990. Nimrods, piscators, pluckers, and planters: the emergence of food production. *Journal of Anthropological Archaeology* 9(1), 31–69.

Heidegger, M. 1927. *Sein und zeit*. Neomarius Verlag, Tübingen.

Helbaek, H. 1964. First impressions of the Çatal Hüyük plant husbandry. *Anatolian Studies* 14, 121–3.

Helmer, D., Gourichon, L. and Stordeur, D. 2004. A l'aube de la domestication animale: imaginaire et symbolisme animal dans les premières sociétés néolithiques du nord du Proche-Orient. *Anthropozoologica* 39, 143–163.

Helms, M. 2003. Tangible materiality and cosmological others in the development of sedentism. Paper presented at conference *Rethinking materiality* (McDonald Institute for Archaeological Research, Cambridge).

Hendon, J. 2000. Having and holding: storage, memory, knowledge, and social relations. *American Anthropologist* 102, 42–53.

Henshilwood, C. S. 2002. Emergence of modern human behavior: Middle Stone Age engravings from South Africa. *Science* 295, 1278–1280.

Heun, M., Schafer-Pregl, R., Klawan, D., Castagna, R., Accerbi, M., Borghi, B. and Salamini, F. 1997. Site of einkorn wheat domestication identified by DNA fingerprinting. *Science* 278, 1312–14.

Hillman, G. 1996. Late Pleistocene changes in wild plant-foods available to hunter-gatherers of the northern Fertile Crescent: possible preludes to cereal cultivation. In Harris, D. R. (ed.) *The origins and spread of agriculture and pastoralism in Eurasia*, pp. 159–203. UCL Press, London.

Hillman, G. and Davies, M. 1990. Measured domestication rates in wild wheats and barley under primitive implications. *Journal of World Prehistory* 4(2), 157–222.

Hodder, I. 1982. *Symbols in action.* Cambridge University Press, Cambridge.

Hodder, I. 1990. *The domestication of Europe.* Blackwell, Oxford.

Hodder, I. (ed.) 1996. *On the surface. Çatalhöyük 1993–95.* McDonald Institute for Archaeological Research/British Institute of Archaeology at Ankara Monograph, Cambridge.

Hodder, I. 1999. *The archaeological process. An introduction.* Blackwell, Oxford.

Hodder, I. (ed.) 2000. *Towards reflexive method in archaeology: the example at Çatalhöyük.* McDonald Institute for Archaeological Research/British Institute of Archaeology at Ankara Monograph, Cambridge.

Hodder, I. 2004. *Archaeology beyond dialogue.* University of Utah Press, Salt Lake City.

Hodder, I. (ed.) 2005a. *Inhabiting Çatalhöyük: reports from the 1995–1999 seasons.* McDonald Institute for Archaeological Research/British Institute of Archaeology at Ankara Monograph, Cambridge.

Hodder, I. (ed.) 2005b. *Changing materialities at Çatalhöyük: reports from the 1995–1999 seasons.* McDonald Institute for Archaeological Research/British Institute of Archaeology at Ankara Monograph, Cambridge.

Hodder, I. (ed.) 2005c. *Çatalhöyük perspectives: themes from the 1995–1999 seasons.* McDonald Institute for Archaeological Research/British Institute of Archaeology at Ankara Monograph, Cambridge.

Hodder, I. 2005d. Memory. In Hodder, I. (ed.) *Çatalhöyük perspectives: themes from the 1995–1999 seasons.* McDonald Institute for Archaeological Research/British Institute of Archaeology at Ankara Monograph, Cambridge.

Hodder, I. (ed.) 2006. *Excavating Çatalhöyük: reports from the 1995–1999 seasons.* McDonald Institute for Archaeological Research/British Institute of Archaeology at Ankara Monograph, Cambridge.

Hodder, I. and Cessford, C. 2004. Daily practice and social memory at Çatalhöyük. *American Antiquity* 69, 17–40.

Hunt, L. 1992. *The family romance of the French Revolution.* Routledge, London.

Ingold, T. 1995. Building, dwelling, living: how animals and people make themselves at home in the world. In Strathern, M. (ed.) *Shifting contexts: transformations in anthropological knowledge,* pp. 57–80. Routledge, London.

Jackson, B. 2005. Report on bead material identification. In Hodder, I. (ed.) *Changing materialities at Çatalhöyük: reports from the 1995–1999 seasons.* McDonald Institute for Archaeological Research/British Institute of Archaeology at Ankara Monograph, Cambridge. (In press).

Jenkins, E. 2005. The Çatalhöyük microfauna: preliminary results and interpretations. In Hodder, I. (ed.) *Inhabiting Çatalhöyük: reports from the 1995–1999 seasons.* McDonald Institute for Archaeological Research/British Institute of Archaeology at Ankara Monograph, Cambridge. (In press).

Johnson, M. 1996. *An archaeology of capitalism.* Blackwell, Oxford.

Jones, M. 2001. *The molecule hunt: archaeology and the search for ancient DNA.* Allen Lane, London.

Joyce, R. 2000. Heirlooms and houses. Materiality and social memory. In Joyce, R. and Gillespie, S. D. (eds.) *Beyond kinship. Social and material reproduction in House Societies,* pp. 189–212. University of Pennsylvania Press, Philadelphia.

Joyce, R. and Gillespie, S. D. (eds.) 2000. *Beyond kinship. Social and material reproduction in house societies.* University of Pennsylvania Press, Philadelphia.

Kenyon, K.M. (T.A. Holland, ed.) 1981. *Excavations at Jericho III.* The British School of Archaeology in Jerusalem and Oxford University Press, Oxford.

Kirch, P. 2000. Temples as 'Holy Houses'. The transformation of ritual architecture in traditional Polynesian societies. In Joyce, R. and Gillespie, S. D. (eds.) *Beyond kinship. Social and material reproduction in House Societies,* pp. 103–114. University of Pennsylvania Press, Philadelphia.

Kirkbride, D. 1968. Beidha 1967: an interim report. *Palestine Exploration Quarterly* 100, 90–96.

Krotschek, U. 2004. Building 49, Space 100. *Çatalhöyük Archive Report 2004.* (http://www.catalhoyuk.com).

Kuijt, I. (ed.) 2000. *Life in Neolithic farming communities: social organization, identity, and differentiation.* Kluwer Academic/Plenum Publishers, New York.

Kuijt, I. 2001. Place, death, and the transmission of social memory in early agricultural communities of the Near Eastern Pre-Pottery Neolithic. In Chesson, M. S. (ed.) *Social memory, identity, and death: anthropological perspectives on mortuary rituals.* Archaeological Papers of the American Anthropological Association 10, 80–99.

Kuniholm, P. I. and Newton, M. W. 1996. Interim dendrochronological progress report 1995/6. In Hodder, I. (ed.) *On the Surface Çatalhöyük 1993–95,* pp. 345–7. McDonald Institute for Archaeological Research/British Institute of Archaeology at Ankara, Monograph, Cambridge.

Kuzucuoğlu, C. 2002. Environmental setting and evolution from the 9th to the 5th millennium cal BC in Central Anatolia: an introduction to the study of relations between environmental conditions and the development of human societies. In Gérard, F. and Thissen, L. (eds.) *The Neolithic of Central Anatolia. Internal* developments and external relations during the 9th–6th millennia cal BC, Proceedings of the International CANeW Round Table, Istanbul 23–24 November 2001, pp. 33–58. Ege Yayınları, Istanbul.

Kuzucuoğlu, C. and Roberts, N. 1997. Évolution de l'environnement en Anatolie de 20,000 á 6,000 BP. Paléorient 23, 7–24.

Lane, P. J. 1994. The temporal structuring of settlement space among the Dogon of Mali: an ethnoarchaeological study. In Parker Pearson, M. and Richards, C. (eds.) Architecture and order, pp. 196–216. Routledge, London.

Last, J. 1996. Surface pottery at Çatalhöyük. In Hodder, I. (ed.) On the surface. Çatalhöyük 1993–95, pp. 115–71. McDonald Institute for Archaeological Research/British Institute of Archaeology at Ankara Monograph, Cambridge.

Last, J. 1998. A design for life. Interpreting the art of Çatalhöyük. Journal of Material Culture 3, 355–378.

Last, J. 2005. Pottery from the East Mound. In Hodder, I. (ed.) Changing materialities at Çatalhöyük: reports from the 1995–1999 seasons. McDonald Institute for Archaeological Research/British Institute of Archaeology at Ankara Monograph, Cambridge. (In press).

Latour, B. 1993. We have never been modern. Harvard University Press, Cambridge.

Latour, B. 1996. Aramis, or, the love of technology. Harvard University Press, Cambridge.

Latour, B. 1999. Pandora's hope: essays on the reality of science studies. Harvard University Press, New York.

Le Goff, J. 1992. History and memory. Columbia University Press, New York.

Leibhammer, N. 2000. Rendering realities. In Hodder, I. (ed.) Towards Reflexive Method in Archaeology: The Example at Çatalhöyük, pp. 129–142. McDonald Institute for Archaeological Research/British Institute of Archaeology at Ankara Monograph, Cambridge.

Lemonnier, P. (ed.) 1993. Technological choices: transformation in material culture since the Neolithic. Routledge, London.

Levi-Strauss, C. 1982. The way of the masks. University of Washington Press, Seattle.

Lewis-Williams, J. D. 2004. Constructing a cosmos: architecture, power and domestication at Çatalhöyük. Journal of Social Archaeology 4, 28–59.

Lloyd, S. 1956. Early Anatolia. Penguin, Harmondsworth.

Lowenthal, D. 1985. The past is a foreign country. Cambridge University Press, Cambridge.

Malhi, R., Van Tuinen, M., Mountain, J., Hodder, I. and Hadly, E. A. 2005. Pilot project: Çatalhöyük ancient DNA study. In Hodder, I. (ed.) Inhabiting Çatalhöyük: reports from the 1995–1999 seasons. McDonald Institute for Archaeological Research/British Institute of Archaeology at Ankara Monograph. (In press).

Martin, L., Russell, N. and Carruthers, D. 2002. Animal remains from the central Anatolian Neolithic. In Gérard, F. and Thissen, L. (eds.) The Neolithic of Central Anatolia. Internal developments and external relations during

the 9th–6th millennia cal BC, Proceedings of the International CANeW Round Table, Istanbul 23–24 November 2001, pp. 193–206. Ege Yayınları, Istanbul.

Matero, F. 2000. The conservation of an excavated past. In Hodder, I. (ed.) Towards Reflexive Method in Archaeology: The Example at Çatalhöyük, pp. 71–88. McDonald Institute for Archaeological Research/British Institute of Archaeology at Ankara Monograph, Cambridge.

Matthews, R. 1996. Surface scraping and planning. In Hodder, I. (ed.) On the surface. Çatalhöyük 1993–95, pp. 79–99. McDonald Institute for Archaeological Research/British Institute of Archaeology at Ankara, Cambridge.

Matthews, R. 2003. The archaeology of Mesopotamia: theories and approaches. Routledge, London.

Matthews, W. 2005a. Micromorphological and microstratigaphic traces of uses and concepts of space. In Hodder, I. (ed.) Inhabiting Çatalhöyük: reports from the 1995–1999 seasons. McDonald Institute for Archaeological Research/British Institute of Archaeology at Ankara Monograph, Cambridge. (In press).

Matthews, W. 2005b. Life-cycle and -course of buildings. In Hodder, I. (ed.) Çatalhöyük perspectives: themes from the 1995–1999 seasons. McDonald Institute for Archaeological Research/British Institute of Archaeology at Ankara Monograph, Cambridge. (In press).

Matthews, W. and Farid, S. 1996. Exploring the 1960s surface – the stratigraphy of Çatalhöyük. In Hodder, I. (ed.) On the surface. Çatalhöyük 1993–95, pp. 271–300. McDonald Institute for Archaeological Research/British Institute of Archaeology at Ankara Monograph, Cambridge.

Matthews, W., French, C. A. I., Lawrence T. and Cutler, D. F., 1996. Multiple surfaces: the micromorphology. In Hodder, I. (ed.) On the surface. Çatalhöyük 1993–95, pp. 301–42. McDonald Institute for Archaeological Research/British Institute of Archaeology at Ankara Monograph, Cambridge.

Mellaart, J. 1959. Archaeological survey of the Konya Plain. Anatolian Studies 9, 31–3.

Mellaart, J. 1962. Excavations at Çatal Hüyük, 1961: First preliminary report. Anatolian Studies 12, 41–65.

Mellaart, J. 1963. Excavations at Çatal Hüyük, 1962: Second preliminary report. Anatolian Studies 13, 43–103.

Mellaart, J. 1964. Excavations at Çatal Hüyük, 1963: Third preliminary report. Anatolian Studies 14, 39–119.

Mellaart, J. 1965. Çatal Hüyük West. Anatolian Studies 15, 135–56.

Mellaart, J. 1966a. Excavations at Çatal Hüyük, 1965: Fourth preliminary report. Anatolian Studies 16, 165–191.

Mellaart, J. 1966b. The leopard shrines of Chatal Huyuk. The Illustrated London News 4th June 1966, 24–25.

Mellaart, J. 1967. Çatal Hüyük: A Neolithic Town in Anatolia. Thames & Hudson, London.

Mellaart, J. 1970. Excavations at Hacilar. Edinburgh University Press, Edinburgh.

Merleau-Ponty, M. 1962. Phenomenology of perception. Routledge, London.

Meskell, L. 2002. *Private life in New Kingdom Egypt.* Princeton University Press, Princeton.

Meskell, L. 2004. *Object worlds in ancient Egypt. Material biographies past and present.* Berg, Oxford.

Middleton, W. D., Douglas Price, T. and Meiggs, D. 2005. Chemical analysis of floor sediments for the identification of anthropogenic activity residues. In Hodder, I. (ed.) *Inhabiting Çatalhöyük: reports from the 1995–1999 seasons.* McDonald Institute for Archaeological Research/British Institute of Archaeology at Ankara Monograph, Cambridge. (In press).

Miller, D. 1987. *Material culture and mass consumption.* Blackwell, Oxford.

Miller, D. (ed.) 1998. *Material cultures.* University of Chicago Press, Chicago.

Mills, B. 2004. The establishment and defeat of hierarchy: inalienable possessions and the history of collective prestige structures in the Pueblo Southwest. *American Anthropologist* 106, 238–251.

Mitchell, T. 2002. *Rule of experts.* University of California Press, Berkeley.

Mithen, S. 1996. *The prehistory of the mind.* Thames & Hudson, London.

Mithen, S. 2003. *After the ice. A global human history, 20,000–5000 BC.* Weidenfeld and Nicolson, London.

Molleson, T., Andrews, P. and Boz, B. 2005. Reconstruction of the Neolithic people of Çatalhöyük. In Hodder, I. (ed.) *Inhabiting Çatalhöyük: reports from the 1995–1999 seasons.* McDonald Institute for Archaeological Research/British Institute of Archaeology at Ankara Monograph, Cambridge. (In press).

Moore, A. M. T., Hillman, G. C. and Legge, A. J. 2000. *Village on the Euphrates: from foraging to farming at Abu Hureyra.* Oxford University Press, Oxford.

Morris, I. 1991. The archaeology of ancestors: the Saxe/Goldstein Hypothesis revisited. *Cambridge Archaeological Journal* 1, 147–69.

Morrison, T. 1990. Site of memory. In Ferguson, R., Gever, M., Minh-ha, T. and West, C. (eds.) *Out there: marginalization and contemporary cultures,* pp. 299–305. MIT Press, Boston.

Morsch, M. G. F. 2002. Magic figurines? Some remarks about the clay objects of Nevali Çori. In Gebel, H. G. K., Hermansen, B. D. and Jensen C. H. (eds.) *Magic practices and ritual in the Near eastern Neolithic,* pp. 145–162. Ex Oriente, Berlin.

Myers, F. (ed.) 2001. *The empire of things: regimes of value and material culture.* School of America Research Press, Santa Fe.

Nadel, D. and Werker, E. 1999. The oldest ever brush hut plant remains from Ohalo II, Jordan Valley, Israel (19,000 BP). *Antiquity* 73, 755–64.

Nakamura, C. and Meskell, L. 2004. Figurines and miniature clay objects. *Çatalhöyük Archive Report* 2004 (www.catalhoyuk.com).

Naveh, D. 2003. PPNA Jericho: a socio-political perspective. *Cambridge Archaeological Journal* 13, 83–96.

Özbaşaran, M. 1999. Musular: a general assessment on a new Neolithic site in Central Anatolia. In Özdoʔan, M. and Baʔgelen, N. (eds.) *Neolithic in Turkey: The cradle of civilization. New discoveries,* pp. 147–56. Arkeoloji ve Sanat Yayınları, Istanbul.

Özbaşaran, M. and Buitenhuis, H. 2002. Proposal for a regional terminology for Central Anatolia, In Gérard, F. and Thissen, L. (eds.) *The Neolithic of Central Anatolia. Internal developments and external relations during the 9th–6th millennia cal BC, Proceedings of the International CANeW Round Table, Istanbul 23–24 November 2001,* pp. 67–77. Ege Yayınları, Istanbul.

Özdoğan, A. 1999. Çayönü. In Özdoʔan, M. and Baʔgelen, N. (eds.) *Neolithic in Turkey: The cradle of civilization. New discoveries,* pp. 35–63. Arkeoloji ve Sanat Yayınları, Istanbul.

Özdoğan, M. 2002. Defining the Neolithic of Central Anatolia. In Gérard, F. and Thissen, L. (eds.) *The Neolithic of Central Anatolia. Internal developments and external relations during the 9th–6th millennia cal BC, Proceedings of the International CANeW Round Table, Istanbul 23–24 November 2001,* pp. 253–261. Ege Yayınları, Istanbul.

Özdoğan, M. and Özdoğan, A. 1990. Çayönü. A conspectus of recent work. *Paléorient* 15, 65–74.

Özdoğan, M. and Başgelen, N. (eds.) 1999. *Neolithic in Turkey, The cradle of civilization, New discoveries,* Arkeoloji ve Sanat Yayınları, Istanbul.

Özdoğan, M. and Özdoğan, A. 1998. Buildings of cult and the cult of buildings. In Arsebük, G., Mellink, M. and Schirmer W. (eds.) *Light on top of the Black Hill. Studies Presented to Halet Cambel,* pp. 581–93. Ege Yayinlari, Istanbul.

Özkan, A. 2002. Kösk Höyük: new contributions to Anatolian archaeology. *Tüba-Ar* 5, 57–72.

Perkins, D. 1969. Fauna of Çatal Hüyük: evidence for early cattle domestication in Anatolia. *Science* 164, 177–9.

Perlès, C. 2001/ *The early Neolithic in Greece.* Cambridge University Press, Cambridge.

Peters, J., Helmer, D., Driesch, A. von den, and Seguí, M. S. 1999. Early animal husbandry in the northern Levant. *Paléorient* 25, 27–47.

Reese, D. S. 2005. The Çatalhöyük shells. In Hodder, I. (ed.) *Inhabiting Çatalhöyük: reports from the 1995–1999 seasons.* McDonald Institute for Archaeological Research/British Institute of Archaeology at Ankara Monograph, Cambridge. (In press).

Renfrew, C. 1987. *Archaeology and language.* Penguin, Harmondsworth.

Renfrew, C. 1998. Mind and matter: cognitive archaeology and external symbolic storage. In Renfrew, C. and Scarre, C. (eds.) *Cognition and material culture: the archaeology of symbolic storage.* McDonald Institute for Archaeological Research, Cambridge.

Renfrew, C. 2001. Symbol before concept. Material engagement and the early development of society. In Hodder, I. (ed.) *Archaeological theory today,* pp. 122–140.

Polity Press, Cambridge.

Renfrew, C. and Scarre, C. (eds.) 1998. *Cognition and material culture: the archaeology of symbolic storage.* McDonald Institute for Archaeological Research, Cambridge.

Richards, M. P., Pearson, J. A., Molleson, T. I., Russell, N. and Martin L. 2003. Stable isotope evidence of diet at Neolithic Çatalhöyük, Turkey. *Journal of Archaeological Science* 30, 67–76.

Richards, M. P. and Pearson, J. A. 2005. Stable isotope evidence of diet at Çatalhöyük. In Hodder, I. (ed.) *Inhabiting Çatalhöyük: reports from the 1995–1999 seasons.* McDonald Institute for Archaeological Research/British Institute of Archaeology at Ankara Monograph, Cambridge. (In press).

Ritchey, T. 1996. Note: building complexity. In Hodder, I. (ed.) *On the surface. Çatalhöyük 1993–95,* pp. 7–17. McDonald Institute for Archaeological Research/British Institute of Archaeology at Ankara Monograph, Cambridge.

Roberts, N. 1995. Climatic forcing of alluvial fan regimes during the late Quaternary in the Konya basin, south central Turkey. In Lewin, J., Macklin, M. G. and Woodward, J. C. (eds.) *Mediterranean Quaternary river environments,* pp. 207–17. Balkema, Rotterdam.

Roberts, N., Black, S., Boyer, P., Eastwood, W. J., Griffiths, H. I., Lamb, H. F., Leng, M. J., Parish, R., Reed, M. J., Twigg D. and Yiğitbaşioğlu, H. 1999. Chronology and stratigraphy of Late Quaternary sediments in the Konya Basin, Turkey: Results from the KOPAL Project. *Quaternary Science Reviews* 18, 611–30.

Roberts, N., Boyer, P., Merrick, J., Eastwood, W. J. and Griffiths, H. I. 2006. The KOPAL research programme at Çatalhöyük (1996–2001). In Hodder, I. (ed.) *Excavating Çatalhöyük: reports from the 1995–1999 seasons.* McDonald Institute for Archaeological Research/British Institute of Archaeology at Ankara Monograph, Cambridge. (In press).

Roberts, N., Boyer, P. and Parish, R. 1996. Preliminary results of geomorphological investigations at Çatalhöyük. In Hodder, I. (ed.) *On the surface. Çatalhöyük 1993–95,* pp. 19–40. McDonald Institute for Archaeological Research/British Institute of Archaeology at Ankara Monograph, Cambridge.

Roberts, N., Reed, J. M., Leng, M. J., Kuzucuoğlu, C., Fontugne, M., Bertaux, J., Woldring, H., Bottema, .S., Black, S., Hunt, E. and Karabiyikoğlu, M. 2001. The tempo of Holocene climatic change in the eastern Mediterranean region: new high-resolution crater-lake sediment data from central Turkey. *The Holocene* 11, 721–36.

Rollefson, G. 1986. Neolithic 'Ain Ghazal (Jordan): ritual and ceremony, II. *Paléorient* 12.1, 45–52.

Rollefson, G. 2000. Ritual and social structure at Neolithic 'Ain Ghazal. In Kuijt, I. (ed.) *Life in Neolithic farming communities,* pp. 163–190. Kluwer, New York.

Rollefson, G. O., Simmons, A. H., and Kafafi, Z. 1992. Neolithic culture at 'Ain Ghazal. *Journal of Field Archaeology* 19, 443–70.

Rosen, A. 2005. Phytolith indicators of plant and land use at Çatalhöyük. In Hodder, I. (ed.) *Inhabiting Çatalhöyük: reports from the 1995–1999 seasons.* McDonald Institute for Archaeological Research/British Institute of Archaeology at Ankara Monograph, Cambridge. (In press).

Rosen, A. and Roberts, N. (2005) The nature of Çatalhöyük: people and their changing environments on the Konya plain. In Hodder, I. (ed.) *Çatalhöyük perspectives: themes from the 1995–1999 seasons.* McDonald Institute for Archaeological Research/British Institute of Archaeology at Ankara Monograph, Cambridge. (In press).

Rosenberg, M. 1999. Hallan Çemi. In Özdoğan, M. and Başgelen, N. (eds.) *Neolithic in Turkey: The cradle of civilization. New discoveries,* pp. 25–34. Arkeoloji ve Sanat Yayınları, Istanbul.

Rowlands, M. 1993. The role of memory in the transmission of culture. *World Archaeology* 25, 141–151.

Rudebeck, E. 2000. *Tilling nature. Harvesting culture.* Acta Archaeologica Lundensia 32. Almquist and Wiksell, Stockholm.

Russell, N. 2005 Çatalhöyük worked bone. In Hodder, I. (ed.) *Changing materialities at Çatalhöyük: reports from the 1995–1999 seasons.* McDonald Institute for Archaeological Research/British Institute of Archaeology at Ankara Monograph, Cambridge. (In press).

Russell, N. and Düring, B. 2005. Worthy is the lamb: a double burial at Neolithic Çatalhöyük. *Antiquity* (forthcoming).

Russell, N. and McGowan, K. J. 2003. Dance of the cranes: crane symbolism at Çatalhöyük and beyond. *Antiquity* 77(297), 445–455.

Russell, N. and McGowan, K. J. 2005. Çatalhöyük bird bones. In Hodder, I. (ed.) *Inhabiting Çatalhöyük: reports from the 1995–1999 seasons.* McDonald Institute for Archaeological Research/British Institute of Archaeology at Ankara Monograph, Cambridge. (In press).

Russell, N and Martin, L. 2005 The Çatalhöyük mammal remains. In Hodder, I. (ed.) *Inhabiting Çatalhöyük: reports from the 1995–1999 seasons.* McDonald Institute for Archaeological Research/British Institute of Archaeology at Ankara Monograph, Cambridge. (In press).

Russell, N. and Meece, S. 2005. Animals representations and animal remains at Çatalhöyük. In Hodder, I. (ed.) *Çatalhöyük perspectives: themes from the 1995–1999 seasons.* McDonald Institute for Archaeological Research/British Institute of Archaeology at Ankara Monograph, Cambridge. (In press).

Scheper-Hughes, N. (ed.) 1987. *Child survival : anthropological perspectives on the treatment and maltreatment of children.* Kluwer, New York.

Schmidt, K. 1999. Boars, ducks and foxes – the Urfa Project. *Neo-Lithics* 3/99, 12–15.

Schmidt, K. 2000. Zuerst kam der tempel, dann die stadt. Vorläufiger bericht zu de grabungen am Göbekli Tepe und am Gürcütepe 1995–1999. *Istanbul Mitteilungen* 50, 5–40.

Schmidt, K. 2001. Göbekli Tepe, Southeastern Turkey: a preliminary report on the 1995–1999 excavations. *Paléorient* 26 (1), 45–54.

Shankland, D. 1996. The anthropology of an archaeological presence. In Hodder, I. (ed.) *On the surface. Çatalhöyük 1993–95*, pp. 218–226. McDonald Institute for Archaeological Research/British Institute of Archaeology at Ankara Monograph, Cambridge.

Shankland, D. 2000. Integrating the past: folklore, mounds and people at Çatalhöyük. In Hodder, I. (ed.) *Towards reflexive method in archaeology: the example at Çatalhöyük*, MacDonald Institute for Archaeological Research/British Institute of Archaeology at Ankara, Cambridge.

Shankland, D. 2005. The socio-ecology of Çatalhöyük. In Hodder, I. (ed.) *Çatalhöyük perspectives: themes from the 1995–9 seasons.* MacDonald Institute for Archaeological Research/British Institute of Archaeology at Ankara, Cambridge. (In press).

Shanks, M. and Tilley, C. 1982. Ideology, symbolic power and ritual communication: a reinterpretation of Neolithic mortuary practices. In Hodder, I. (ed.) *Symbolic and structural archaeology*, pp. 129–54. Cambridge University Press, Cambridge.

Shell, C. A. 1996. Magnetometric survey at Çatalhöyük East. In Hodder, I. (ed.) *On the surface. Çatalhöyük 1993–95*, pp. 101–13. McDonald Institute for Archaeological Research/British Institute of Archaeology at Ankara Monograph, Cambridge.

Sherratt, A. G. 1972. Socio-economic and demographic models for the Neolithic and Bronze Ages of Europe. In Clarke, D. L. (ed.) *Models in archaeology*, pp. 477–542. Methuen, London.

Sherratt, A. G. 1980. Water, soil and seasonality in early cereal cultivation. *World Archaeology* 11, 313–30.

Sidell, J. and Scudder, C. 2005. The eggshell from Çatalhöyük; a pilot study. In Hodder, I. (ed.) *Inhabiting Çatalhöyük: reports from the 1995–1999 seasons.* McDonald Institute for Archaeological Research/British Institute of Archaeology at Ankara Monograph, Cambridge. (In press).

Silistreli, U. 1991. 1989 Köşk Höyük kazısı. *XII Kazı Sonuçları Toplantısı* 1, 95–104.

Silverblatt, I. 1988. Women in states. *Annual Review of Anthropology* 17, 427–60.

Simmons, A. H. and Najjar, M. 2000. Preliminary report of the 1999–2000 excavation season at the Pre-Pottery Neolithic settlement at Ghwair I, southern Jordan. *Neo-Lithics* 1, 6–8.

Solecki, R. 1977. Predatory bird rituals at Zawi Chemi Shanidar. *Sumer* 33, 42–7.

Spence, J. D. 1985. *The memory palace of Matteo Ricci.* Penguin, New York.

Stevanovic, M. and Tringham, R. 1998. The BACH 1 Area. *Çatalhöyük Archive Report 1998.* (http://catal.arch.cam.ac.uk/catal/Archive_rep98/steva novic98.html).

Stordeur, D., Helmer D. and Wilcox, G. 1977. Jefrel Ahmar: un nouveau site de l'Horizon PPNA sur le Moyen

Euphrate Syrien. *Bulletin de la Société Préhistorique Française* 94, 282–85.

Stordeur, D., Benet, M., der Aprahamian, G. and Roux, J.-C. 2000. Les bâtiments communautaires de Jerf el Ahmar et Mureybet Horizon PPNA (Syrie). *Paléorient* 26, 29–44.

Strathern, M. 1988. *The gender of the gift: problems with women and problems with society in Melanesia.* University of California Press, Berkeley.

Swogger, J. 2000. Image and interpretation: the tyranny of representation? In Hodder, I., (ed.) *Towards Reflexive Method in Archaeology: The Example at Çatalhöyük*, pp. 143–152. McDonald Institute for Archaeological Research/British Institute of Archaeology at Ankara, Cambridge.

Testart, A. 1982. *Les chasseurs-cueilleurs ou l origine des inégalités.* Klincksieck, Paris.

Thomas, J. 1996. *Time, culture and identity.* Routledge, London.

Thomas, N. 1991. *Entangled objects.* Harvard University Press, Cambridge.

Thomas, N. and Humphrey, C. 1996. *Shamanism, history and the state.* University of Michigan Press, Ann Arbor.

Tilley, C. 1994. *A phenomenology of landscape.* Berg, Oxford.

Tilley, C. (ed.) 1999. *Metaphor and material culture.* Blackwell, Oxford.

Tilley, C. 2004. *The materiality of stone: explorations in landscape phenomenology.* Berg, Oxford.

Todd, I. 1976. *Çatal Hüyük in perspective.* Cummins, Menlo Park, California.

Tringham, R. 2000. The continuous house. A view from the deep past. In Joyce, R. and Gillespie, S. D. (eds.) *Beyond kinship. Social and material reproduction in House Societies*, pp. 115–134. University of Pennsylvania Press, Philadelphia.

Tung, B. 2005. A preliminary investigation of mudbrick in Çatalhöyük. In Hodder, I. (ed.) *Changing materialities at Çatalhöyük: reports from the 1995–1999 seasons.* McDonald Institute for Archaeological Research/British Institute of Archaeology at Ankara Monograph, Cambridge. (In press).

Turnbull-Kemp, P. 1967. *The leopard.* Bailey, London.

Turner, V. 1969. *The ritual process: structure and anti-structure.* Routledge and Kegan Paul, London.

Türkcan, A. 2005. Some remarks on Çatalhöyük stamp seals. In Hodder, I. (ed.) *Changing materialities at Çatalhöyük: reports from the 1995–1999 seasons.* McDonald Institute for Archaeological Research/British Institute of Archaeology at Ankara Monograph, Cambridge. (In press).

Valla, F. 1994. The first settled societies – Natufian (12,500–10,200 BP). In Levy, T. E. (ed.) *The archaeology of society in the Holy Land*, pp. 170–87. Leicester University Press, London.

Vedder, J. F. 2005. The obsidian mirrors of Çatalhöyük. In Hodder, I. (ed.) *Changing materialities at Çatalhöyük: reports from the 1995–1999 seasons.* McDonald Institute for

Archaeological Research/British Institute of Archaeology at Ankara Monograph, Cambridge. (In press).

Verhoeven, M. 2000. Death, fire and abandonment: ritual practice at Late Neolithic Tell Sabi Abyad, Syria. *Archaeological Dialogues* 7, 46–83.

Verhoeven, M. 2002. Ritual and ideology in the Pre-Pottery Neolithic B of the Levant and southeast Anatolia. *Cambridge Archaeological Journal* 12/2, 233–258.

Voigt, M. M. 2000. Çatalhöyük in context. Ritual at Early Neolithic sites in Central and Eastern Turkey. In Kuijt, I. (ed.) *Life in Neolithic farming communities: social organization, identity, and differentiation,* pp. 253–93. Kluwer Academic/Plenum, New York.

Wasson, P. 1994. *The archaeology of rank.* Cambridge University Press, Cambridge.

Weiner, A. 1992. *Inalienable possessions: the paradox of keeping-while-giving.* University of California Press, Berkeley.

Weinstein-Evron, M. 1998. *Early Natufian el-Wad revisited.* Etudes et Recherches Archéologiques de l'Université de Liège 77.

Wendrich, W. 2005. Specialist report on the Çatalhöyük basketry. In Hodder, I. (ed.) *Changing materialities at Çatalhöyük: reports from the 1995–1999 seasons.* McDonald Institute for Archaeological Research/British Institute of Archaeology at Ankara Monograph, Cambridge. (In press).

Whitley, J. 2002. Too many ancestors. *Antiquity* 76, 119–26.

Whittle, A. 1996. *Europe in the Neolithic. The creation of new worlds.* Cambridge University Press, Cambridge.

Wiessner, P. and Tumu, A. 1998. *Historical vines. Enga networks of exchange, ritual and warfare in Papua New Guinea.* Smithsonian Institution Press, Washington.

Winnicott, D. W. 1958. *Collected papers.* Tavistock Publications, London.

Wobst, H. 1974. Boundary conditions for Paleolithic social systems, *American Antiquity* 39, 147–78.

Woodburn, J. 1980. Hunters and gatherers today and reconstruction of the past. In Gellner, E. (ed.) *Soviet and western anthropology,* pp. 95–117. Duckworth, London.

Wright, G.A. 1978. Social differentiation in the Early Natufian. In Redman, C., Berman, M. J., Curtin, E. V., Langhorne Jr, W. T., Versaggi, N. M. and Wanser, J. C. (eds.) *Social archaeology. Beyond subsistence and dating,* pp. 201–23. Academic Press, New York.

Wright, K. 2000. The social origins of cooking and dining in early villages of western Asia. *Proceedings of the Prehistoric Society* 66, 89–121.

Yalman, N. 2005. Settlement logic studies as an aid to understand prehistoric settlement organization: ethnoarchaeological research in Central Anatolia. In Hodder, I. (ed.) *Inhabiting Çatalhöyük: reports from the 1995–1999 seasons.* McDonald Institute for Archaeological Research/British Institute of Archaeology at Ankara Monograph, Cambridge. (In press).

Yeomans, L. 2005. Discard and disposal practices at Çatalhöyük. In Hodder, I. (ed.) *Inhabiting Çatalhöyük: reports from the 1995–1999 seasons.* McDonald Institute for Archaeological Research/British Institute of Archaeology at Ankara Monograph, Cambridge. (In press).

Acknowledgments

Çatalhöyük was first excavated by James Mellaart in 1961–1965. Renewed excavations under my direction began there in 1993 and have continued every year since then. This book has been written as the result of the excavations that took place between 1995 and 1999, and as a result of post-excavation analysis and research conducted between 2000 and 2003. Some reference is made to excavations conducted by other teams from 2000 to 2004, but the main body of work referred to in this volume was carried out by those listed below, and with the financial and other support of the listed individuals and institutions. I have been lucky enough to work at a remarkable site, which itself has attracted a remarkable group of people who have worked with great energy and commitment. Simply to list their involvement can in no way express my indebtedness and my respect and admiration.

Individual contributions by those involved in the project over this period are presented in a series of edited volumes (Hodder 1996, 2000, 2005a, b, c, 2006). A publication by Michael Balter (2005) also deals with the project in the same period. I have tried within the text to indicate the contributions of individuals and laboratories within the overall team. But this does not adequately express the ways in which the ideas I present here are the results of many hours and years of discussion and debate within a large community – mainly the team itself, but also others that have been involved with it. While what I say in this volume is my own version and my own take on a complex set of data, and while I do not want to implicate any of those listed here in my claims and interpretations, I do want to emphasise how much I depend on and have learnt from them. I have provided here a summary based on a large amount of specialist research. Those interested in exploring the data on which my general claims are based should consult the edited volumes and the project website at www.catalhoyuk.com.

Funding for the field research was provided by a wide variety of corporate and academic bodies. Academic bodies include the British Academy/Arts and Humanities Research Board, the British Institute of Archaeology at Ankara, the Turkish Ministry of Culture and Tourism, the Newton Trust, the McDonald Institute for Archaeological Research, the European Union, the National Geographic Society, Kress Foundation, the Heber-Percy Trust, Lloyd Cotsen, Dayton Foundation, the Flora Family Foundation, Stanford University, National Science Foundation and the Polish Academy of Sciences.

Corporate sponsorship without which the Çatalhöyük Research Project would be impossible has included generous contributions from Koçbank, Boeing, Koçsistem, Visa International, Fiat, Merko, Glaxo-Wellcome, British Airways, Thames Water and Shell. Other support has been provided by IBM, Pepsi, Eczacıbaşı, Arup, Meptur and the Turkish Friends of Çatalhöyük, especially Reşit Ergener. Substantial personal donations have been made by Mr John Coker, and other donations were made by Mrs Dorothy Cameron and Mary Settegast.

The main institutional partners of the Çatalhöyük Research Project have been Cambridge University, Stanford University, University of California at Berkeley, University College London, Liverpool University, Middle East Technical University, Poznan University and the University of Thessaloniki. Many other institutions have supported or contributed to the project in some way. In particular, I would like to mention the Science Museum of Minnesota, Museum of London, Museum of London Archaeology Service, University of Pennsylvania, University of Sheffield, University of Wales at Cardiff, the Museum of Natural History, Selcuk University, Istanbul University and Karlsruhe Media-Technology Institute.

In particular I wish to thank Ömer Koç for his continued support of the project in many ways.

The project works in Turkey with a permit from the Ministry of Culture and Tourism, General-Directorate of Cultural Heritage and Museums. Over the period covered by these publications much support and advice was given by the department and I would particularly like to thank the Director Generals M. Akif Işık, Engin Özgen, Kenan Yurttagül, Ender Varinlioğlu, Dr Alpay Pasinli, Nadir Avcı and the Assistant Director Generals Ömer Yiğit Sayılgan, Necati Ayaz, M. Aykut Özet, Abdülkadir Karaoğlu, Kenan Yurttagül and İlhan Kaymaz.

The project works under the auspices of the British Institute of Archaeology in Ankara. I would like to thank Sir Timothy Daunt and the directors David French, acting director David Shankland, Roger Matthews and

Hugh Elton as well as the administrators Gülgün Girdivan (formerly Kazan), Yaprak Eran in Ankara and Gina Coulthard in London. Additionally I am grateful for the support of the BIAA committee members for continued support, the Ambassadors Özdem Sanberk, Korkmaz Haktanir, Akın Alptuna and staff at the Turkish Embassy and consulate in London and the Ambassadors Kieran Prendergast, David Logan and Peter Westmacott, and staff at the British Embassy in Ankara. The patrons of the project are Professor Lord Renfrew of Kaimsthorn and Sir David Attenborough. Board members have included Sir Mark Russell, George Warren, John Curtis, Nicholas Postgate, Lady Diana Daunt, Andrew Sherratt, Trevor Watkins, Malcolm Wagstaff, Christopher Stevenson, Charly French, Martin Jones, Chris Scarre and Sevket Sabancı.

Special thanks must be made to the government temsilci (representatives) who were Ali Önder (1995), Baykal Aydınbek and Osman Ermişler (1996), İlhame Öztürk and Gülcan Küçükkaraaşlan (1997), Edip Özgür (1998), Osman Ermişler, Recep Okçu, Edip Özgür and Candan Nalbantoğlu, (1999), Vahap Kaya and Enver Akgün (2000), Dursun Çağlar and Nejat Atar (2001), Rahmi Asal and Yaşar Yılmaz (2002 and 2004) and Belma Kulaçoğlu (2003). The Museum of Anatolian Civilisations at Ankara, especially the director Ilhan Temiszoy, have also been consistently helpful. I am indebted and ever grateful to Erdoğan Erol the director of the Konya Museums Services and his staff, in particular Kazim Mertek who is curator of the Çatalhöyük artifacts stored in the Archaeological Museum.

In Konya help and support was provided at many levels. The Vali Ahmet Kayhan, the Cultural Directors Osman Siviloğlu and Necip Mutlu, the Director of the Koruma Korulu Ayhan Alp, the DSI (Turkish Water Authority), officers at the Emniyet, our bank managers Aydın Kimyonşen and Arif Kutluca, our accountant Ahmet İçyer. In the local town of Çumra I am much appreciative of the help of the Kaymakams Bülent Savur, Abdullah Aslan, İbrahim Öğüz, Adem Yılmaz, Osman Bilgen, Osman Taşkan and the Belediye Başkans Recip Konuk, the late Abidin Ünal and Zeki Türker. I would also like to extend my thanks to İbrahim Gökce from the local fire brigade who provided water on 'dry days,' our local doctor Ömer Yıldırım, health officer Abdullah Akpınar and the Jandarma commitants. At our local store Abdullah Yetiş has always been on hand to help and metal workers Ayhan and Musa Veziroğlu and carpenters Sami Güdül and sons have produced some of our more challenging constructions on site.

I am also grateful for the support of the members of Atolye Mimarlık – Ridvan Övünç, Ceren Balkir, Sinan Omacan and Didem Teksoz. The Hilton Hotel in Konya, in particular Emrullah Akçakaya. The Büyük Londra Hotel in Istanbul, the late Roger Short and Asim Kaplan from Karavan.

From the local village of Küçükköy I would like to thank the people and their muhtar Huseyin Ceviz. The work would be impossible without the local men and women who work with us at the site. The excavations were ably assisted by Ismail Yaşli who was our site foreman from 1995 to 1999 and Arif Arslan, Ridvan Büyüktemiz, Riza Büyüktemiz, Mehmet Çağlar, Kemal Fati, Ahmet Kayserlı, Hakan Kılıçarslan, Mehmet Kuşçuoğlu, Taner Kuşçuoğlu, Marem Köse, Galip Kiraz, Halil Nurkoyuncu, Osman Özdil, Mehmet Salmancı, Metin Yilmaz, Mevlut Sivas, Mustafa Sivas, Mustafa Yaş, Gazi Yaşlı, Hülusi Yaşlı, Hasan Yaşlı, Hüseyin Yaşlı, Hüseyin Veli Yaşlı, Mustafa Veli Yaşlı, Osman Yaşlı, Paşa Yaşlı, Veli Yaşlı, Tamer Yiğit, Mustafa Zetin. A team of women have the laborious task of sorting through heavy residue samples which they do with amazing enthusiasm, Dane Gökdağ, Nesrin Günaşık, Ayfer Kiraz, Hafize Sarıkaya, Saliha Sivas, Gülcan Tüfekçi, Fadimana Yaşlı, Fatima Yaşlı, Hatice Yaşlı, Hülya Yaşlı, Rabiya Yaşlı, Saliha Yaşlı, Şenay Yaşlı and Suna Yaşlı.

The teams at the site have been fed and watered by our cook Ismail Salmancı and kept in comfort by our house staff who have been Rükiye Salmancı, Nevriye Şener, Necati and Nazmiye Terzioğlu and their daughter Nefise, Mavili Tokyağsun and Teslime Tüfekçi. Our camp managers who undertook momentous bureaucratic procedures as well as many thankless tasks for the smooth running of the camp and project. They were Özgür Özdilsiz, Özkan Köse, Murat Ufuk Kara, Cinar Dirim, Tolga Pekperdahçı, Melih Pekperdahçı and Hüsnü Tayanç. The site has been ably protected by the local guards Mustafa and Hasan Tokyağsun, Sedrettin Dural, Sadet Kuşçuoğlu, and Ibrahim Eken.

During the period in question the project was ably administered by Amanda Cox, Josephine Stubbs, Becky Coombs, Christina Clements, Jackie Ouchikh and Katerina Johnson with support from Colin Lomas of the McDonald Institute. Anja Wolle provided invaluable computer support. The site directors were Roger Matthews (1993 to 1996) and Shahina Farid (1997 to present), to whom I and the entire project are deeply indebted. None of the research of the project, and none of the words written here would have been possible without Shahina. Her dedication, remarkable field skills, social tact and patience in managing large numbers of people remain a wonder to me and they are the basis for my work. I dedicate this book to her as her friend and admirer.

I wish to thank all those who worked at the site in the main period covered by this volume 1995 to 1999. Their names include the following: Meltem Ağcabay, Engin Akdeniz, Göze Akoğlu, Ali Akin Akyol, Mary Alexander, Peter Andrews, Steve Archer, Başak Arda, Michael Ashley-Lopez, Eleni Asouti, Sonya Atalay (Suponcic), Meral Atasağun, Banu Aydinoğluğil, Douglas Baird, Michael Balter, Jason Bass, Adnan Baysal, Harriet Beaubien, Åsa Berggren, Zeynep Beykont, Nurhayat Bilge, Hatice Bilgiç, Ömer Bilgin, Catherine Bonner, Dusan Boric, Peter Boyer, Başak Boz, Mehmet Bozdemir, Keith Bradflaad, Jenny Bredenberg, Dorothée Brill, Jasmina Brinkhuizen, Deniz Bulak, Ann Butler, Ivan Butorac, Ayfer Bartu Candan, Can Candan, Tristan Carter, Thomas Cawdron, Dagmar Cee, Serdar Cengiz, Craig Cessford, Adrian Chadwick, Adam Cohen, James Conolly, Anwen Cooper, Bruno Coppola, Chris Cumberpatch, Aylin Çavdar, Predrag Dakic, Daniela Delfs, Meltem Delibaşı, Burghard Detzler, Jo Deverenski, Clark Dobbs, Linda Donley-Reid, Louise Doughty, Miriam Doutriaux, Warren Eastwood, Makbule Ekici, Martin Emele, Aylan Erkal, Amanda Erwin, Arturo Escobar, Freja Evans-Swogger, Andrew Fairbairn, Lindsay Falck, Shahina Farid, Lu'chen Foster, Sheelagh Frame, Alexander Gagnon, Duncan Garrow, Adriana Garza, Robert Geiger, Soultana Geroussi, Catriona Gibson, Caitlin Gordon, Atakan Güven, Lori Hager, Carolyn Hamilton, Charlotte Hamilton, Naomi Hamilton, Christine Hastorf, Stamatis Hatzitoulousis, Margaret Hauselt, Lucy Hawkes, Emily Hayes, Chris Hills, Ayşe Hortacsu, Liz Hunt, Vladimir Ilic, Ioannis Imamidis, Brian Jackson, Emma Jenkins, Don Johnson, Azize Kadayifci, Elif Kavas, Nurcan Kayacan, Amanda Kennedy, Kathryn Killackey, the late Heinrich Klotz, Mark Knight, Afriditi Konstantinidou, Evan Kopelson, Kostas Kotsakis, Perihan Kösem, Esin Kuleli, Aslı Kutsal, Emine Küçük, Evangelia Kyriatzi, Despina Lahandiou, Paul Lapinski, Jonathan Last, Su Leaver, Leola Leblanc, Nessa Leibhammer, Sara Leuke, Tonya Van Leuvan-Smith, Claudia Lopez, Gavin Lucas, the late Maria Magkafa, Tona Majo, Harpreet Malhi, Louise Martin, Daniéle Martinoli, Sabrina Maras, Frank Matero, Roger Matthews, Wendy Matthews, Stephanie Meece, David Meiggs, Sinan Mellaart, Jamie Merrick, Boris Michalski, William Middleton, Arlene Miller Rosen, Dragana Milosevic, Slobodan Mitrovic, Theya Molleson, Caitlin Moore, Peter Moore, Joseph Mora, Rachel Moritz, Elizabeth Moss, Cassie Myers, Julie Near, Charlie Newman, Aglaia Nitsou, Vladimir Novakovic, Aylin Orbaşlı, Emin Murat Özdemir, Serap Özdöl, Latif Özen, Jessica Pearson, Paolo Pelegatti, Don Pohlman, Tom Pollard, Dietmar Puttman, Tiffany Raszick, Tim Ready, David Reese, Roddy Regan, Michael Richards, Tim Ritchey, Neil Roberts, Celia Rothmund, Natalie Rusk, Nerissa Russell, Andy Schoenhofer, Joshua Seaver, Kent Severson, Orrin Shane, David Shankland, Julia Shaw, Colin Shell, Connie Silver, David Small, Lothar Spree, Laura Steele, Mirjana Stevanovic, John-Gordon Swogger, Robert Symmons, Jez Taylor, Jo Taylor, Vuk Trifkovic, Ruth Tringham, Sybilla Tringham, Burcu Tunc, Richard Turnbull, Catherine Turton, Ali Türkcan, Mustafa Türker, Asuman Türkmenoğlu, Katheryn Twiss, Mehmet Uluceviz, Heidi Underbjerg, Anne Marie Vandendriesch, James Vedder, Dimitrios Vlachos, Margarete Vöhringer, Thomas Vollherbst, Barbara Voss, Trevor Watkins, Sharon Webb, Willeke Wendrich, Fabian Winkler, Anja Wolle, Michelle Wollestonecroft, Martin Wrede, Nurcan Yalman, Lisa Yeomans, Çiçek Yildu and Levent Zoroğlu.

Team members who worked on publication material off-site included: Erhan Akça, Alexander Bentley, Wendy Birch, Petya Blumbach, Céline Bressy, Ian Bull, Kate Clark, Mark Copley, Sarah Cross, Şahinde Demirci, Mohammed Elhmmali, Begumşen Ergenekon, Richard Evershed, Cemal Göncüoğlu, Tom Higham, Huw Griffiths, Elizabeth Hadly, John Hather, Gordon Hillman, David Jenkins, Selim Kapur, Asena Kızılarslanoğlu, Peter Kuniholm, Ripan Malhi, Sturt Manning, Kevin McGowan, Joanna Mountain, Wim van Neer, Maryanne Newton, Mustafa Özbakan, Thomas Higham, Aymelek Özer, Nicholas Pearce, Vincent Perret, Gérard Poupeau, Douglas Price, David Roberts Claire Scudder, Musa Serdem, Jane Sidell, Marcel van Tuinen, Vedat Toprak, Asuman Türkmenoğlu, John Williams and Katherine Wright.

The volumes produced between 2000 and 2003, and referred to above, would not have been produced without the work of Craig Cessford. The project, and I particularly, owe him an enormous debt in pulling the reports and work together into these volumes. Assistance in publication has also been given by Louise Doughty, Shahina Farid, Katerina Johnson and Anja Wolle, Helen Jones, Sophie Lamb, Duncan Lees, Margaret Matthews. Reconstructions used in this volume are the work of John Swogger and photographic images were taken by project members unless cited.

I also wish to thank Douglas Baird, Lynn Meskell, Andrew Sherratt, Nerissa Russell, Colin Ridler, Mirjana Stevanovic and an anonymous reviewer for their comments and suggestions on an earlier draft of this book. In particular I wish to thank Colin Ridler for his long-term support of the project and this endeavour to produce a text from it. His detailed comments have certainly improved the book.

As always it is a special pleasure to acknowledge the continuing input of James and Arlette Mellaart and their son Alan. The continued work at the site would not have been possible without their understanding and kindness.

It cannot have been easy to hand over such a remarkable site to a new team. I am deeply grateful to them for continuing to support our work and for having the generosity of spirit to remain as advisors and mentors for us. It was a particular pleasure to have James and Arlette's grandson Sinan Mellaart work with us at the site in 2001. Much of this book builds directly on the work of James Mellaart and his team, and I am very much indebted to him and them.

Sources of Illustrations

TEXT FIGURES: Chapter openers drawn by Ali Türkcan; 1 Arlette and James Mellaart; 2 Arlette and James Mellaart; 3 Arlette and James Mellaart; 4 Çatalhöyük Research Project (CRP); 5 Ben Plumridge; 6 Ian Todd; 7 John Swogger; 8 Eastman Kodak Company; 9 Paul Lane; 10 Ian Hodder; 11 Firth (1936, 77), redrawn by John Swogger; 12 Arlette and James Mellaart; 13 Arlette and James Mellaart; 14 Nurcan Yalman; 15 CRP; 16 CRP; 17 CRP; 18 Cessford (2005a); 19 Cessford (2005a); 20 CRP; 21 Arlette and James Mellaart; 22 Arlette and James Mellaart; 23 Cessford and Mitrovic (2005); 24 Hodder and Cessford (2004); 25 CRP; 26 CRP with reconstructions by Lucy Walker; 27 Ian Todd; 28 Wendy Matthews (2005a); 29 CRP; 30 CRP; 31 CRP; 32 Asouti 2005 with additions; 33 Fairbairn *et al* (2005b); 34 John Swogger; 35 Arlette and James Mellaart; 36 Mellaart (1967); 37 Mellaart (1967); 38 Mellaart (1966); 39 John Swogger; 40 CRP; 41 CRP; 42 John Swogger; 43 John Swogger; 44 John Swogger; 45 CRP; 46 John Swogger; 47 CRP; 48 CRP; 49 CRP; 50 CRP; 51 CRP; 52 Wendy Matthews; 53 Cessford 2006; 54 CRP; 55 DAI, Berlin; 56 Arlette and James Mellaart; 57 Mellaart (1967); 58 Ian Todd; 59 CRP; 60 CRP; 61 CRP; 62 CRP; 63 CRP; 64 Tim King; 65 CRP and Tim Ritchey; 66 Ian Todd; 67 Mellaart (1967); 68 CRP; 69 CRP; 70 CRP; 71 CRP; 72 CRP; 73 CRP; 74 John Swogger; 75 CRP; 76 CRP; 77 CRP; 78 Mellaart (1967); 79 Wendrich (2005); 80 Katie Killackey based on Mellaart (1967); 81 Cessford (2006); 82 CRP; 83 John Swogger; 84 Mellaart (1966); 85 Hauptmann (1999); 86 Hauptmann (1999); 87 Arlette and James Mellaart; 88 D. Johannes/DAI, Berlin; 89 DAI, Berlin; 90 CRP; 91 Mellaart (1967); 92 Richards and Pearson (2004); 93 CRP; 94 Arlette and James Mellaart; 95 Cessford (2006); 96 Hodder and Cessford (2004); 97 CRP; 98 CRP; 99 CRP; 100 CRP; 101 John Swogger; 102 Arlette and James Mellaart; 103 CRP; 104 CRP; 105 (upper) Mira Stevanovic and Ruth Tringham; (lower) Mellaart (1967); 106 Arlette and James Mellaart; 107 CRP; 108 CRP; 109 Arlette and James Mellaart; 110 Arlette and James Mellaart; 111 CRP.

PLATES: 1 Mellaart (1967); 2 CRP; 3 John Swogger; 4 CRP, photo Michael Ashley and Jason Quinlan; 5 CRP; 6 CRP; 7 Mira Stevanovic and Ruth Tringham, photo Michael Ashley and Jason Quinlan; 8 John Swogger; 9 Arlette and James Mellaart; 10 Arlette and James Mellaart; 11 CRP; 12 Wendy Matthews; 13 CRP, photo Jason Quinlan and Michael Ashley; 14 CRP, reconstruction by John Swogger; 15 Ian Todd; 16 Ian Todd; 17 Arlette and James Mellaart; 18 Mellaart (1963; 1967); 19 CRP; 20 Mellaart (1967); 21 CRP; 22 CRP; 23 CRP; 24 Arlette and James Mellaart.

Index